To Jill and Walter
With love
From Mom Lem-
pert

Good birding!

Birding in Ohio

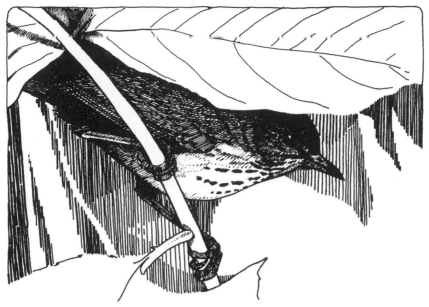

Birding in Ohio

TOM THOMSON

with the assistance of 38 Regional Contributors

WITH A FOREWORD BY **ROGER TORY PETERSON**,
PREFACE BY **RICHARD B. PIERCE**,
AND DRAWINGS BY **CHARLES W. GAMBILL**

Indiana University Press   *Bloomington & Indianapolis*

The paper used in this publication meets the minimum requirements of
American National Standard for Information Sciences–Permanence of
Paper for Printed Library Materials, ANSI Z39.48-1984.

Manufactured in the United States of America

Library of Congress Cataloging-in-Publication Data

Thomson, Tom
    Birding in Ohio / by Tom Thomson with the assistance of 24
    regional contributors ; with a foreword by Roger Tory Peterson ;
    preface by Richard B. Pierce ; and drawings by Charles W. Gambill.–
    2nd ed.
        p.   cm.
    Includes bibliographical references (p.   ) and indexes.
    ISBN 0-253-35995-3 (cloth). – ISBN 0-253-20874-2 (paper).
    1. Bird watching–Ohio.   2. Birds–Ohio.   I. Title.
QL684.03T48   1994
598'.07234771–dc20   94-2448

1 2 3 4 5   00 99 98 97 96 95 94

On the previous page: Gray-cheeked Thrush
Shown on the title pages for Parts I–IV are, respectively, Double-crested
Cormorants, Yellow-bellied Sapsucker, Hooded Warbler, and Shorebirds in Flight.

To Jan, Jeff, and James

I can predict the hour and the minute when the sun will cross the equator, but not the exact day of the wood thrush. I can fore-tell many of the birds that will be on the list of visitors, but not all—and among them will be some it never occurred to me I might see. I set out each morning not knowing what surprise and new delight may be in store for me.

—Louis J. Halle, *Spring in Washington*

Contents

Maps

Foreword: On Birding in Ohio

ROGER TORY PETERSON

I count myself fortunate to have spent most of my life portraying birds on canvas, on film, and in words. But, on reflection, it has been equally rewarding to have had the opportunity to meet so many others with similar interests.

Thus it was a joy and a privilege for me to have known some of the finest naturalists who ever studied the birdlife of Ohio.

I am speaking of people like Edward S. Thomas, Lawrence E. Hicks, Donald Borror, Irv Kassoy, and Milton Trautman.

For many years Ed Thomas was Curator of Natural History at the old Ohio State Museum in Columbus. He was a nature columnist for the *Columbus Dispatch* for 57 years.

Lawrence E. Hicks was a Fellow of the American Ornithologists' Union and in 1930 he was the United States delegate to the International Ornithological Congress at Louen, France, where he presented a paper on the European Starling. In 1935, the Ohio Biological Survey published his monograph, *Distribution of the Breeding Birds of Ohio*. Until 1945, he was the first head of the Cooperative Wildlife Research Station at The Ohio State University.

Donald J. Borror was a professor of zoology and ornithology at the Ohio State University. He became widely known for his recordings of bird songs, which resulted in nine phonograph records and over 25 scientific publications.

By good fortune, the above three men were mentors of Tom Thomson and major influences in his interest in birds from the time he was 15 years old. By the time he was a sophomore in high school he was sitting in on university seminars, going on field trips, and drawing books from departmental libraries.

Later in life, he got to know Milton B. Trautman, the author of *The Birds of Buckeye Lake, Ohio* and *The Fishes of Ohio,* and Irving Kassoy, whom I had known as a young man when we were both members of the legendary Bronx Bird Club. As some of you may know, Irv was an authority on owls, especially the Barn Owl.

I'm not sure I knew Dr. Carl Reese, professor emeritus of zoology and ornithology at OSU, but his teaching also influenced the young Tom Thomson.

And, of course, everybody knows Ernie Limes, that indefatigable chaser

of birds and friend of birders. Tom and Ernie have been birding pals for more
years than either one of them cares to admit.

In 1983, when Thomson's *Birding in Ohio* was first released, it was pro-
claimed as one of the finest state birding guides published up to that time. This
new edition, with the input of regional contributors, is sure to please even more
people. It contains many revised site descriptions and an appreciable number
of totally new ones.

The cult of birdwatching continues to grow. It is said that there are now
more birders than either hunters or fisherfolks. Crowds of birders descend on
hot spots like the boardwalk in Magee Marsh, which is just a feather less
spectacular than famed Point Pelee in Ontario.

Enjoy this book. The volunteers made invaluable contributions and the
author poured his heart and soul into it.

Preface

RICHARD B. PIERCE, CHIEF
OHIO DIVISION OF WILDLIFE

Birdwatching is an increasingly important activity for the Ohio Division of Wildlife. Recent survey figures show that Ohioans spend more than $125,000,000 annually on binoculars, cameras, film, birdseed, and birdhouses. Forty percent of this total is for birdseed alone. An additional $250,000,000 per year is spent on travel to take advantage of wildlife viewing opportunities. In terms of numbers of people, nearly 80% of Ohioans 16 years of age or older participate in some form of wildlife observation. These are impressive numbers and they continue to grow.

We are trying to help meet the demands created by an active and knowledgeable birding public. Programs and projects start with protecting and enhancing the avian resource itself. This means population monitoring, habitat protection, and active management projects such as our work with Ohio's nesting bald eagles and peregrine falcons. I am also grateful to the hundreds of Ohio birders who have volunteered time to work with us on these projects, and who are partly responsible for the successes we have seen.

Another important part of our effort is to provide opportunities for citizens to observe, study, and appreciate wildlife. In recent years, facilities have been improved in wildlife areas, such as the boardwalks at Magee Marsh and Spring Valley. These projects would not have been possible without the support shown by Ohioans for the Endangered and Wildlife Diversity Program Checkoff, and I am certain that birders are disproportionately represented among those who contribute.

And ultimately, it is a resource like *Birding in Ohio* that helps bring it all together. No one in Ohio is more familiar with areas to bird than Tom Thomson, and he has pulled this knowledge together to make birding more accessible and enjoyable for everyone. And that's important, because the long term health and viability of a diverse avian population will depend on the number of people who know about it, and who have developed a personal interest in it.

Introduction

Birding in Ohio, first published in 1983, described over 200 good birding spots scattered about the state. This revised edition of the book includes most of those locations, plus an additional 100 sites, making a grand total of over 300 places to go looking for birds. Much of this new material, plus updates on previously mentioned sites, has been submitted by regional editors and volunteer contributors. For brief biographies of these dedicated birders and a complete list of the volunteers, see "About the Contributors." I am especially indebted to John Schrader and the experts he recruited for their outstanding contribution in adding to and updating sites in southwest Ohio. I also want to thank the following regional editors whose offerings proved invaluable to the completeness of this undertaking: Tom Kemp, Pete and Bill Whan, Bruce Stehling, Gildo Tori, John Pogacnik, Lynn Barnhart, Charles Bombaci, Elsie and Harry Knighton, Marcella and Howard Meahl, Tod Dawson, Ned Keller, Jay Stenger, and Glen Kitson. A special word of thanks to Wildlife Biologist Denis Case of the Ohio Division of Wildlife for his contribution on the status of Peregrine Falcons in the state. Thanks also to Charles H. Gambill, who illustrated the first edition and created a number of new line drawings for this book.

In the 11 years since the first edition of *Birding in Ohio* was published, there have been a number of site changes, the creation or rediscovery of additional sites, and significant and quickening trends in the distribution and status of some bird species.

As in the first edition, some of the described sites are extensive natural areas of many square miles, others are renowned for large concentrations of birds or rare breeding species, and still others are out-of-the-way spots relatively uninvestigated ornithologically where opportunities abound for adding to our knowledge of the distribution and breeding ranges of Ohio birds. Some sites, because they are representative of the regions in which they are located, are discussed in greater detail than others, and it can be assumed there are often similar birds in nearby areas not treated as thoroughly in the text.

Part I directs the birder to sites in the northern tier of counties, where in many cases birding is influenced by Lake Erie. Part II investigates the west-central counties, and Part III explores the unglaciated Allegheny Plateau counties of southern and eastern Ohio. In each part, the sites are presented in alphabetical order and keyed to section maps. In the site descriptions, the birds and seasons of the year discussed in the greatest detail are those considered most important ornithologically at that particular location.

Part IV is an expanded checklist of the birds of Ohio with symbols denoting geographical locations, seasons of the year, and numerical status. Because the annotations were deleted in this edition to accommodate the added birding sites, a brief mention of how some species are faring follows.

Double-crested Cormorants continue to increase in numbers. They are currently breeding on West Sister Island in Lake Erie and might well be discovered nesting in other locations before the century is over.

In the spring, small numbers of Snowy Egrets and Little Blue Herons continue to be rare visitors to suitable locations in the state and fairly regular summer residents in the western Lake Erie marshes with two or three pairs of each species nesting on West Sister Island since 1983. Tricolored Herons have been rare but nonbreeding visitors to the Lake Erie marches since about 1979. During the first two-thirds of this century, Snowy Egrets and Little Blue Herons usually appeared in Ohio during late summer dispersals from their breeding grounds in the south.

Occurrences of extralimital Black Vultures are becoming more commonplace with some individuals being recorded as far north as Lake Erie. Ospreys are increasing in numbers: there are more records of summering individuals, and it is probably only a matter of time before they reestablish themselves in Ohio as nesting birds.

Piping Plovers continue to decline, but most other shorebirds seem to be maintaining their populations. Populations of gulls continue to proliferate with a corresponding increase in the sightings of rarities and strays. Ring-billed Gulls have become more common in the interior of the state and in some places are becoming urbanized. The number of gull species recorded for the state now stands at 18.

The last recorded nesting of Bewick's Wrens in Ohio was of a pair in Pike County in 1987. Loggerhead Shrikes have continued their decline, probably because of the loss of suitable habitat. The few pairs that now nest are mostly in western counties. Other species that have suffered from changes in agricultural practices and diminishing habitat are Upland Sandpipers, Barn Owls, Vesper Sparrows, and Eastern Meadowlarks. From all existing evidence, the Bachman's Sparrow seems to have been extirpated from Ohio.

In the years since 1983, almost all observers reported a gradual decline in the numbers of many neotropical songbird migrants. Transient flycatchers, thrushes, vireos, warblers, tanagers, grosbeaks, and orioles all seemed to be passing through Ohio in reduced numbers. Yet, paradoxically, the 1993 spring migration, after getting off to a late start, surpassed all expectations with the numbers of many of these species rebounding magnificently. It is entirely possible that when a species is faced with dwindling numbers, genetic factors trigger a response that results in more vigorous reproductive activity.

The results of a breeding bird census I have done over the past 23 years in the seven-and-a-half-mile-long Clear Creek Valley in Hocking County indicate that some of the neotropical breeders might be in a period of decline. Sometimes, as is the case with American Redstarts and Yellow-breasted Chats, the declines have been precipitous. A few other warblers seem to be slipping but the evidence is hard to read because many species regularly pendulate between minimum and maximum populations.

In addition to cormorants, most birds of prey, shorebirds, and gulls, many other species appear to be maintaining or increasing their populations. Wild Turkeys continue to prosper in many of the hill counties. All of the woodpeckers, with the exception of the Red-headed, are maintaining stable populations. Common Ravens are being seen more often and a pair that was recorded in the Clear Creek Valley for three years was seen feeding a fledgling in 1987. Most permanent residents are doing well and, of course, the ubiquitous House Finches completed their unprecedented occupation of much of the Eastern United States, including Ohio.

Because we study birds, many of us are particularly sensitive to environmental changes going on around us—and that is good. As Roger Tory Peterson has noted many times, wild birds are to the environment what canaries were for many years to miners: an early warning system against disaster.

Map Credits

Ohio Department of Natural Resources, Ohio Department of Transportation, The Nature Conservancy, Hamilton County Park District, Lake Metroparks, Miami County Park District, Metroparks of Butler County, Dayton-Montgomery County Park District, Cleveland Museum of Natural History, Columbus and Franklin County Park District, Ohio Agricultural Research and Development Center, Oxbow, Inc., U.S. Fish and Wildlife Service, U.S. Army Corps of Engineers, Gilmore Ponds Conservancy, Inc., Ohio Historical Society. County location maps by Kent D. King.

PART I

The Northern Tier of Counties

LAKE ERIE

WILLIAMS | FULTON | LUCAS
WOOD | OTTAWA
HENRY | SANDUSKY | ERIE | LORAIN | CUYAHOGA
DEFIANCE | SENECA | HURON | MEDINA | SUMMIT | PORTAGE
PAULDING | HANCOCK
PUTNAM | WYANDOT | CRAWFORD | RICHLAND | ASHLAND | WAYNE
VAN WERT | ALLEN

LAKE | ASHTABULA
GEAUGA | TRUMBULL
MAHONING

A | L | B

NORTHERN OHIO is blessed with both a diversity and a plenitude of favorable bird habitats. Its riches include the oak openings of Lucas County, the great complex of marshes that stretches from Toledo to Sandusky, the many fine lookout points along the Erie shore from Huron to Cleveland and on east to Conneaut, the flat farmland and woodlots of northwestern Ohio, and the rolling, often rugged terrain of the northeastern counties with their many reservoirs and large lakes. Fortunately, significant portions of these natural areas are being saved for future generations—not only for people, but for birds, animals, plants, and all the other life forms that cohabit the earth with us. State and metropolitan parks, national refuges, state wildlife areas, nature preserves, and sanctuaries all contribute to this life-saving process. Part I describes well over 100 birding sites in the 31 counties of the northern tier. The westernmost counties, shown on Map A, are Allen, Ashland, Crawford, Defiance, Erie, Fulton, Hancock, Henry, Huron, Lucas, Ottawa, Paulding, Putnam, Richland, Sandusky, Seneca, Van Wert, Williams, Wood, and Wyandot counties. The northeastern section, shown on Map B, includes Ashtabula, Cuyahoga, Geauga, Lake, Lorain, Mahoning, Medina, Portage, Summit, Trumbull, and Wayne counties. Descriptions of and directions to the birding spots are presented in alphabetical order.

Amann Reservoir   *In Crawford County, take U.S. 61 south*
                                     from Galion to County Line Road.
                                     (Map A–1)

In March and April, this 156-acre park and reservoir is always worth checking for American Black Ducks, Mallards, Blue-winged Teals, American Wigeons, Redheads, Ring-necked Ducks, Lesser Scaups, and Hooded Mergansers. Trails through the surrounding beech woods can aid in compiling a good list of land birds.

Ashtabula Harbor/Walnut Beach   *Take Ohio 531 to Lake Avenue and turn*
                                     north to Walnut Boulevard and the beach.
                                     (Map B–2)

Check the phragmites and brush that border the downhill road to the beach for migratory sparrows, then follow the road to the right until you come to a large sandbar that extends out into the lake. If conditions are right, you can

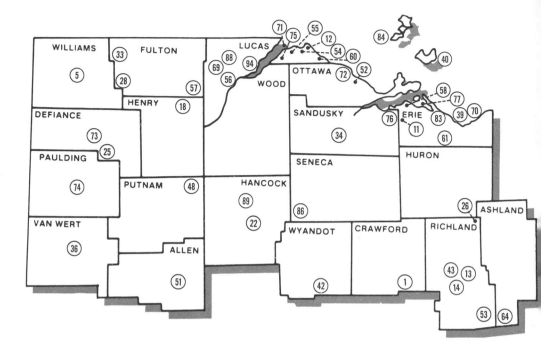

MAP A

1 Amann Reservoir
5 Beaver Creek State Wildlife Area
11 Castalia Pond
12 [Little] Cedar Point National Wildlife Refuge
13 Charles Mills Lake
14 Clear Fork Reservoir
18 Dry Creek Access
22 Findlay Reservoirs
25 Five Mile Creek Access
26 Fowler Woods
28 Goll Woods Nature Preserve
33 Harrison Lake State Park
34 Hayes State Memorial
36 Hiestand Woods Park
39 Huron Harbor and Breakwater
40 Kelley's Island
42 Killdeer Plains Wildlife Area
43 Kingwood Center
48 Leipsic Reservoir
51 Lost Creek Reservoir
52 Magee Marsh Wildlife Area
53 Malabar Farm
54 Mallard Club Marsh Wildlife Area

55 Maumee Bay State Park
56 Maumee River Rapids
57 Maumee State Forest
58 Medusa Marsh
60 Metzger Marsh Wildlife Area
61 Milan Wildlife Area
64 Mohican State Park and State Forest
69 Oak Openings
70 Old Woman Creek
71 Oregon Power Plant/Bay Shore Power Plant
72 Ottawa National Wildlife Refuge
73 Oxbow Lake Wildlife Area
74 Paulding Ponds
75 Pearson Metropolitan Park
76 Pickerel Creek Wildlife Area
77 Pipe Creek Wildlife Area
83 Sheldon Marsh State Nature Preserve
84 South Bass Island
86 Springville Marsh State Nature Area
88 Toledo Express Airport
89 Van Buren State Park
94 Woodlawn Cemetery

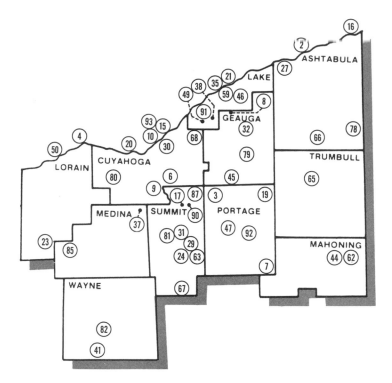

MAP B

2 Ashtabula Harbor
3 Aurora Pond and Bog
4 Avon Lake Power Plant
6 Bedford Reservation/Tinkers Creek Gorge
7 Berlin Reservoir
8 Big Creek Park
9 Brecksville Reservation
10 Burke Lakefront Airport
15 Cleveland Waterfront/Winter Birding
16 Conneaut Harbor
17 Deep Lock Quarry Metro Park
19 Eagle Creek Nature Preserve
20 Edgewater Park/Perkins Beach
21 Fairport Harbor
23 Findley State Park
24 Firestone Metro Park
27 Geneva State Park
29 Goodyear Heights Metro Park
30 Gordon Park
31 Gorge Metro Park
32 Hambden Orchard Wildlife Area
35 Headlands Beach State Park
37 Hinkley Reservation
38 Holden Arboretum/Stebbins' Gulch
41 Killbuck Marsh Wildlife Area

44 Kyle Woods
45 La Due Reservoir
46 Lake County Parks
47 Lake Rockwell
49 Little Mountain
50 Lorain Harbor
59 Mentor Marsh State Nature Preserve
62 Mill Creek Park
63 Mogadore Reservoir
65 Mosquito Creek Reservoir
66 New Lyme Wildlife Area
67 Nimisila Reservoir/Portage Lakes
68 North Chagrin Reservation
78 Pymatuning State Park
79 River Park
80 Rocky River Reservation
81 Sand Run Metro Park/Seiberling Nature Center
82 Secrest Arboretum
85 Spencer Lake Wildlife Area
87 Tinkers Creek Nature Preserve and State Park
90 Virginia Kendall Metro Park
91 Waite Hill
92 West Branch State Park
93 White City Park

Snowy Owl

drive farther; if not it would be better to walk. During winter months, check the breakwater for Snowy Owls. In late November and December, the chances are fairly good of finding a Purple Sandpiper. The inner harbor might provide a resting place for a few grebes and ducks. Scan the entire sandbar for migrant shorebirds. This is the area where a Rufous-necked Stint was found several years ago. Other rare and unusual birds seen here include Golden Eagle, Willet, Baird's Sandpiper, Franklin's, Little, Iceland, and Glaucous gulls. In the spring, look for migrating raptors. Hidden in the phragmites south of the sandbar, there is a pond that sometimes attracts Least Bitterns and Marsh Wrens. Return to Walnut Boulevard, turn left and drive to the park at the end of the road for another good view of the harbor.

Go back to Ohio 531 and head east. Just past Ohio 11 at Minnesota Avenue, turn left and proceed to Lakeshore Park. The park is closed in the winter, but you can park your car, enter on foot, and obtain a good view of the east harbor. Here again, look for Purple Sandpipers and Snowy Owls on the breakwaters. The east end of the park in the spring can be good for migrant warblers and other passerines.

Return to Ohio 531 and head east. The two power plants you pass have been visited by Peregrine Falcons and, on one occasion, by a gray-phased Gyrfalcon. Just beyond the easternmost power plant there is a small pulloff on the north side of the road. You can get out here and walk along the east side of the fence for a view of the hot water outlet. Do not go beyond the fence as the area is off limits and patrolled. Some of the good birds that have been found here include: Harlequin Duck, Oldsquaw, all three scoters, Purple Sandpiper, and California Gull. After you are through with this area, you can head east on Ohio 531 to Conneaut Harbor, another great birding location.

Aurora Pond and Bog   *Take Ohio 14 south of Cleveland to*
Twinsburg, then Ohio 82 east to Aurora,
and Ohio 43 north to the pond.
(Map B–3)

In addition to migratory waterbirds in the spring and fall, this unique spot boasts an impressive list of nesting birds. Summer visitors and breeding birds include American and Least bitterns, Great Blue Heron, Great Egret, Green-backed Heron, Wood Duck, American Black Duck, Mallard, Sharp-shinned Hawk, Virginia Rail, Sora, Common Moorhen, Black Tern, Brown Creeper, Sedge and Marsh wrens, Veery, Yellow-throated Vireo, Yellow and Prothonotary warblers, Northern Waterthrush, and Scarlet Tanager.

Avon Lake Power Plant   *In Lorain County, along U.S. Route 6 in*
the town of Avon Lake, enter the
municipal park just west of the power
plant. (Map B–4)

This small area is of most interest during the colder months when warm outflows from the power plant keep adjacent Lake Erie waters from freezing. Good views can sometimes be had of rafts of ducks, along with loons and grebes, by a stealthy approach to the chain-link fence at the top of the bluff. Oldsquaws and all three scoters can be seen here during winter months, and such rarities as Red-throated Loon, Red-necked Grebe, Eared Grebe, King Eider, Harlequin Duck, and Brant have been seen here.

At the northeast corner of the fence is a vantage point for scanning the breakwater and a sandy cove to the east where large numbers of gulls often congregate. Bonaparte's, Ring-billed, Herring, and Great Black-backed gulls are common. Little, Thayer's, Lesser Black-backed gulls, and Black-legged Kittiwakes are sometimes seen and, during the coldest months, Iceland and Glaucous gulls are possible. There are records for Mew and California gulls. Purple Sandpipers and Snowy Owls have been seen on the rocks of the breakwater in winter.

Bay Shore Power Plant   *See Oregon Power Plant.*

Beaver Creek State Wildlife Area   *On Ohio 15 6 miles north of Bryan in*
Williams County. (Map A–5)

If you want to find a representative sample of the birds that breed in extreme northwestern Ohio, this 153-acre wildlife tract can be extremely rewarding. There is a 40-acre beech-maple woods, the creek, brushy areas, and fields.

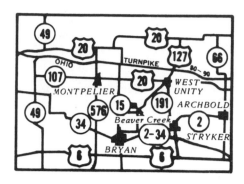

Near the entrance, look for Eastern Kingbirds, Indigo Buntings, and Field Sparrows. A Belted Kingfisher is often present along the creek; in the woods there are Eastern Wood-Pewees, Tufted Titmice, House Wrens, Gray Catbirds, Brown Thrashers, Red-eyed Vireos, Cerulean Warblers, Ovenbirds, and Rufous-sided Towhees. Red-tailed Hawks can be seen in the vicinity, and Barred Owls nest in the woods.

Bedford Reservation and Tinkers Creek Gorge   *Take Ohio 14 south of Cleveland to Egbert Road. (Map B–6)*

This 1,335-acre tract is an important part of Cleveland's Emerald Necklace system of metropolitan parks. Rugged hiking trails, a deep gorge, and beautiful scenery make this a delightful place to visit any time of the year. Upland forests are beech-maple, oak, hickory, and ash, while mountain maple, yellow birch, and hemlock are found in the floodplain. There are bridle paths and several picnic areas.

Rewards of a hike into the gorge area during the breeding season will include the discovery of the Winter Wren, Solitary Vireo, Magnolia and Canada warblers. Other breeding birds found on the reservation include the Broad-winged Hawk, Great Horned Owl, Pileated Woodpecker, Acadian and Least flycatchers, Cerulean Warbler, American Redstart, Ovenbird, Louisiana Waterthrush, and Scarlet Tanager. Black-throated Green and Blackburnian warblers have also been known to nest.

Berlin Reservoir State Wildlife Area   *Located midway between Youngstown, Akron, and Canton, the area can best be reached on U.S. 224, which crosses the reservoir. (Map B–7)*

This 6,763-acre impoundment attracts large numbers of waterbirds in March and the first two weeks of April. Loons and grebes are frequently seen along

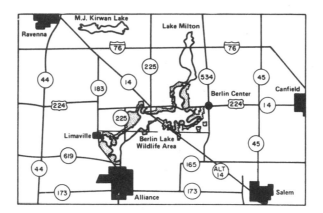

with considerable numbers of Canada Geese, occasional flocks of Tundra Swans, and a few Snow Geese. Large concentrations of American Black Ducks and Mallards are sometimes present, as well as lesser numbers of Green-winged Teal, Northern Pintail, Blue-winged Teal, Gadwall, American Wigeon, Redhead, Ring-necked, and Lesser Scaup ducks, Common Goldeneye, Bufflehead, all three mergansers, and Ruddy Duck. During the fall, lowered water levels sometimes create mudflats which attract a variety of shorebirds.

Big Creek Park   *On old Ohio 44 in Geauga County .75 mile north of Chardon. (Map B–8)*

Large upland woods, stands of hemlock in shaded valleys, and small lakes create a diversity of habitats attractive to a large variety of birds. Broad-winged Hawks and Ruffed Grouse nest here along with Pileated Woodpeckers and, possibly, Long-eared Owls.

    Other nesting birds include the Black-capped Chickadee, Veery, Yellow-throated Vireo, Cerulean and Black-and-white warblers, American Redstart, Ovenbird, Hooded Warbler, Scarlet Tanager, and Rose-breasted Grosbeak. Blackburnian Warblers are a possibility in the hemlocks, and Chestnut-sided Warblers may be found along some of the woods' brushy edges. Wood Ducks, Blue-winged Teals, and American Wigeons are counted among the waterfowl that occur on the lakes. In winter, look for Red and White-winged crossbills, Common Redpolls, and Pine Siskins, especially in the hemlocks.

Brecksville Reservation   *From Cleveland, take I-77 south to the Brecksville exit and go east on Ohio 82 or turn south on U.S. 21. (Map B–9)*

This 2,768-acre tract of oak-hickory, beech-maple, and hemlock relict forests is another important link in Cleveland's Emerald Necklace system of metropolitan parks. The area is outstanding geologically for its exposed faces of Mississippian age Berea sandstone, Bedford shale, Cleveland shale (containing fragments of giant armored fish), and fossil-rich Chagrin shale. There is a trailside museum, a labeled nature trail, and an asphalt-paved Trail for All People designed for the handicapped.

Migration time, especially in the spring, produces hordes of transient birds. Hawks are apt to be seen soaring overhead (a few species nest), various waterbirds are seen along the Cuyahoga River, and flycatchers, thrushes, vireos, warblers, and finches seem to be everywhere on a good day.

Birds breeding at Brecksville include the Red-tailed Hawk, American Kestrel, Eastern Screech-Owl, Great Horned and Barred owls, Ruby-throated Hummingbird, Belted Kingfisher, Red-headed, Downy, and Hairy woodpeckers, Northern Flicker, Eastern Wood-Pewee, Eastern Phoebe, Purple Martin, and Northern Rough-winged and Barn swallows. Also the Blue Jay, American Crow, Black-capped Chickadee, Tufted Titmouse, White-breasted Nuthatch, House Wren, Blue-gray Gnatcatcher, Eastern Bluebird, Veery, Wood Thrush, American Robin, Gray Catbird, Brown Thrasher, Cedar Waxwing, European Starling, Yellow-throated, Warbling, and Red-eyed vireos, Yellow, Cerulean, and Black-and-white warblers, American Redstart, Ovenbird, Louisiana Waterthrush, Scarlet Tanager, Northern Cardinal, Rose-breasted Grosbeak, Indigo Bunting, Rufous-sided Towhee, and Chipping, Field, and Song sparrows.

To find Yellow-throated Warblers during May and June, from the town of Brecksville take State Route 82 east to the intersection with Riverview Road. Turn right (south) and proceed down the hill, turn right on Chippewa Creek Drive, go about half a mile to bridge, and park. Look and listen for the birds in the big sycamore trees.

Burke Lakefront Airport   *Leave Ohio 2 at East Ninth Street in downtown Cleveland (just east of the municipal stadium) and follow North Marginal Road. (Map B–10)*

An unusual number of rare birds have been attracted to this pocket-sized airport in the heart of downtown Cleveland. Good views of the field can be obtained by following the drive east along the fence. Shorebird rarities frequently put down here during their migrations in the spring, summer, and fall. Species observed have included the Black-bellied Plover, Lesser Golden-Plover, Piping Plover, Willet, Upland Sandpiper, Whimbrel, Hudsonian Godwit, Marbled Godwit, Buff-breasted Sandpiper, and Wilson's and Red-necked phalarope.

Even more unexpected have been records such as the Lark Sparrow, Sharp-tailed Sparrow, and Western Meadowlark. The airport is one of the best

Whimbrel

places in Ohio to find Snowy Owls during the winter months. Look for them on nearby breakwaters and retaining walls along the lake. Snow Buntings are found from late fall to early spring, and Water Pipits are frequently seen from October into December and again in March and April.

Castalia Pond   *Take either U.S. 20 or U.S. 6 to Ohio*
101, which goes through the small town
of Castalia, southwest of Sandusky.
(Map A–11)

The pond is in the middle of town; it is fed by a steady flow of water from springs associated with the Blue Hole. (The Blue Hole, also in Castalia, is a beautiful, seemingly bottomless 10-acre pool. Every day nearly 2 million gallons of water well up in it from a vast network of underground limestone channels nearly 100 square miles in area, most of it lying south of Castalia.) Water in this 12-acre pond remains open during the winter and attracts large numbers of waterfowl, which can be observed and photographed at extremely close range.

Some of the birds that can be seen here between December and March include the Pied-billed Grebe, Horned Grebe, Canada Goose, Wood Duck, Green-winged Teal, American Black Duck, Mallard, Northern Pintail, Blue-winged Teal, Northern Shoveler, Gadwall, American Wigeon, Canvasback, Redhead, Ring-necked Duck, Lesser Scaup, Common Goldeneye, Bufflehead,

Hooded Merganser, and Ruddy Duck. Rarer species have included the Mute
Swan and Snow Goose.

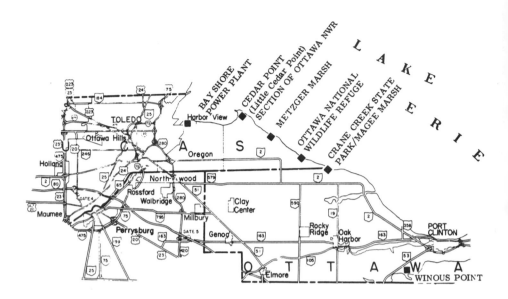

Cedar Point National Wildlife
Refuge (Little Cedar Point)

East of Toledo, turn off Ohio 2 onto
Decant Road (10.9 miles west of Crane
Creek State Park) and proceed north to
Cedar Point Road. Look for the sign
marking the new entrance to the refuge
which is off Corduroy Road and leads onto
a scenic drive atop new dikes that encircle
the entire marsh. (Map A–12)

Administered by and part of the Ottawa National Wildlife Refuge Complex,
this 2,245-acre marsh is one of the best all-round birding areas in the state.
Permission to enter the area is difficult to obtain, but a bird census is taken the
first Sunday of each month. Organized groups are conducted on tours of the
refuge. For further information, write Refuge Manager, Ottawa National Wildlife Refuge Complex, 14000 W. State Route 2, Oak Harbor, Ohio 43449, or
phone (419) 897-0211.

One of the ornithological attractions at Cedar Point NWR is the possibility of seeing large numbers of migrating Blue Jays. On favorable days in late
April and early May, as flock after flock pass overhead, several thousand can
be seen in an hour or two. An even more interesting spectacle is provided by

the jays engaged in reverse migration when the flocks stream by in a southeast-erly direction.

When walking along the dikes, keep a sharp lookout for migrating hawks. The westward movement of raptors around the end of Lake Erie is an almost daily occurrence from March until the middle of May, and includes birds that have arrived along the lakeshore from as far east as Port Clinton. During the spring months, the numerous woodlots along Ohio 2 and south of that high-way often harbor many hawks seeking food and a place to rest until conditions are favorable for continuing their migration. Species most often seen, when they take to the air, are Sharp-shinned and Broad-winged hawks. Some North-ern Harriers, Cooper's, Red-shouldered, and Red-tailed hawks will also be observed during a good flight. Turkey Vultures and American Kestrels com-monly follow the same flightline. Rough-legged Hawks are decidedly scarce, and Merlins and Peregrine Falcons are rare, although a few are seen each year.

Most birders enter the refuge to see a diversity of waterbirds–bitterns, herons, egrets, geese, ducks, rails, and shorebirds. Landbirds, however, are frequently an equal if not greater attraction in late April and May, when prodi-gious concentrations sometimes occur wherever there are trees or adequate cover. Open expanses of water and marsh are visible from many vantage points. The deeper pools are a stopping place for most of the duck species and many other waterbirds. In March, Tundra Swans are almost always present, sometimes in the hundreds. Ospreys investigate the marsh during their migra-tions, but seldom remain for any length of time. One or two Great Horned Owls can usually be flushed out of the trees any time of the year.

Birds that nest or spend the summer at Cedar Point NWR include the Pied-billed Grebe, American and Least bitterns, Great Blue Heron, Great Egret, Cattle Egret, Green-backed Heron, Black-crowned Night-Heron, Can-ada Goose, Wood Duck, Green-winged Teal, American Black Duck, Mallard, Northern Pintail, Blue-winged Teal, Northern Shoveler, Gadwall, American Wigeon, Redhead, Hooded Merganser, Ruddy Duck, Turkey Vulture, Bald Eagle, Northern Harrier, Cooper's, Red-shouldered, and Red-tailed hawks, American Kestrel, Ring-necked Pheasant, King and Virginia rails, Sora, Com-mon Moorhen, and American Coot.

Also Killdeer, Spotted Sandpiper, Herring and Ring-billed gulls (occa-sional breeders, sometimes in goose tubs), Caspian, Common, and Black terns, Mourning Dove, Yellow-billed Cuckoo, Eastern Screech-Owl, Great Horned Owl, Chimney Swift, Ruby-throated Hummingbird, Belted Kingfisher, Red-headed (irregular) and Downy woodpeckers, Northern Flicker, Eastern Wood-Pewee, Acadian and Willow flycatchers, Eastern Phoebe, Great Crested Flycatcher, Eastern Kingbird, Horned Lark, Purple Martin, Tree, Northern Rough-winged, and Bank swallows, Blue Jay, American Crow, Tufted Tit-mouse, White-breasted Nuthatch (irregular), House, Sedge, and Marsh wrens (rare and irregular), Eastern Bluebird, American Robin, Gray Catbird, Brown Thrasher, Warbling Vireo, Yellow Warbler, Common Yellowthroat, Northern Cardinal, Indigo Bunting, Dickcissel (irregular), Chipping, Field, Savannah, Song, and Swamp sparrows (rare), Red-winged Blackbird, Eastern Meadowlark, Northern Oriole, and American Goldfinch.

The fall migration of landbirds lacks the dramatic impact of the northward movement in the spring, but there can be moments of excitement. Tree Swallows seem to be everywhere and from midsummer on there are wandering bands of Bobolinks and other early migrants to look for, not to speak of shorebird arrivals and increased numbers of Cattle Egrets and other nomads among the heron tribe. Rarely, the Sharp-tailed Sparrow invades the Lake Erie marshes in late September and October, but by then there are plenty of other things to look for, including the first returning waterbirds.

Charles Mills Lake

Take Ohio 30 8 miles east of Mansfield.
(Map A–13)

This large lake (1,350 acres) attracts significant numbers of waterbirds in both spring and fall; in the latter season, many linger until the water freezes. In spring, scan the water for Gadwalls, American Wigeons, and rafts of diving ducks composed of Canvasbacks, Redheads, Ring-necked Ducks, Lesser Scaups, and Buffleheads. In fall, good numbers of Red-breasted Mergansers have been seen here, along with Hooded and Common mergansers.

Surrounding woods, in spring and summer, provide breeding habitats for Red-headed Woodpeckers, Great Crested Flycatchers, Wood Thrushes, Cerulean Warblers, Ovenbirds, Scarlet Tanagers, and Northern Orioles.

Clear Fork Reservoir

Take I-71 in Richland County to Ohio
97; proceed west 1 mile past Lexington.
(Map A–14)

Ohio 97 closely follows the south shore of this 1,000-acre reservoir surrounded by beech-maple woods. There are numerous vantage points to look over the water for migrant waterfowl. Ospreys are sometimes seen in April and May and again from late August to mid-October. Common Loons, Pied-billed and Horned grebes, Double-crested Cormorants (becoming more common in Ohio), American Coots, gulls, and terns can all be found in season. A few of the summer residents are Cooper's Hawk, Eastern Kingbird, Carolina Chickadee, Wood Thrush, Cedar Waxwing, Yellow-throated Vireo, Cerulean Warbler, American Redstart, Ovenbird, Summer Tanager (occasionally), Scarlet Tanager, and Rose-breasted Grosbeak.

Special regional insert

Cleveland Waterfront   *(Map B-15)*
Winter Birding

Winter birding along urban shorelines of Lake Erie in the Greater Cleveland area can offer special thrills. The deeper waters of the lake's central basin are preferred by many species, but the area's man-made facilities—warm-water outflows from power plants and other industries, offshore breakwaters, harbors, marinas, and piers—also attract by offering open water, shelter, and resting places during the colder months. Here the intrepid birder can find vagrants from east and west, wintering boreal species, and more southerly inclined birds that have been induced to linger.

Nowhere else in Ohio can so many interesting species be seen from Thanksgiving to the first part of March. Many of the most common waterbirds are often present in huge aggregations, but it is the hope of finding rare and accidental species that adds real gusto to the birder's quest. Such birds include Red-throated and Pacific loons, Red-necked, Eared, and Western grebes, Northern Gannet, Brant, Eurasian Wigeon, Common and King eiders, Harlequin Duck, Oldsquaw, all three scoters, Barrow's Goldeneye, Gyrfalcon, Purple Sandpiper, Red Phalarope, all three jaegers, Black Guillemot, Snowy Owl, Northern Hawk-Owl, Northern Shrike, winter finches, and the following gulls: Little, Common Black-headed, Heermann's, Mew, California, Thayer's, Iceland, Lesser Black-backed, Glaucous, Black-legged Kittiwake, Sabine's, and Ivory. Winter sightings elsewhere on the Great Lakes of Yellow-billed Loon, Ross's Gull, and Ancient Murrelet have raised hopes of those and other rare species turning up sooner or later.

Lakeside winds can be bitter, a test of one's will as much as one's clothing, and all those birds bobbing in the waves or wheeling overhead are a great test of one's identification skills. The variety of immature and non-breeding plumages, particularly among the gulls, presents a nearly inexhaustible series of challenges. Eventually one can be proud of distinguishing the differences between female and immature scoters and eiders and, once learned, how easy it is to pick out a Black-legged Kittiwake from multitudes of resting Bonaparte's Gulls by its short legs. Such cold-weather birding experiences are exhilarating and make up for aching fingers and frozen noses.

Other field tips to bear in mind: Harlequin Ducks usually occur singly or in pairs in rough water near breakwaters. Scoters are often seen in rafts of Greater or Lesser Scaups. Loons tend to be more solitary. Purple Sandpipers

Observation Sites in the Cleveland Region

1 Location of observation sites
*Restricted access

⊞ Urban areas

🝙 Metropolitan par[k]

--- County lines

1. Akron Lakes
2. Avon Lake Power Plant
3. Bedford Reservation
4. Brecksville Reservation
5. Burke Lakefront Airport
6. Cuyahoga Valley National Recreation Area
7. East 72nd Street
   (Cleveland Lakefront State Park)
8. Eastlake Power Plant
9. Edgewater Park & Perkins Beach
   (Cleveland Lakefront State Park)
10. Euclid Creek Reservation
11. Findley State Park
12. Headlands Beach State Park
13. Hinckley Reservation
14. Holden Arboretum
15. LaDue Reservoir
16. Lake Isaac
17. Lake Rockwell

18. Lake View Cemetery
19. Little Mountain*
20. Lorain Lakefront & Power P[lant]
21. Mentor Marsh
22. North Chagrin Reservation
23. Rocky River Reservation
24. Shaker Lakes
25. Sims Park
26. Stebbins Gulch*

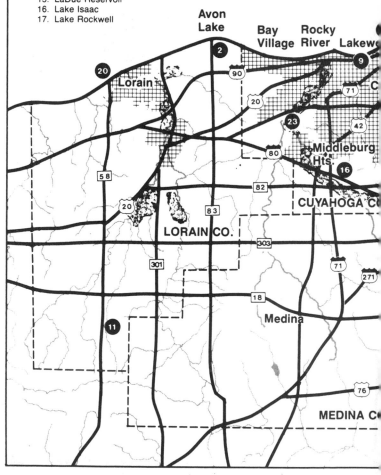

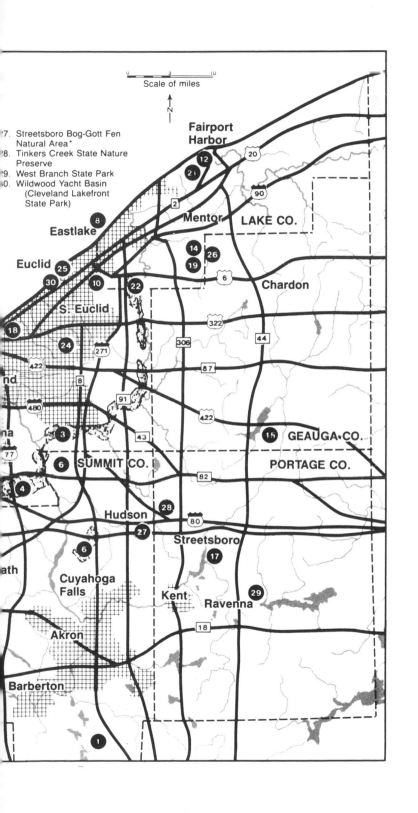

7. Streetsboro Bog-Gott Fen
   Natural Area*
8. Tinkers Creek State Nature
   Preserve
9. West Branch State Park
0. Wildwood Yacht Basin
   (Cleveland Lakefront
   State Park)

Scale of miles

N

Fairport
Harbor

Mentor   LAKE CO.

Eastlake

Euclid

S. Euclid

Chardon

Cleveland

SUMMIT CO.

GEAUGA CO.

PORTAGE CO.

Hudson

Streetsboro

Cuyahoga
Falls

Kent   Ravenna

Akron

Barberton

Little Gulls

are found on rocky breakwaters, nonchalantly feeding just beyond breaking waves.

The old axiom, "the worse the weather, the better the birding" is often true. Strong northerly winds and drifting ice tend to bring many waterbirds closer to shore. During long periods of extremely cold weather as well as late in the winter, populations thin out and the remaining individuals concentrate near unfrozen water. These are the times when Thayer's, Iceland, and Glaucous gulls are most often found near the power plants at Eastlake, East 72nd Street, Avon Lake, and Lorain. Following are brief descriptions of smaller sites worth investigating, listed from east to west.

Eastlake Power Plant   *In Eastlake along Ohio 283, turn north*
on Erie Street to a parking area.

If the parking lot is iced over and closed, pull off along the road near the entrance and walk in; otherwise the area is accessible to wheelchairs. This small site offers an excellent vantage point which has provided many sightings of rare birds. Waterfowl and gulls gather near the plant's warm-water discharge.

Sims Park   *In Euclid, take Babbitt Road north from*
I-90, then east on Lakeshore Boulevard to
the entrance at East 231st Street.

Good views of waterfowl and smaller numbers of offshore gulls from the bluff
and a pier.

Wildwood Park   *In Cleveland, take Neff Road from I-90*
north to the entrance.

A small harbor with a walkable breakwater, in addition to a creek estuary.
Look for waterfowl and gulls both in the harbor and out on the lake.

Euclid Beach Park   *In Cleveland, located off Lakeshore*
Boulevard just west of Wildwood Park.

Presents a wider expanse of lakefront than Wildwood Park, with good views of
the lake from bluffs and a pier.

Marginal Road   *In Cleveland, from the East 55th Street*
exit off I-90, take North Marginal Road
to the east.

After pulling off the road at safe points, small coves can be scanned for waterfowl. The marinas in the area often host thousands of resting gulls on their
piers. Check the distant breakwaters for Snowy Owls, Purple Sandpipers, and
Harlequin Ducks in nearby choppy waters.

Areas East of Edgewater Park   *Within Edgewater Park, at the Park's*
northeasternmost corner.

At the northeast corner of the parking lot, a paved walkway on a breakwater
leads east toward the water treatment plant. Huge flocks of gulls and some
waterfowl are often seen here, and Snowy Owls can sometimes be found on
the remote breakwaters. Another vantage point can be reached by going east
toward the Yacht Club to a parking lot next to the plant. Walk out the pier into
the basin.

Lakewood Park   *Off Lake Avenue in Lakewood.*

A large area of the lake can be scanned from behind the fence on the high
bluff.

Rocky River Park   *In Rocky River, take Morewood Road*
                                        north off Rte. 6 to the entrance.

This tiny park's overlook platform, accessible to wheelchairs, affords a good view of the lake. Large rafts of ducks are often within spotting scope range. This has been one of the best spots to find all three scoters.

> End of regional insert

Conneaut Harbor   *In Conneaut, follow Ohio 531 to where it*
                                        ends at Broad Street. Turn left and
                                        proceed to the harbor. (Map B–16)

Drive down the hill and turn left toward the boat launch area. You can stop anywhere along here to view the harbor and the sandbar. You can then follow the road that goes west along the base of the hill to the sandbar. If you decide to drive out to the sandbar be careful to stay on the roadway and check conditions before driving onto the sandbar. This road is closed in the winter, but there is a little pulloff in front of the gate that provides a good view of the sandbar.

Areas to check: the sandbar for shorebirds and gulls, the channel south of the sandbar for waterfowl, the cattail area to the west for herons, and the inner harbor and breakwater for odds and ends.

The list of rare and unusual birds is extensive and varied. Included are Eared Grebe, American White Pelican, Brown Pelican, Snowy Egret, Little Blue Heron, Brant, Oldsquaw, all three scoters, Osprey, Bald Eagle, Peregrine Falcon, Piping Plover, American Avocet, Willet, Hudsonian and Marbled godwits, Purple Sandpiper, Wilson's and Red phalaropes, Laughing, Franklin's, Little, Common Black-headed, Iceland, and Glaucous gulls, Snowy Owl, Northern Mockingbird, and LeConte's Sparrow. It is also worth checking the marina area which can be reached by returning to the main road and turning left. Conneaut Park can be good for an overview of the harbor and for migrating songbirds. The park is reached by going back to Ohio 531 and driving west about one mile to the entrance.

Crane Creek State Park   *See Magee Marsh Wildlife Area.*

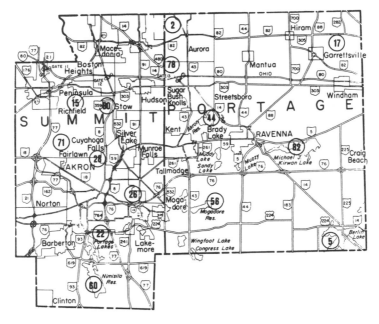

Akron Area

Deep Lock Quarry Metropolitan Park

Take I-77 in Summit County to the village of Peninsula; the park is located on Riverview Road south of town.
(Map B-17)

Once a Berea sandstone quarry shipping millstones and grindstones around the world, this 191-acre park was also the site of a lock in the canal between Akron and Cleveland. Now there is a pleasant woodland, with nature trails, plus many mementos of days gone by.

During May migration, flycatchers, thrushes, vireos, tanagers, finches, and swarms of warblers pass among the trees and shrubs. On a red-letter day, you may see twenty or more warbler species.

In early summer, trails along the old canal and the Cuyahoga River can be especially rewarding. One should see or hear Wood Ducks, both cuckoos, Ruby-throated Hummingbirds, Belted Kingfishers, five woodpecker species, Eastern Wood-Pewees, Eastern Phoebes, Great Crested Flycatchers, Eastern Kingbirds, Northern Rough-winged and Barn swallows, Black-capped Chickadees, Tufted Titmice, White-breasted Nuthatches, House Wrens, Wood Thrushes, Gray Catbirds, Cedar Waxwings, Warbling and Red-eyed vireos, Yellow and Cerulean warblers, Common Yellowthroats, Northern Cardinals, Indigo Buntings, Chipping and Song sparrows, Northern Orioles, and American Goldfinches.

Dry Creek Access   *On U.S. 24 1 mile west of the village of*
                                         Texas in Henry County. (Map A–18)

This pocket park along the Maumee River is always worth checking for waterbirds in spring and fall. There are apt to be some surface feeding ducks along with Common Goldeneyes, Buffleheads, and Common Mergansers. Warbling Vireos and Northern Orioles nest in sycamores along the river, and Ospreys frequently patrol the river during their migrations.

Eagle Creek Nature Preserve   *From the intersection of Ohio 88 and Ohio*
                                       82 in Garrettsville, go east on 82 for 2
                                       blocks to the flashing light. Turn left
                                       (north) at the light onto Center Road.
                                       Follow Center Road for 2.3 miles to
                                       Hopkins Road and turn right (south).
                                       Visitors' parking lot is on Hopkins Road.
                                       (Map B–19)

These 441 acres are unique in the variety of habitats they offer. A glacial stream cut through Mississippian rock to create a south-facing slope with an inspiring forest featuring huge white oaks and a north facing slope of beech-maple forest. There is also a floodplain with attendant buttonbush swamp, a number of small peat bogs, and marshland. Beaver ponds, fox dens, and a fine assortment of breeding birds attest to the wilderness aspects of this spot. A few of the breeding birds are the Wood Duck, Red-tailed Hawk, Yellow-billed Cuckoo, Eastern Screech-Owl, five species of woodpeckers, five flycatcher species, including the Willow Flycatcher, Black-capped Chickadee, Carolina Wren (cyclic), Veery, Wood Thrush, Yellow-throated and Red-eyed vireos, Blue-winged, Yellow, and Cerulean warblers, Ovenbird, Common Yellowthroat, Scarlet Tanager, Rufous-sided Towhee, Chipping, Field, and Song sparrows, and Northern Oriole.

Edgewater Park and Perkins Beach   *Take U.S. 20 to the Edgewater Park exit at West 70th Street in Cleveland. (Map B–20)*

An excellent point along Cleveland's lakeshore for observing a fine variety of loons, grebes, diving ducks, and gulls during the fall, winter, and early spring. This locality includes a wooded drive high atop a bluff that affords an out-standing view of the waters offshore, and a small park at water level combining a small beach and a breakwater. Except in the coldest winters, there is usually some open water. Many rare species have been reported in the vicinity.

Look for Red-throated (rare) and Common loons, Pied-billed and Horned grebes, occasional puddle ducks, Canvasbacks, Redheads, Ring-necked Ducks, Greater and Lesser scaups, Common Goldeneyes, Buffleheads, Red-breasted Mergansers (often the most common duck in early winter), American Coots, and Bonaparte's, Ring-billed, and Herring gulls.

Among the decidedly unusual birds that have been observed are the Glossy Ibis, Brant, Common and King eiders, Black, Surf, and White-winged scoters, Sandhill Crane, Red-necked Phalarope, Franklin's, Little, Iceland, and Glaucous gulls, Black-legged Kittiwake, and Snowy Owl. In December 1963, a Rock Wren was identified in the area. Look for rare Purple Sandpipers along breakwaters and rocky retaining walls.

During March and April, migrating Blue Jays, Mourning Doves, Northern Flickers, and other landbirds sometimes stream by in impressive numbers. At this time, too, hawks are frequently seen flying eastward along the lakeshore. During the height of the spring migration, the trees and bushes are often alive with warblers.

Fairport Harbor   *Take I-90 east of Cleveland, exit onto Ohio 44, and proceed north. (Map B–21)*

From October to April, this is an excellent place to find Common Loons, Horned Grebes, a variety of puddle ducks, and most of the diving ducks. Large numbers of gulls gather here in this area of protected water, especially in the late fall and early spring.

Some of the rare species that have been encountered in the harbor and vicinity include the Eared Grebe, Northern Gannet, Black and White-winged scoters, Whimbrel, Purple Sandpiper, Pomarine and Parasitic jaegers, Laughing, Iceland, and Glaucous gulls, Black-legged Kittiwake, and Roseate Tern.

Findlay Reservoirs

Take Ohio 37 southeast of Findlay about 3 miles to Township Road 234; proceed north to either Township Road 205 or 207 and turn east. Both roads circle the reservoirs and provide access to two ramp areas. (Map A–22)

These sizeable upground reservoirs are excellent for waterfowl after the ice has broken up in the early spring and from October to freezeup. Geese, ducks, and a few Tundra Swans stop over in the spring, but most of the rarities are seen in the fall. Then be on the lookout for the Red-throated Loon, Red-necked Grebe, Double-crested Cormorant, and rafts of diving ducks that might contain Oldsquaws and Black, Surf, or White-winged scoters. After rainy weather, wet spots in nearby fields attract shorebirds such as the Black-bellied Plover, Lesser Golden-Plover, Greater and Lesser yellowlegs, Pectoral Sandpipers, Short-billed Dowitchers, and small peeps. Laughing and Franklin's gulls have been recorded here along with flocks of graceful Bonaparte's Gulls, Herring Gulls, and Ohio's most common gull, the Ring-billed.

Findley State Park

On Ohio 58, in Lorain County, 4 miles south of Wellington. (Map B–23)

A 93-acre lake surrounded by beech-maple woods and pine trees attracts a few waterbirds in the spring and from October to freezeup. In winter, half a dozen bird feeders are in operation and can be observed from the roadways. At these times, Downy and Hairy woodpeckers, Blue Jays, Black-capped Chickadees, Tufted Titmice, White-breasted Nuthatches, Rufous-sided Towhees, Tree and Song sparrows, Dark-eyed Juncos, and American Goldfinches can be seen to good advantage. A Varied Thrush visited one of these feeders during the winter of '79–'80.

Purple Finches, Red and White-winged crossbills, Common Redpolls, Pine Siskins, and Evening Grosbeaks are possible in the winter, especially in the area of pine trees. Some of the country roads a few miles north of the park are well worth investigating in winter for the Cooper's Hawk, Horned Larks, Northern Shrike (rare), Lapland Longspurs, and Snow Buntings.

Breeding birds in the park include the Wood Duck, Sharp-shinned Hawk, American Woodcock, Yellow-billed Cuckoo, Barred Owl, Belted Kingfisher, Eastern Wood-Pewee, Veery, Wood Thrush, Yellow and Cerulean warblers,

American Redstart, Ovenbird, Hooded Warbler, Scarlet Tanager, Rose-breasted Grosbeak, and Rufous-sided Towhee.

Firestone Metropolitan Park   *South of Akron, take I-224 to South Main Street, then south to Swartz Road, east to Harrington Road and the Tuscarawas parking lot on the northwest side of Harrington Road. (Map B-24)*

The Tuscarawas River flows through this 250-acre swamp forest of oak, tulip, cherry, ash, elm, and alder trees. Red-shouldered and Broad-winged Hawks probably nest here, in addition to Red-headed and Pileated woodpeckers, Willow Flycatchers (in areas of shrub and alder), Black-capped Chickadees, Veeries, Cedar Waxwings, Yellow-throated, Warbling, and Red-eyed vireos, Blue-winged and Cerulean warblers, American Redstarts, Ovenbirds, Scarlet Tanagers, Northern Cardinals, Rufous-sided Towhees, Chipping, Field, and Song sparrows, and Northern Orioles.

Five Mile Creek Access   *On Ohio 111, 5 miles south of Defiance. (Map A-25)*

This pocket park on the Auglaize River provides a view of the water above the power dam. Small numbers of waterfowl stop here in spring and late fall including the Canada Goose, American Black Duck, Mallard, Northern Pintail, American Wigeon, Redhead, Ring-necked Duck, Lesser Scaup, Common Goldeneye, Common Merganser, and Ruddy Duck. On cool days in April and May, look for Chimney Swifts and all the swallow species skimming low over the water.

Fowler Woods   *Take Ohio 13, in Richland County, 6 miles northwest of Olivesburg to Noble Road. Proceed east on Noble Road to the intersection with the Olivesburg-Fitchville Road. (Map A-26)*

With trees undisturbed for well over 100 years, this preserve has 80 acres of forest, about 50 acres in near-virgin condition. Another part of the area is swamp forest, with beech-maple woods on higher ground. Surrounding fields are in various stages of natural succession and should yield Horned Larks, Field, Vesper, Savannah, and Grasshopper sparrows, and Bobolinks.

Barred Owls, Pileated Woodpeckers, Yellow-throated Vireos, Blue-winged, Yellow, and Cerulean warblers, American Redstarts, Ovenbirds, Kentucky

Warblers, Scarlet Tanagers, Rose-breasted Grosbeaks, and Northern Orioles are among the nesting birds.

Geneva State Park

In Ashtabula County, just west of Geneva-on-the-Lake and the intersection of Ohio 531 and 534. (Map B–27)

Near the intersection of Routes 531 and 534 there is a small parking area that affords a good view of Lake Erie. All three scoter species and Eared Grebe have been seen here. Traveling south on Ohio 534 from the intersection and taking the first road west will take you to the main park entrance.

The road to the marina is good for woodland breeders such as Ovenbirds and Hooded Warblers. At the east end of the marina parking lot an area of dead trees is a good place to look for migrant flycatchers and woodpeckers. Red-headed Woodpecker, Olive-sided Flycatcher, and Western Kingbird have been seen here. Check the gravel parking area for Water Pipits, Lapland Longspurs, and Snow Buntings, in season, then look over the marina for waterfowl and Snowy Owls. From mid-November through December especially, look the breakwater over for Purple Sandpipers.

The large building north of the marina plays host to a few Cliff Swallows and large numbers of nesting Barn Swallows. Scan the surrounding grassy areas for anything unusual. Brant and Whimbrel have been found feeding here. If you leave the main entrance and travel west, you will come to a beach parking lot (closed in the winter) and another smaller lot farther west that are good places to observe passing waterfowl. The lakeside trail has yielded Long-eared and Northern Saw-whet owls and congregations of migrant passerines. Still farther west is a small stream which attracts occasional herons and rails. The entire area is good for migrating hawks in the spring.

Goll Woods Nature Preserve

Take Ohio 66 2.5 miles north of Archbold in Fulton County; turn west on Township Road F and proceed 2.9 miles to the third crossroad, then turn south to the parking lot entrance. (Map A–28)

The 320 acres of this preserve constitute one of the best remnants of the Black Swamp Forest in Ohio. Bur oaks, white oaks, and yellow oaks achieve sizes of five feet or more in diameter and are estimated to be 400 to 500 years old. Other sections of the woods contain beech-maple, elm, red oak, basswood, and ash trees.

At the parking lot, look and listen for Northern Flickers, Eastern Kingbirds, House Wrens, American Robins, Cedar Waxwings, Field Sparrows, and Eastern Meadowlarks.

Nesting birds include Red-shouldered and Red-tailed hawks, American Woodcock, Yellow-billed Cuckoo, Red-headed and Hairy woodpeckers, Acadian, Willow, and Great Crested flycatchers, Eastern Kingbird, Black-capped Chickadee, White-breasted Nuthatch, Eastern Bluebird, Veery, Wood Thrush, Brown Thrasher, Yellow-throated and Red-eyed vireos, Chestnut-sided Warbler (edges), Cerulean and Black-and-white warblers, American Redstart, Ovenbird, Scarlet Tanager, Northern Cardinal, Rose-breasted Grosbeak, and Northern Oriole.

Goodyear Heights Metropolitan Park
Located on the east side of Akron at Darrow Road and Newton Street, west of Ohio 9, north of I-76. (Map B–29)

This 372-acre park is an excellent place to see large numbers of spring and fall migrants right in the city of Akron. Grass recreation areas are interspersed with wooded slopes of beech-maple and pine; there is a 15-acre lake, a marshy spot, and numerous thick shrub plantings.

Overwintering birds include Downy and Hairy woodpeckers, Northern Flicker, Black-capped Chickadee, Tufted Titmouse, White-breasted Nuthatch, Brown Creeper, Golden-crowned Kinglet, Northern Cardinal, Song and White-throated sparrows, and Dark-eyed Junco.

Gordon Park (72nd Street, Cleveland Lakefront State Park)
On the near east side of Cleveland, take I-90 to the Liberty Boulevard exit and turn left at the stop sign. (Map B–30)

Located on the lakeshore on Cleveland's near east side, the park benefits in the winter from the warm water outflow of the power plant. In the fall, winter, and early spring, this is a particularly good spot to observe waterbirds that have sought the protection of the breakwaters, and they can often be seen at close range.

Rare bird records include Red-throated Loon, Northern Gannet, Brant, Harlequin Duck, King Eider, Black, Surf, and White-Winged scoters, Sharp-tailed and Curlew sandpipers, Little and Glaucous gulls, Black-legged Kittiwake, Pomarine and Parasitic jaegers, Snowy Owl, Northern and Loggerhead shrikes, and Smith's Longspurs.

Other birds found during the cold months include Common Loon, Pied-billed and Horned grebes, Mallard, American Wigeon, Canvasback, Redhead, Ring-necked Duck, Greater and Lesser scaups, Oldsquaw (scarce), Common Goldeneye, Bufflehead, Common and Red-breasted mergansers, Bonaparte's, Ring-billed, and Herring gulls. The three latter species sometimes occur in the tens of thousands. Also search the shore and breakwaters for Snow Buntings.

Gorge Metropolitan Park

Located on Front Street between Cuyahoga Falls and Akron, north of the Cuyahoga River, west of North Main Street, and west of Route 8 and the Route 59 expressway. (Map B–31)

Pileated Woodpeckers range through this dramatic 250-acre park where the Cuyahoga River tumbles and splashes over several miles of falls and rapids. There are also nesting Cooper's and Red-shouldered hawks, Great Horned and Barred owls, Belted Kingfishers, Red-bellied and Hairy woodpeckers, Black-capped Chickadees, Chestnut-sided, Black-throated Green, Cerulean, and Black-and-white warblers, American Redstarts, Ovenbirds, Common Yellowthroats, Hooded Warblers, Scarlet Tanagers, Rose-breasted Grosbeaks, and Rufous-sided Towhees.

Hambden Orchard Wildlife Area

On Ohio 608 3 miles south of the village of Hambden in Geauga County. (Map B–32)

Beech-maple and oak-hickory woods dominate this 841-acre tract which also includes two pools, fields, and an old orchard. Wood Ducks, Mallards, and Blue-winged Teals feed and rest on the ponds; Ruffed Grouse, American Woodcocks, Eastern Screech-Owls, and Barred Owls inhabit the woods. In spring and summer, look and listen for the Red-headed Woodpecker, Hairy Woodpecker, Eastern Wood-Pewee, Acadian and Great Crested flycatchers, Black-capped Chickadee, Tufted Titmouse, White-breasted Nuthatch, House Wren, Wood Thrush, Brown Thrasher, Veery, Yellow-throated and Red-eyed vireos, Cerulean Warbler, American Redstart, Ovenbird, Hooded Warbler, Scarlet Tanager, and Rose-breasted Grosbeak.

Purple Martins and Tree and Northern Rough-winged swallows skim over the ponds; flocks of Cedar Waxwings can be found along the forest edges along with Gray Catbirds, Common Yellowthroats, and Chipping, Field, and Song sparrows.

Harrison Lake State Park

Take U.S. 20 west from Toledo approximately 30 miles; turn south on Fulton County Road 26. (Map A–33)

Beech woods, pine trees, and old fields surround this 105-acre lake in northwestern Ohio. When winter ice breaks up, flocks of American Black Ducks, Mallards, Northern Pintails, American Wigeons, Common Goldeneyes, and Common Mergansers can be seen here to good advantage. Blue-winged Teals and American Coots feed close to the shore and around the marshy end of the lake. Close scrutiny of the neighboring fields should yield Horned Larks and Vesper and Savannah sparrows.

Hayes State Memorial   *Take U.S. 6 in Fremont to the intersection*
of Buckland and Hayes avenues.
(Map A–34)

This 25-acre wooded estate was the home of Rutherford B. Hayes, 19th president of the United States. There are walks, driveways, and paths that enable one to explore the gardens, cool wooded slopes, and broad lawns.

In late March and early April, there are Yellow-bellied Sapsuckers, Black-capped Chickadees, Tufted Titmice, Red- and White-breasted nuthatches, Brown Creepers, Winter Wrens, Golden- and Ruby-crowned kinglets, Hermit Thrushes, Solitary Vireos (late April), Yellow-rumped Warblers, Northern Cardinals, White-throated Sparrows, Dark-eyed Juncos, and Pine Siskins. Later in the spring, large hemlock trees attract migratory Northern Parulas, Cape May, Black-throated Green, and Bay-breasted warblers.

Headlands Beach State Park   *Take U.S. 90 east from Cleveland; exit*
onto Ohio 44 North and follow it to the
park. (Map B–35)

This 120-acre parcel of land embraces a beach, a small amount of marsh habitat, picnic facilities, and a bit of swamp forest. The park is near Mentor Marsh and Fairport Harbor. Loons, grebes, and diving ducks are frequently seen offshore, including rarities such as the Oldsquaw and all three scoters. A surprising number of rare shorebirds turn up here in the spring migration and a few less in the summer and fall. Read the account on Mentor Marsh State Nature Preserve for additional birds found in the vicinity.

Hiestand Woods Park   *Off Ohio 127 on Hospital Drive at the*
edge of Van Wert. (Map A–36)

This pleasant little park has hiking trails through a wooded area and along a small stream. There are picnic tables set amid large oak and honey locust trees that attract numerous warblers and other birds during the spring migration. There are also Red-headed and Pileated woodpeckers, Eastern Wood-Pewees, Eastern Kingbirds, Northern Rough-winged and Barn swallows, Warbling Vireos, Common Yellowthroats, Indigo Buntings, Song Sparrows, and Northern Orioles.

Hinkley Reservation   *Take I-71 in Cleveland to Ohio 303;*
                                     proceed east, then turn south on Bellus
                                     Road and drive to a park road on the
                                     right that leads to the dam on Hinkley
                                     Lake. (Map B–37)

Famous for its roost of Turkey Vultures, the reservation is the southernmost
unit of the Cleveland Metropolitan Park District's Emerald Necklace. The region offers hillside woods of beech, oak, maple, and chestnut, and spectacular
outcroppings of Pennsylvanian period conglomerate rock.

Among the birds that can be found during the late spring and summer (in
addition to permanent residents) are the Great Blue Heron, Green-backed
Heron, Wood Duck, Mallard, Turkey Vulture, Cooper's, Red-shouldered,
Broad-winged, and Red-tailed hawks, American Kestrel, Killdeer, Spotted
Sandpiper, Mourning Dove, Black-billed Cuckoo, Eastern Screech-Owl, Great
Horned and Barred owls, Ruby-throated Hummingbird, Belted Kingfisher,
Red-headed, Downy, and Hairy woodpeckers, Northern Flicker, Eastern
Wood-Pewee, Acadian Flycatcher (infrequent), Purple Martin, Tree, Northern
Rough-winged, and Barn swallows, Blue Jay, Common Crow, and Black-
capped Chickadee.

Also the Tufted Titmouse, White-breasted Nuthatch, House Wren, Blue-
gray Gnatcatcher, Eastern Bluebird, Veery (uncommon), Wood Thrush, American Robin, Gray Catbird, Brown Thrasher, Cedar Waxwing, Solitary, Yellow-
throated, Warbling, and Red-eyed vireos, Blue-winged, Yellow, Cerulean, and
Black-and-white warblers, American Redstart, Ovenbird, Louisiana Waterthrush, Kentucky Warbler, Common Yellowthroat, and Hooded Warbler.

Investigate the woods near the boathouse for nesting Red-breasted Nuthatches, Golden-crowned Kinglets, Solitary Vireos, Magnolia and Blackburnian warblers.

Additional summer birds include the Scarlet Tanager, Northern Cardinal,
Rose-breasted Grosbeak, Indigo Bunting, Rufous-sided Towhee, Chipping,
Field, and Song sparrows, and Northern Oriole. During the summer and early
fall, scan the lakeshore for Great Egrets and occasional shorebirds. In spring
and fall, the entire area is good for migrating landbirds.

Holden Arboretum   *Located on Sperry Road north of U.S. 6*
                                  near Mentor. (Map B–38)

A delightful place to visit any time of the year, the arboretum features over
5,000 different kinds of cultivated woody plants, flowering trees, and shrubs.
Its scenic nature trails meander along the east branch of the Chagrin River past
ponds and through wooded ravines. One trail leads to ornithologically interest-

ing Stebbins' Gulch, which is described later in this account. Other trails wind through a beech-maple climax forest, which also includes oak, sassafras, sour gum, and dogwood trees. Nature courses are offered; there are guided tours and nature walks.

The impressive list of birds seen here includes most of the warblers that occur in Ohio. During the spring and fall migrations, Corning Lake attracts good numbers of waterfowl, including Tundra Swans. Aeration keeps the water open, and Canada Geese and a variety of ducks stay through the winter.

Some of the rare and unusual species that have been observed at the arboretum include the Eared Grebe, Least Bittern, Yellow-crowned Night-Heron, Greater White-fronted and Snow geese, Eurasian Wigeon, Barrow's Goldeneye, Peregrine Falcon, Yellow Rail, Northern Saw-whet Owl, Pileated Woodpecker, Western Kingbird, and Black-throated Gray Warbler. One of the first House Finch incursions into Ohio was in this region.

Summer birds include the Pied-billed Grebe, Green-backed Heron, Canada Goose, Wood Duck, Mallard, Turkey Vulture, Cooper's, Red-shouldered, Broad-winged, and Red-tailed hawks, American Kestrel, Spotted Sandpiper, Yellow-billed and Black-billed cuckoos, Eastern Screech-Owl, Great Horned and Barred owls, Ruby-throated Hummingbird, Belted Kingfisher, Red-headed, Red-bellied, Downy, and Hairy woodpeckers, Northern Flicker, and Eastern Kingbird.

Also look for the Eastern Wood-Pewee, Willow Flycatcher, Eastern Phoebe, Great Crested Flycatcher, Purple Martin, Tree, Northern Rough-winged, Bank, and Barn swallows, Blue Jay, American Crow, Black-capped Chickadee, Tufted Titmouse, Red-breasted (rare) and White-breasted nuthatches, House Wren, Eastern Bluebird, Veery, Wood Thrush, American Robin, Gray Catbird, and Brown Thrasher.

Other breeding species are the Yellow-throated, Warbling, and Red-eyed vireos, Yellow, Magnolia (rare), and Cerulean warblers, American Redstart, Ovenbird, Common Yellowthroat, Scarlet Tanager, Northern Cardinal, Rose-breasted Grosbeak, Indigo Bunting, Rufous-sided Towhee, Eastern Meadowlark, and Northern Oriole.

Stebbins' Gulch is just off Mitchell Mills and Wisner roads north of Route 6. This rugged little gorge was formed by erosion many eons ago and was named after Hosea Stebbins, who purchased the property in 1860. The gulch and adjoining land was given to the Holden Arboretum in 1958. In places the steep walls rise several hundred feet above the streambed. Along one section, the stream drops almost 300 feet in a mile and is festooned with numerous falls and cascades along its course. In the deeper parts of the gulch, the temperature seldom rises above 75° on the hottest summer days; thus trees and plants of more northern climes thrive here. The gulch contains a mixed hardwood forest of mature hemlocks and white pines on the north-facing slopes.

Among the bird specialties found nesting here or present during the breeding season are: Acadian and Least flycatchers, Black-capped Chickadee, Brown Creeper, Winter Wren, Solitary Vireo, Brewster's Warbler (hybrid), Nashville, Magnolia, Black-throated Green, and Blackburnian warblers, Louisiana Waterthrush, Mourning and Canada warblers, and Dark-eyed Junco.

Huron Harbor and Breakwater

Take Ohio 6 into the center of Huron and turn north at the intersection with Ohio 13. (Map A–39)

Impressive numbers of rare birds are observed here with remarkable regularity, especially since dredging spoil has been pumped into a large circular area bounded by steel walls and a breakwater on the west side of the pier. To the east of the pier parking lot, a wide channel is a favorite concentration point for Bonaparte's, Ring-billed, and Herring gulls. Gulls and waterfowl also frequent a bay to the west, which can be viewed from a small municipal park. Depending on their seasonal movements along the lake—east in fall and early winter, west in late winter and spring—thousands of gulls frequently fill the air, with additional large numbers resting on nearby sand and coal piles. At other times, additional concentrations of gulls may be found resting on shoals in the Huron River just north of the U.S. 2 bridge, or wheeling over marinas closed for the winter.

A veritable forest of phragmites separates the pier from the dredge spoil area favored by shorebirds. Trails through this labyrinth of reeds are difficult to negotiate and, even when present, do not last for long. The only sure way to make a close approach to the area is to rock-hop along the southern side of the breakwater, a journey to be cautiously undertaken, especially with a scope and tripod. Within the enclosure, pools and mudflats (usually best in the southwest corner) invite gulls, terns, and shorebirds. In late summer and fall, even grass-loving Buff-breasted Sandpipers can be found on the drier portions of the flats. Scan carefully through the assorted peeps for rare species such as Red Knot, Western, White-rumped, and Baird's sandpipers. In wet places and in shallow water along the edges of the mudflats, look through flocks of yellowlegs for the methodically probing motions of Stilt Sandpipers searching for food. Short-billed and Long-billed dowitchers and Common Snipe also favor such watery habitat. In even deeper water, look for the pirouetting of winter-plumaged Wilson's or Red-necked phalaropes. In late fall and early winter, Snow Buntings sometimes feed along the shore.

Cottonwoods and willows near the pier sometimes yield migrant passerines and, during the winter months, there is always the possibility of finding a Northern Shrike or a small flock of Common Redpolls. Persistent *spishing* might even produce a rare Sharp-tailed Sparrow.

Out by the lighthouse at the pier's end, survey the lake in appropriate seasons for loons, grebes, cormorants, and diving ducks. If the going gets tough in cruel weather, the rule along the lake is that the worst weather often produces the most interesting birds.

Rare birds seen in the area include: Pacific Loon, Northern Gannet, Oldsquaw, all three scoters, Piping Plover, American Avocet, Spotted Redshank, Whimbrel, Hudsonian Godwit, Red Phalarope, Pomarine and Parasitic jaegers, and the following gulls: Laughing, Franklin's, Little, Common Black-headed, Mew, California, Thayer's, Glaucous, Sabine's, and Black-legged Kittiwake. A Least Tern and carefully authenticated Arctic Tern have been seen here. One or more Snowy Owls occur during most winters.

Kelley's Island

Reached by plane via Island Airlines in Port Clinton, or by ferry from Marblehead or Sandusky. (Map A–40)

A unique and relaxing birding area unlike anyplace else in Ohio where you can rent a bicycle in the summertime or hoof it any time of the year. The island is in a comparatively wild state and interesting birds can be found almost anywhere. Some of the better places, however, are the State Wildlife Area in the east-central part of the island, the State Park, the marsh south of the camping area (home to the rare Lake Erie water snake), and the rocky outcroppings along the north shore. From this location, you can watch passing waterbirds and, in the fall when there is a north wind blowing, watch passerine birds fly in off the lake from the direction of Pelee Island. Observers in the past have witnessed impressive diurnal migrations of such birds as Black-capped Chickadees and Golden-crowned Kinglets. Hawk-watching is good to the west and northwest of the campground.

Christmas Bird Counts done on the island are interesting. Rock Doves and House Sparrows are scarce and are outnumbered by Hermit Thrushes (counts of 50 to 60 are not unusual), hundreds of Black-capped Chickadees, and Yellow-rumped Warblers. Wintering birds find plentiful food and cover in the island's cedars and shrubby dogwoods.

Some of the interesting breeding birds include: Green-backed Heron, Wood Duck, Herring Gull, Yellow-billed Cuckoo, Ruby-throated Hummingbird, Belted Kingfisher, Least Flycatcher, Great Crested Flycatcher, all of the Ohio swallows with the possible exception of Cliff Swallow, Black-capped Chickadee, House Wren, Gray Catbird, Brown Thrasher, Cedar Waxwing, White-eyed and Red-eyed vireos, Yellow Warbler, American Redstart, Common Yellowthroat, Yellow-breasted Chat, Northern Cardinal, Indigo Bunting, Rufous-sided Towhee, Chipping, Field, and Song sparrows, Orchard Oriole, possibly the Northern Oriole, Purple Finch, House Finch, and American Goldfinch.

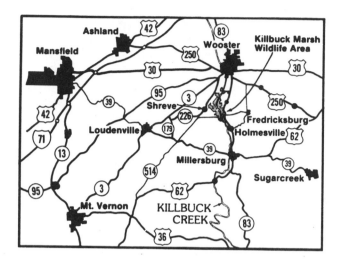

Killbuck Marsh Wildlife Area

From Ohio 83 approximately 6 miles south of Wooster, turn west onto Clark Road, or proceed farther south and turn west onto Force or Harrison roads.
(Map B–41)

The largest remaining inland marsh in Ohio, this state wildlife area extends along Killbuck Creek for some eight miles. The region combines the creek and adjacent large tracts of marsh, ponds, woodland, and fields. There are a number of off-road parking spots that make it easier to explore this fine natural area. Prothonotary Warblers can be found along Clark Road and, a bit farther west, along Willow Road. If they cannot be found in these locations, go about a mile south on Route 83 to Force Road and try there, or go another mile south to Harrison Road and check out the area around the parking spaces and the bridge over the creek.

Bird highlights, in season, include American and Least bitterns, Great Blue Heron, Great Egret, Cattle Egret, Green-backed Heron, Canada Goose, Tundra Swan (occasional), Wood Duck, Blue-winged Teal, a scattering of other surface-feeding ducks, Northern Harrier, Red-shouldered and Red-tailed hawks, Ring-necked Pheasant, King Rail (rare), Virginia Rail (uncommon), Sora, Common Moorhen, American Coot, Greater and Lesser yellowlegs, Solitary and Spotted sandpipers, Common Snipe, and American Woodcock.

In late spring and summer, the Yellow-billed Cuckoo is fairly common, as are the Red-headed Woodpecker and Eastern Kingbird. Listen for the distinctive *fitz-bew* song of the Willow Flycatcher. Tree, Northern Rough-winged, and Barn swallows nest and Marsh Wrens breed in the dense cattails.

In sycamore and cottonwood trees, look and listen for Warbling Vireos and Northern Orioles. Yellow Warblers and Common Yellowthroats are common, and in late summer Cedar Waxwings become abundant. Swamp Sparrows nest in the marsh and a few can probably be found year-round.

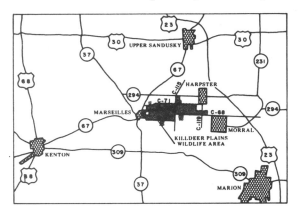

Killdeer Plains Wildlife Area

From U.S. 23 about 14 miles northwest of Marion, turn west onto Ohio 294; continue through the village of Harpster to County Road 115, then drive south for about 1 mile. (Map A–42)

Over 8,000 acres of impoundments, cropland, fields in various stages of succession, and woods are included in this valuable state wildlife area. Large numbers of Canada Geese and numerous duck species are present in early spring, late fall, and early winter. Small numbers of blue-phased Snow Geese are frequently seen from late October through November. Canada Geese and half a dozen kinds of ducks nest in the area. Good observation points are from atop the earthen mound south of the residence on County Road 115, and along the embankment on the north side of County Road 68. A pair of Bald Eagles has nested in the area during the past several years.

During the colder half of the year, the area is famous for attracting a wonderful variety of hawks and owls. Cruise the little country roads looking for Northern Harriers, Cooper's, Red-tailed and Rough-legged hawks, American Kestrels, and, more rarely, Red-shouldered Hawks. Snowy Owls are rare winter visitors, and Short-eared Owls occur regularly, most often in the fields south and west of the headquarters building. Some years a few pairs remain to nest. Investigate stands of pine trees for Barred, Long-eared, and Northern Saw-whet owls.

Representative summer residents are the Pied-billed Grebe, American Bittern, Great Blue Heron, Green-backed Heron, Canada Goose, Wood Duck, American Black Duck, Mallard, Blue-winged Teal, Turkey Vulture, Northern Harrier (scarce), Cooper's, Red-shouldered, and Red-tailed hawks, American Kestrel, Ring-necked Pheasant, Northern Bobwhite, Sora, Killdeer, American Woodcock, Spotted Sandpiper, Yellow-billed Cuckoo, Great Horned and Barred owls, Belted Kingfisher, Red-headed Woodpecker, Horned Lark, Purple Martin, Tree, Northern Rough-winged, and Barn swallows, Carolina Chickadee, Sedge Wren (erratic), Marsh Wren, Eastern Bluebird, Loggerhead Shrike (rare), Warbling Vireo, Prothonotary Warbler (scarce), Yellow Warbler, Common Yellowthroat, Scarlet Tanager, Summer Tanager (uncommon), Dickcissel (erratic), Chipping, Field, Vesper, Savannah, Grasshopper, Henslow's (erratic), and Song sparrows, Bobolink, Orchard Oriole (uncommon), and Northern Oriole.

During winter months, Killdeer Plains is an excellent place to see flocks of Horned Larks and Snow Buntings, and smaller numbers of Lapland Longspurs.

Rare birds observed have included American White Pelican, Snowy Egret, Glossy Ibis, Mute Swan, White-fronted Goose, Fulvous Whistling-Duck, Golden Eagle, Peregrine Falcon, Sandhill Crane, Marbled Godwit, and Lark and Sharp-tailed sparrows.

Kingwood Center
900 West Park Avenue in Mansfield.
(Map A–43)

This delightful arboretum and garden covers 47 acres and includes a trail that meanders through a woods and meadow. In April and May, many migrant landbirds pass through the trees and shrubs—thrushes and vireos, a colorful variety of warblers, tanagers, grosbeaks, and buntings.

Kyle Woods
On Ohio 224, in Mahoning County,
about 1.5 mile east of Canfield.
(Map B–44)

This 53-acre swamp forest contains sugar maple, black gum, black cherry, oak, and ash trees. Springtime pools of water are alive with salamanders and several species of frogs. A large log house near the preserve was a stopping place on the Underground Railway during the Civil War.

Though modest in size, the preserve offers plenty of food and cover for both migratory and nesting birds. The Winter Wren, Hermit Thrush, Fox Sparrow, Rusty Blackbird, and Purple Finch can be seen here in early spring and again in the fall; Northern Waterthrushes and many of the northern warblers pass through in May.

Breeding birds include the Red-headed Woodpecker, Eastern Wood-Pe-wee, Black-capped Chickadee, House Wren, Gray Catbird, Cedar Waxwing, Yellow-throated Vireo, Yellow Warbler, American Redstart, Ovenbird, Common Yellowthroat, Scarlet Tanager, Indigo Bunting, Rufous-sided Towhee, Field and Song sparrows.

La Due Reservoir   *On U.S. 422 about 10 miles southeast of*
Chagrin Falls. (Map B–45)

This reservoir is the stopping place for a wide variety of waterbirds during the spring and fall migrations. Among these transients, look for the Common Loon, Pied-billed and Horned grebes, Bonaparte's, Ring-billed, and Herring gulls, and most of the duck species commonly seen in Ohio. If water levels are down during the late summer and fall, a variety of shorebirds are apt to be found.

Some of the more unusual occurrences have been a Common Loon in July, Greater White-fronted Goose, Oldsquaw, Yellow Rail, Common Moorhen (nested), Willet, and Sandhill Crane.

Special regional insert

LAKE COUNTY METROPOLITAN PARKS AND NATURE PRESERVES (MAP B–46)
[Chagrin River, Hell's Hollow Reserve, Riverview, Hidden Valley, Hogback Ridge, Lakeshore, Girdled Road, Chapin Forest, and Penitentiary Glen Park and Nature Center]

Chagrin River   *Take State Route 2 east toward Eastlake*
and exit north (left) onto Lost Nation
Road. Go to the second traffic light, turn
west (left) onto Reeves Road, and proceed
to the park sign, where there is a small
parking lot. (Not mapped)

This brand-new Metro Park combines riparian habitat, woods, and fields. Some of the best birding is along a gravel path that follows the river, continues past a picnic area, and enters the woods. Birds seen during the spring of 1994

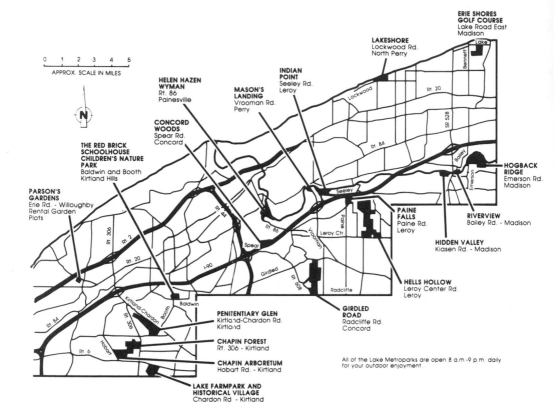

included Olive-sided Flycatcher, Bell's Vireo, and Kirtland's, Connecticut, and Mourning warblers.

Hell's Hollow Reserve

Located in Leroy Township, Lake County. Take Ohio 528 to Thompson. From the town square, go west on Leroy-Thompson Road approximately 4¹ miles to Leroy-Center Road. Proceed west until you arrive at the park.

One of the Lake Metro Parks' largest tracts (708 acres), noted for spectacular views and a dropoff of over 100 feet to the Paine Creek valley. Trails start north of the parking lot. A short loop will take you along the rim of the gorge. A longer, more strenuous trail descends to the creek valley where you can hike through the shade of hemlocks to the music of waterfalls.

Dark-eyed Juncos are rather common during the breeding season (as many as 16 pairs have been counted). Other interesting nesters are: Winter Wren (rare), Solitary Vireo, Black-throated Green and Cerulean warblers, Louisiana Waterthrush, Hooded Warbler, and Canada Warbler (rare).

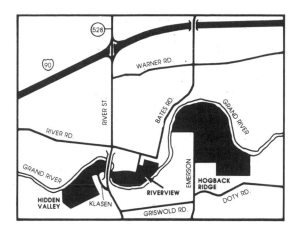

**Riverview/Hidden Valley/
Hogback Ridge**

In Lake County, from Ohio 528: To get to Riverview Park, turn east on River Road, go about 0.5 mile, then turn right and proceed to the entrance. To get to Hidden Valley Park, drive south on 528 across the Grand River and turn west on Klausen Road. The road goes down the hill into the park. To get to Hogback Ridge Park, go south another 0.25 mile and turn east on Griswold Road. Proceed about 1.5 mile to the end of the road and turn left onto Emerson Road, which goes into the park.

Riverview Park has nesting Eastern Phoebes, Carolina Wrens, and Hooded Warblers. At Hidden Valley Park, there is a trail that follows the river west into an area of hemlocks. Breeding birds here include Black-throated Green, Cerulean, and Hooded warblers, Louisiana Waterthrushes, and Dark-eyed Juncos. A Yellow-throated Warbler was found during the summer of 1992. Northern Waterthrushes have been known to nest just past the lavatories. Northern Saw-whet Owls sometimes occur in the winter. Hogback Ridge has many of the same breeding birds as the other two parks, plus Ruffed Grouse and Wild Turkey. A boardwalk makes part of this area wheelchair-accessible.

Lakeshore Metro Park

*In Lake County, off U.S. 20 in North
Perry. Take Antioch Road (the first road
past the Perry Power Plant) about 2 miles
to its end, then turn right on Lockwood
Road and proceed to the park entrance.*

An outstanding area for year-round birding. In spring, the cliffs offer an excellent spot for viewing migrating waterfowl and gulls. The large open field at the west end of the park is equally good for watching migrant raptors and passerines. On favorable May and September mornings, the woods and brushy areas can be alive with warblers and other birds of passage. Summer can also produce late and early stragglers, not to speak of a nice list of nesting birds which include Magnolia, Blackburnian, and Hooded warblers and Pine Siskins. Numerous coniferous trees sometimes attract winter finches.

Some of the unusual and interesting birds that have been seen here include: Red-throated Loon, Red-necked Grebe, Brant, King Eider, Harlequin Duck, Oldsquaw, Bald Eagle, Northern Goshawk, Red Phalarope, Pomarine and Parasitic jaegers, Franklin's, Little, Thayer's, Iceland, and Glaucous gulls, Long-eared, Short-eared, and Northern Saw-whet owls, Connecticut Warbler, Dickcissel, Clay-colored and Henslow's sparrows.

Girdled Road Park

*In Lake County, take Ohio 608 to the
Lake-Geauga county line, then proceed east
on Radcliffe Road to the park entrance.*

A large park of 744 acres with a parking area surrounded by fields of nesting Prairie Warblers, Savannah and Henslow's sparrows, and Bobolinks. Trails through the woods lead to ravines where Wild Turkeys and Black-and-white and Canada warblers nest. Northern Shrikes are occasionally found in winter.

Chapin Forest

*In Lake County, off Ohio 306 just south
of Kirtland. Another entrance is found by
taking 306 to U.S. 6, then traveling west
about 2 miles to Hobart Road and
turning right to the entrance.*

A 331-acre park with scenic overlooks that are good hawk-spotting sites. Some of the breeding birds include: Red-shouldered Hawk, Pine, Black-and-white, and Kentucky warblers, and Dark-eyed Junco. There is a summering record of a Blue Grosbeak. The Hobart Road entrance is sometimes called **Chapin Arboretum** because of the extensive plantings of pines and other evergreens.

Other activities and facilities include cross-country skiing, snowshoeing, playgrounds and athletic fields.

**Penitentiary Glen Park and
Nature Center**   *In Lake County, take Ohio 306 north of
                                   Kirtland to Kirtland-Chardon Road and
                                   proceed south to the entrance.*

A popular park of 328 acres offering a nature interpretive center, feeders, a rehab center, and a small man-made marsh. The field south of the nature center has nesting Eastern Meadowlarks and Bobolinks. There are nesting Sharp-shinned Hawks and other woodland birds typical of the area. A deep gorge can be visited on one of the organized hikes.

End of regional insert

Lake Rockwell   *Take County Road 797, in Portage
                                   County, about 2 miles north of Kent, or
                                   Ohio 14 where it crosses the upper end of
                                   the reservoir. (Map B-47)*

Originally a swamp forest with glacial bog plants, this 800-acre site with its large lake provides the city of Akron with water. Surrounding woods are beech-maple, oak-hickory, and pine. Tundra Swans and Canada Geese linger here in March along with good numbers of surface-feeding and diving ducks, gulls and terns. Breeding birds are representative of Portage and Summit counties and include nesting records for Red-breasted Nuthatches, Pine Warblers, and Northern Waterthrushes.

Leipsic Reservoir   *On Ohio 613 3 miles east of Leipsic in
                                   Putnam County. (Map A-48)*

This modest-sized 30-acre reservoir was built on a branch of Beaver Creek. The groves and thickets around it attract a variety of spring and fall migrants. Late March and early April arrivals include the Belted Kingfisher, Northern Flicker, Eastern Phoebe, Tree Swallow, Eastern Bluebird, Hermit Thrush, Yellow-rumped Warbler, Field and White-throated sparrows.

A few waterbirds, mostly Mallards and Blue-winged Teals, and occasional Pied-billed Grebes pay brief visits to the lake. By the first of May, Spotted

Sandpipers are teetering along the shore, and small troupes of vireos, warblers, and orioles can be found in the surrounding trees.

Little Mountain   *South of Mentor, take Sperry County*
                                                       Road north of U.S. 6. (Map B-49)

Part of Holden Arboretum, this 65-acre site has a stand of white pine and hemlock at an elevation of 1,200 feet. This delightful spot is famed as the nesting locale for a number of species that rarely nest elsewhere in Ohio. These elite birds include the Least Flycatcher, Red-breasted Nuthatch, Solitary Vireo, and Blackburnian Warbler. Pine, Wilson's, and Canada warblers are probable nesters. The Black-throated Green Warbler is an abundant breeder on Little Mountain. Each year from 1933 to 1938, B. P. Bole, Jr., found 10 to 19 of these warblers nesting in a 75-acre tract. He also counted 15 pairs of Oven-birds in the same area in 1939. Other breeding warblers include the Cerulean, Black-and-white, American Redstart, and Hooded. Broad-winged Hawks have been found nesting, and the Ruffed Grouse is an annual breeding bird.

Red-breasted Nuthatch

Little Mountain is an exceptionally fine place to find transient landbirds during the spring and fall migrations. On May 4, 1936, a migrating flock of approximately 200 Black-throated Blue Warblers was encountered by one observer.

Lorain Harbor and Breakwater
Take U.S. 6 to Oberlin Avenue in downtown Lorain, turn north, and go to First Street, which parallels the lakeshore. The municipal pier is between the power plant and the coal dock. (Map B–50)

Thanks to a warm water outflow from the Ohio Edison Power Plant, a sizeable area of the inner harbor never freezes over. One can see a multitude of waterbirds in midwinter without even getting out of the car at dockside.

Search all of the breakwaters and jetties with a spotting scope, especially at the water's edge; sometimes in midwinter a Great Blue Heron or a Black-crowned Night-Heron can be found. Other birds to look for are American Black Ducks, Mallards, Canvasbacks, Redheads, Greater and Lesser scaups, Common Goldeneyes, Buffleheads, and an occasional Oldsquaw. A few Common Mergansers are apt to be present along with larger numbers of Red-breasted Mergansers. Among the gulls, there should be thousands of Bonaparte's and Ring-billed and smaller numbers of Herring gulls. Rarer species of *Laridae* are discussed later in this account.

To get to the breakwater, return to Route 6, proceed east across the bridge on Erie Avenue, turn toward the lake on Arizona Avenue, then drive left one block to Lakeside Avenue. Park along the street and walk down the incline to the breakwater, which is at least half a mile long and angles off into the lake. During the winter months, be sure to bring along plenty of warm clothing, because this can be one of the coldest and windiest places anywhere.

When landbirds are migrating, check out the trees along Lakeside Avenue. Also, at the bottom of the incline, there is a thicket that is an excellent trap for warblers, sparrows, and a variety of other birds.

Once out on the breakwater, look for Common Loons and Horned Grebes, all of the ducks mentioned above, plus additional numbers of Greater Scaups, Oldsquaws, occasional scoters, and Common and Red-breasted mergansers. In winter, there is always a chance of seeing a Purple Sandpiper; during the spring and fall, a few shorebirds frequent the puddles and pools of water that are sometimes present atop the breakwater.

The list of rare birds seen at Lorain, mainly in the two areas described, is impressive. Count among them the Red-throated Loon, Red-necked Grebe, Northern Gannet, Brant, Greater White-fronted Goose, Common and King eiders, Harlequin Duck, all three scoter species, jaegers, and the following gulls: Laughing, Franklin's, Little, Common Black-headed, Heermann's, Mew, California, Thayer's, Iceland, Lesser Black-backed, Glaucous, Black-legged Kittiwake, and Sabine's. Though not rare, the Great Black-backed Gull is seen with regularity during the winter months. A Snowy Owl or two are seen most winters, usually perched on a breakwater.

Lost Creek Reservoir   *Drive 1 mile east of Lima on High Street*
Road. (Map A–51)

This 112-acre reservoir is owned by the city of Lima. The main avian attraction here is the early spring and late fall migration of waterfowl. Species that occur with a fair degree of regularity include Pied-billed and Horned grebes, Canada and Snow (uncommon) geese, Green-winged Teal, American Black Ducks, Mallards, Northern Pintails, Blue-winged Teal, Gadwalls, Canvasbacks, Redheads, Lesser Scaups, Common Goldeneyes, Buffleheads, Hooded Mergansers, and Ruddy Ducks.

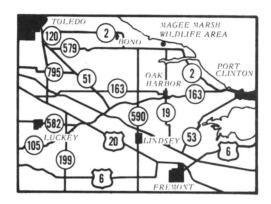

Magee Marsh Wildlife Area   *In Ottawa and Lucas counties, 10 miles*
north of Oak Harbor. The entrance is on
Ohio 2, 17 miles west of Port Clinton and
2 miles west of Ohio 19. (Map A–52)

This wonderful mosaic of marsh, impounded ponds, swamp forest, and the waters of Lake Erie is one of the premier birding locations in the United States. The area includes the Crane Creek State Park beach. The marsh was purchased by the state in 1951, and in 1956 the Crane Creek Wildlife Experiment Station was established. Taken together, the area comprises 1,821 acres of extensive marshes, ponds, woods, Lake Erie beach, and fields. An attractive nature center is located a short drive from the entrance, and a paved road crosses the width of the marsh to the lakeshore, where there are beaches, woods, picnic facilities, and a fine nature trail.

Considerable numbers of Canada Geese have been induced to nest in the area. With the addition of migrants, many thousands of these birds are present in late October and November and again in March. In May and June, proud parent birds shepherd their goslings about the refuge, even up onto the roads, where it is a common sight to see families of geese holding up traffic.

During the greater part of the year, there is good birding from the moment one enters the wildlife area. A roadside pond just inside the entrance frequently overflows its banks during wet weather and attracts shorebirds, geese, gulls, egrets, and an occasional rail. In spring and summer, there are Purple Martins and Tree Swallows flying about the Visitors Center and there is always the possibility of seeing one of the Yellow-headed Blackbirds that have nested nearby in recent years. The shallow ponds behind the center should be searched for shorebirds such as the Dunlin, a common late spring migrant.

From the Visitors Center, turn left and continue down the road to the east, take the bend to the north and slowly follow the road as it intersects the vast width of Magee Marsh. The water levels vary greatly from year to year and season to season, affecting the ease with which one can see appreciable numbers of birds. When the water is low, mudflats are exposed and the wading birds tend to concentrate in a few favored places. From April through October, there should be good numbers of Great Blue Herons, plenty of Great Egrets (sometimes very close to the road), a few Green-backed Herons, and lesser numbers of the more secretive Black-crowned Night-Herons. In March and April, ducks are plentiful, along with large flocks of American Coots, and a sprinkling of Pied-billed Grebes. Tundra Swans are a possibility during the first part of the period. Ring-billed and Herring Gulls will be liberally scattered about the marsh, and there's always a good chance of finding a little flock of Water Pipits along the water's edge. Look for migrating hawks in the skies.

Toward the end of April, when many of the waterfowl have departed, there are still some birds that stay behind to nest. A few other waterbirds arrive daily as the season progresses into May. Coots abound; every once in a while, an American Bittern will flounder into the air on its bicolored wings and flap across the marsh; and there's always a chance of seeing a King, Virginia, or Sora rail. Every other willow seems to have its Yellow Warbler, and their *sweet-sweet-sweet tsee tsee* songs fill the air with music.

Continuing out the causeway, check the dredged channels on either side of the road for White-rumped Sandpipers, Dunlin, and other small peeps. Wilson's Phalaropes are sometimes seen in this area. Be on the lookout for Bonaparte's Gulls and Forster's Terns. Each species shows flashes of silvery white in their wings. Caspian, Common, Forster's, and Black terns are sometimes seen over the marsh or migrating along the shore. As the road nears the lake, it turns left through an area that was once used for parking. Pull off here and climb up on the retaining wall along the lake. Scan the slabs of concrete for Ruddy Turnstones and Sanderlings and search the lake for additional gulls and terns. Sometimes Palm Warblers and White-crowned Sparrows will be feeding in the protective shelter provided by the wall.

When a good migration is underway, hundreds of swallows can be observed flying westward along the shore, and during the early morning hours

many other species can be seen engaged in a similar migration. From April 25
to May 15, migrating flocks of Blue Jays in a single morning sometimes total
thousands of individuals (and sometimes reverse their migration). Also look
for migrating flocks of Cedar Waxwings, Indigo Buntings, Goldfinches, and
smaller numbers of other species. Here also is a section of relatively undisturbed beach sometimes visited by Bald Eagles. Look for Ruddy Turnstones,
Sanderlings, and other shorebirds. Scan the offshore waters for passing
waterbirds.

After returning to the car, carefully look over the old parking lot—which is
now mostly grown up in grass—for shorebirds. Then proceed west to the new
parking area, paying particular attention to the elongated pond on the left side
of the road. When the water is down, look for shorebirds; when the water is
up, look for Common Moorhens and Least Bitterns. A boardwalk built with
tax check-off funds circles part of this pond so you will have a second opportunity to look it over when you are on foot.

Entrances to the boardwalk bird trail are located at the west and east ends
of the parking lot. The boardwalk is handicapped-accessible and was built to
provide a safe, clean circuit of the area—a fine example of a "migrant trap."
Surrounded by marsh on three sides and the lake on the fourth, this bit of
swamp forest attracts huge numbers of passerine birds during the spring migration and only slightly fewer numbers in the fall. On days after heavy nocturnal
migration, many species concentrate here and continue to build up even during
the daylight hours. The fact that the lake lies just beyond undoubtedly tempts
many spring arrivals to rest and feed here before continuing their journeys.
Conversely, in the autumn, for many birds this is the first landfall after crossing
the lake.

The mature cottonwoods found here, along with numerous willows,
snarls of grapevines, and dense thickets of underbrush are frequently swarm-
ing with warblers and other migrants. During late April and May, 20 to 30
warbler species are often found within a few hours. Scarlet Tanagers, Rose-
breasted Grosbeaks, and Northern Orioles are usually present in good numbers. Every bend in the boardwalk is apt to reveal a new surprise: young Great
Horned Owls, looking like balls of yarn, a Whip-poor-will or woodcock almost
at one's feet.

In late March and April, grapevines and red cedars are favorite hiding
places for Northern Saw-whet Owls. Eastern Screech-Owls are permanent residents but difficult to find. Great Horned Owls start nesting in February and
March, often utilizing goose nesting tubs that have been erected about the
swampy woodland. The boardwalk winds past various inundations, ponds,
inlets, and rivulets that honeycomb the entire area. From March to April,
Rusty Blackbirds frequent these wet places, and there is always a chance of
seeing a Brewer's Blackbird. May specialties include several pairs of nesting

Prothonotary Warblers, migrant Northern Waterthrushes, and Mourning, Hooded, Wilson's, and Canada warblers.

Over 300 species of birds have been recorded at Magee Marsh. Cattle Egrets have increased in numbers, Glossy Ibis show up more frequently, and a few Sandhill Cranes are seen almost every year. The list of western strays grows more impressive with each passing year.

Other rarities include: American White Pelican, Little Blue and Tricolored herons, White-faced Ibis, Fulvous Whistling-Duck, Mute Swan, Greater White-fronted Goose, Brant, Cinnamon Teal, Eurasian Wigeon, Common Eider, King Eider, Golden Eagle, Merlin, Peregrine Falcon, Gyrfalcon, Yellow and Black rails, Wilson's and Piping plovers, Black-necked Stilt, American Avocet, Willet, Whimbrel, Hudsonian and Marbled godwits, Buff-breasted Sandpiper, Ruff, all three phalaropes, Groove-billed Ani, Snowy Owl, Western Kingbird, Northern Shrike, Townsend's Warbler, Kirtland's Warbler, Clay-colored, Lark, LeConte's, Sharp-tailed, and Harris' sparrows, and Western Meadowlark.

Malabar Farm   *Take Ohio 95, in Richland County, about*
                                5 miles northeast of Butler; follow the
                                signs to Bromfield Road. (Map A–53)

This lovely home surrounded by rolling hills and green fields was the dream and joy of author and environmentalist Louis Bromfield, who converted four worn-out and eroded farms into an agricultural Eden. A tour of the house with its fine furniture, artwork, and memorabilia is highly recommended.

Someone once said that Bromfield was as big as all outdoors. Not only did he stand 6'1" in his stocking feet, but, even more important, friends and acquaintances were impressed with his deep convictions—amounting almost to a religious fervor—about the proper use of land.

Thousands of people visited Malabar during his lifetime, including many celebrities. Proudly Bromfield would show his visitors his thousand-acre farm, including sleek herds of Holsteins, and tell them how he reclaimed marginal hillside fields by nourishing the soil with humus and using new methods of disking and plowing. He would point out the luxuriant multiflora rose hedge-rows, which he said served as the perfect fence, windbreak, and refuge for wildlife.

Summer bird residents include the Ruby-throated Hummingbird, Eastern Phoebe, Eastern Kingbird, Northern Rough-winged and Barn swallows, House Wren, Eastern Bluebird, Gray Catbird, Northern Mockingbird, Cedar Wax-wing, Yellow Warbler, Northern Yellowthroat, sometimes the Summer Tanager, Indigo Bunting, Chipping, Field, and Song sparrows, Eastern Meadowlark, and Northern Oriole. In the cultivated fields, look for Vesper, Savannah, and Grasshopper sparrows.

Bald Eagle on Nest

Mallard Club Marsh Wildlife Area

In Lucas County, 3 miles east of Bono on Ohio 2, turn north on Decant Road until it dead-ends at Cedar Point Road. There is a parking lot off Decant Road and two more along Cedar Point Road. (Map A-54)

This 410-acre marsh, located between Cedar Point NWR and Maumee Bay State Park, is one of Ohio's newest wildlife areas. Neglected in recent years, the area is being restored by the Division of Wildlife to its once productive state.

Year-round access is allowed on walking trails atop dikes that surround the marsh units. The dike along the western border and Cusino Ditch provides a path to Maumee Bay, where good waterfowl and gull watching opportunities exist. The dike bordering the Cedar Point unit of the Ottawa National Wildlife Refuge is off limits and is signed as such.

This is great birding country. King Rails can be found fairly regularly in the marsh unit northwest of the Decant Road parking lot. Bald Eagles can be seen soaring overhead and, from March to the first part of May, on favorable days impressive numbers of raptors can be seen turning the corner of Lake Erie.

Maumee Bay State Park   *In Lucas County, east of Toledo, drive
                                      north from Ohio 2 on either Norden or
                                      North Curtice Road approximately 2 miles.
                                      (Map A–55)*

In winter, look for Northern Harriers, Red-tailed and Rough-legged hawks, Short-eared and occasional Snowy Owls. From the shore, scan the bay for diving ducks and walk the beach for Snow Buntings.

During the spring, a large hill provides a fine observation point to look for migrating raptors that traditionally fly around the western end of Lake Erie. March and April days with a southwest wind are the best. Maximum numbers are usually seen from mid-morning to mid-afternoon. Surrounding fields are good for open-country birds and often attract Western Meadowlarks. A board-walk winding through a lakeside swamp forest is an excellent viewing area for migrant songbirds, as well as providing a passageway to the haunts of Long-eared and Northern Saw-whet owls. East of the golf course along Cedar Point Road, just west of the entrance to Little Cedar Point NWR, is a marshy area worth checking for bitterns, moorhens, and rails.

Maumee River Rapids   *Follow U.S. 24 southwest from Toledo.
                                      (Map A–56)*

This is a favorite place to find waterfowl during the winter months, and shore-birds in late summer and fall when the water is low. The best birding area is between the community of Maumee and the Providence Dam.

During winter the water remains open, attracting large numbers of ducks, including many American Black Ducks, Mallards, American Wigeons, and Common Goldeneyes. Among these, look for Green-winged Teals, Northern Pintails, and Gadwalls. Diving ducks are sometimes found in the deeper pools of the rapids; in addition to Common Goldeneyes, there may be Canvasbacks,

Redheads, Ring-necked Ducks, and Common Mergansers. Ring-billed Gulls, along with a few Herring Gulls, are seen almost year-round.

Many species of shorebirds have been found in the rapids, especially during the southward movement extending from July through October. Commonly seen species are the Killdeer, Greater and Lesser yellowlegs, Solitary and Spotted sandpipers, Ruddy Turnstone, Sanderling, Semipalmated, Least, White-rumped, and Pectoral sandpipers, Dunlin, and Common Snipe. Other birds to look for include herons and egrets, geese, Ospreys, rails, terns, Belted Kingfishers, swallows, pipits, sparrows, and Rusty Blackbirds.

Medusa Marsh   *In Erie County, located on the south side of Sandusky Bay. Take Ohio 2 to Ohio 269 South. Go north at that exit until the road dead-ends at Barrett Road (about 1 mile). Go east on Barrett Road another mile to the marsh. (Map A–58)*

Medusa Marsh is actually a series of privately owned marshes located between Sandusky Bay and Route 2. Originally owned by the Medusa Cement Company, all are now in private hands and are closed to the public. However, from the side of Barrett Road you can see a good portion of the whole area. A car makes an excellent blind; stay in it to avoid scaring the birds.

Parts of the road are sometimes posted against stopping when a pair of Bald Eagles nests nearby, and this regulation should not be taken lightly. It is strictly enforced. There is also a Great Blue Heron colony that due to its age might soon be abandoned. Because of the buildup of droppings, most colonies will last just so long before the nesting trees die and the birds are forced to find a new site.

A good viewing area for waterfowl in the spring is at the intersection of Routes 269 and 2. A pair of Mute Swans summers at this location. A large expanse of open march on the south side of Barrett Road is probably most productive and is noted for the large numbers of Northern Shovelers that it attracts. If it is a year when they are drawing down the marsh, good numbers of shorebirds can be found. It is a good idea also to look north along the bay. Ospreys and Bald Eagles frequently perch in the trees, and cormorants can sometimes be found sitting on protruding rocks.

A few of the rare birds that have been found here include Little Blue and Tricolored heron, Glossy Ibis, Eurasian Wigeon, Peregrine Falcon, California Gull, and Snowy Owl.

Mentor Marsh State Nature
Preserve

Exit I-90 at Ohio 44 and proceed
through Painesville, then turn west on Ohio
283. Continue about 0.5 mile and turn
right onto Corduroy Road to the Marsh
House. (Map B–59)

Jointly owned by the Ohio Department of Natural Resources and the Cleveland Museum of Natural History, this 619-acre preserve has ponds and adjoining marshy areas bordered by sand dunes and a beech-maple forest. In the early spring, transient waterfowl throng to the preserve: Wood Ducks, Green-winged Teal, American Black Ducks, Mallards, Northern Pintails, Blue-winged Teal, Gadwalls, American Wigeons, Ring-necked Ducks, Lesser Scaups, Hooded Mergansers, and Ruddy Ducks can be found, along with Canada Geese and a few Pied-billed and Horned grebes.

By mid-April, new arrivals include American and Least bitterns, Great Blue Herons, occasional Great Egrets, and Black-crowned Night-Herons. Marshy edges yield Virginia Rails, Soras, Common Moorhens, and American Coots. By the first week in May, all of the swallow species found in Ohio can be seen winging over the ponds. As the spring progresses, migrant landbirds are sometimes present in impressive numbers.

On May 1, 1976, a John Carroll University ornithology class, using tape-recorded calls on the Becker Trail, attracted 100–200 Virginia Rails and Soras. Prothonotary Warblers nest in the area every year.

A few of the rare birds recorded in the vicinity, including the municipality of Mentor, are Northern Goshawk, Merlin, Brunnich's Murre, Black and King rails, Short-eared Owl, Violet-green Swallow, Western Tanager, Blue Grosbeak, Clay-colored and Lark sparrows, and Red Crossbill.

Metzger Marsh Wildlife Area

On Ohio 2, about 7 miles west of Magee
Marsh Wildlife Area, or 1 mile east of
Reno. (Map A–60)

An eroded cove abutting the western edge of Ottawa National Wildlife Refuge, this area features a marina, a wooded point with a breakwater and pier, and extensive marshlands. The trees and brush on the point can attract migrant landbirds, and Bald Eagles sometimes perch in the cottonwoods or soar over the marsh. Gulls and terns rest on sandbars in the inlet and out in the lake and a few shorebirds frequent the rocky breakwater. Geese, swans, and ducks use the marsh in season—in greater numbers when northerly winds deepen the water. On favorable days in March and April, the point is a strategic place to

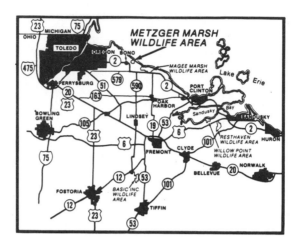

watch migrating flocks of ducks and other waterbirds heading northwest toward their traditional nesting grounds. In spring, summer, and fall, bitterns, herons, egrets, and rails are frequently seen.

The 500-acre marsh is quite shallow, and changes in the wind, especially when it blows from the south or west, can expose extensive mudflats. At such times, a good viewing area is across the road from the marina parking lot where a creekbed and shallow pools of water create varying habitat for a great variety of shorebirds. Other views can be obtained at several pulloffs along the road to the point. A hundred yards or so north of the marina parking lot, a path leads out into the marsh on a brushy finger of higher land with additional views of the marsh and mudflats to the south.

Milan Wildlife Area

Take Ohio 113, in Erie County, 3 miles west of Milan. (Map A–61)

A 200-acre woods of oak, hickory, ash, cottonwood, and maple is transected by the cliff-lined Huron River, providing habitat for a considerable number of nesting birds. Turkey Vultures, Cooper's Hawks, and Red-tailed Hawks nest in or near the area. Other breeding birds include the Yellow-billed Cuckoo, Barred Owl, Red-headed and Pileated woodpeckers, Acadian Flycatcher, Black-capped Chickadee, Veery, Wood Thrush, Brown Thrasher, Yellow-throated Vireo, Black-and-white and Cerulean warblers, Ovenbird, Scarlet Tanager, Rose-breasted Grosbeak, Rufous-sided Towhee, and Song Sparrow.

Mill Creek Park

*Entrances to this park in Youngstown are
at the Mahoning Avenue Bridge at
Glenwood and Falls avenues, and at
Canfield Road, which is also U.S. 62.
(Map B–62)*

The park commences where Mill Creek joins the Mahoning River and then extends southward along a picturesque gorge for seven miles. There are roadways along both sides of the creek. Oak, walnut, sugar maple, and hickory trees cover the hillsides and gorge. Hemlocks grace the slopes of some of the cool, moist spots in the gorge. In addition to the stream, there are three lakes, numerous ponds, and several swamps.

Several productive trails start at the Old Mill on Canfield Road. During the latter part of April and throughout May, large numbers of migrant landbirds can be found in many parts of the park. The vicinity of the lakes, and almost anywhere along the gorge, are especially good areas. Boardman Woods and Flats is relatively undisturbed and can yield hours of enjoyable hiking and birding. It is located at the southern end of the park.

A surprising number of birds nest in the park, including the Green-backed Heron, Red-shouldered Hawk, American Kestrel, American Woodcock, Yellow-billed Cuckoo, Eastern Screech-Owl, Barred Owl, Chimney Swift, Ruby-throated Hummingbird, Belted Kingfisher, Red-headed, Red-bellied, Downy, Hairy, and Pileated woodpeckers, Acadian and Willow flycatchers, Eastern Phoebe, Eastern Kingbird, and Northern Rough-winged and Barn swallows.

Also the Black-capped Chickadee, House Wren, Veery, Wood Thrush, Gray Catbird, Brown Thrasher, Yellow-throated, Warbling, and Red-eyed vireos, Blue-winged, Yellow, Cerulean, and Black-and-white warblers, American Redstart, Ovenbird, Louisiana Waterthrush, Common Yellowthroat, Yellow-breasted Chat, Scarlet Tanager, Northern Cardinal, Rose-breasted Grosbeak, Indigo Bunting, Rufous-sided Towhee, Chipping, Field, Henslow's, and Song sparrows, Orchard and Northern orioles, and Purple Finch.

Mogadore Reservoir

*Take Ohio 43 about 3 miles south of
I-76 just east of Akron. (Map B–63)*

This 1,015-acre site contains a large reservoir partly surrounded with pine plantations, beech-maple and oak-hickory woods. Wood Ducks, Mallards, and probably Blue-winged Teals nest.

From mid-March to early April, Tundra Swans are frequently present, along with large flocks of ducks: Green-winged Teal, American Black Ducks, Mallards, Blue-winged Teal, American Wigeons, Canvasbacks, Redheads, Ring-necked Ducks, Lesser Scaups, Common Goldeneyes, Red-breasted and Hooded mergansers, and Ruddy Ducks. In the fall, before the water freezes, Horned Grebes are sometimes plentiful and there is a chance to see rarities such as the Oldsquaw and all three scoters.

Mohican State Park and State Forest

Take I-71 to the Ohio 97 exit and proceed east to Loudonville, then go 2 miles south on Ohio 3. (Map A–64)

Together, Mohican State Park and the forest which surrounds it make up a scenic and wooded recreation area of over 5,000 acres. The park features a lodge, dining facilities, meeting rooms, gift shop, indoor and outdoor pools, tennis courts, a beach, boating, fishing, hiking trails—and birding.

The Lyons Falls hiking trail affords spectacular views of a Black Hand sandstone (see Black Hand Gorge State Nature Preserve) overhang, great stands of oak-hickory and beech-maple forest, and an abundance of wild-flowers. There are also extensive pine plantations, as well as native pines, and giant hemlocks along many of the rugged slopes.

Pleasant Hill Lake is reached by taking Ohio 95 northeast from Butler. Extending two or more miles from Pleasant Hill Dam to the Mohican River is beautiful Clear Fork Gorge, which may be explored by a nature trail on the north side. Along its banks can be found red maple, Canadian yew, and a stand of virgin white pine and hemlock. The sunny northern slope provides suitable habitat for red and white oaks, tulip trees, beech, and magnificent sycamores.

Birds that are permanent residents include Cooper's and Red-tailed hawks, American Kestrel, Ring-necked Pheasant, Ruffed Grouse, Mourning Dove, Eastern Screech-Owl, Great Horned and Barred owls, Belted Kingfisher, Red-headed, Red-bellied, Downy, Hairy, and Pileated woodpeckers, Blue Jay, American Crow, Black-capped Chickadee, Tufted Titmouse, White-breasted Nuthatch, Carolina Wren, Eastern Bluebird, Northern Cardinal, Rufous-sided Towhee, and Song Sparrow.

Summer residents and nesting birds include a wide variety of attractive species, many of which can be seen and heard by canoeing through the region. Wood Ducks inhabit the Mohican River; Northern Rough-winged, Bank, and Barn swallows skim over the fields; and Northern Orioles and attendant War-bling Vireos are abundant in the streamside sycamores. In 1974, I counted 36 pairs of Warbling Vireos and 30 pairs of Northern Orioles along a six-mile stretch of the river.

In the more open, brushy areas, there is a chance of finding a Golden-winged Warbler among the numerous Blue-winged Warblers. Yellow Warblers and Common Yellowthroats are common. Once in a while, a Yellow-breasted Chat squawks and chatters; Summer Tanagers are possible, and Indigo Buntings and Chipping, Field, and Song sparrows are almost always within earshot. Blue-gray Gnatcatchers and Cedar Waxwings ply the areas between open spaces and wooded edges.

Where there are deeper woods and gorges, look and listen for the many Wood Thrushes present, plus Northern Parulas in the hemlocks, Cerulean and Black-and-white warblers, American Redstarts, Ovenbirds, and Scarlet Tanagers. A Solitary Vireo was once observed along the river in late May, and a Lawrence's Warbler, the rare recessive hybrid of the Golden- and Blue-winged warblers, was observed once in June. Further investigation of the region should reveal additional breeding birds.

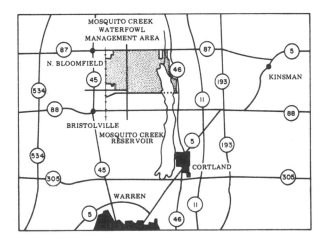

Mosquito Creek Reservoir

Take the Ohio 5 Outerbelt northeast of Warren and exit at Ohio 46 or 305.
(Map B–65)

The 11,857-acre state park and wildlife area that surrounds the reservoir is a first-rate spot for observing waterfowl and shorebirds in season. The reservoir covers 7,850 acres and attracts numerous ducks and geese in the spring and fall. Most of the puddle ducks are common, and rafts of diving ducks are often seen on the wider expanses of water. Canada Geese are common and flocks of Tundra Swans stop over in March and November. On the south side of the reservoir is the park, which combines a beech-maple forest, a swamp, and old fields. Canada Geese now nest here as a result of a program started in 1957.

Shorebirding is good in the summer and fall if the water level drops enough to create mudflats. Among the species seen at such times are the Black-bellied Plover, Lesser Golden-Plover, Semipalmated Plover, Killdeer, Greater and Lesser yellowlegs, Solitary and Spotted sandpipers, Ruddy Turnstone, Western, Least, White-rumped, Baird's, Pectoral, and Stilt sandpipers, Short-billed Dowitcher, Common Snipe, and Red-necked Phalarope. Ospreys are regular migrants, and Bald Eagles are seen occasionally. Common Loons, Horned Grebes, and increasing numbers of Double-crested Cormorants occur in migration. Glossy Ibis, Snow Goose, Oldsquaw, Merlin, Whimbrel, Buff-breasted Sandpiper and Long-billed Dowitcher are among the rare birds that have been recorded.

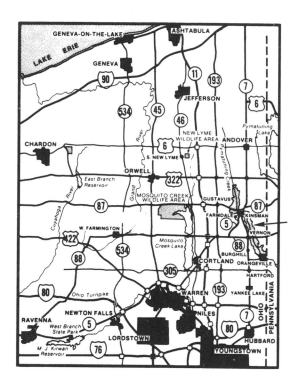

New Lyme Wildlife Area   *On Ohio 46 1 mile east of South New Lyme, in Ashtabula County. (Map B–66)*

This 529-acre swamp forest is composed of pin oak, swamp oak, ash, and elm on ground that stays wet until midsummer. There are fine opportunities here for finding nesting birds rare in other parts of Ohio.

During the spring, Ruffed Grouse can often be heard drumming, and American Woodcocks can be observed performing their nuptial sky dances. In June, this is a breeding place for the Least Flycatcher, Black-capped Chickadee,

Veery, Solitary Vireo (rare), Nashville Warbler (rare), Rose-breasted Grosbeak, Rufous-sided Towhee, and Purple Finch.

Nimisila Reservoir/Portage Lakes   *Take Ohio 619 south from Barberton, or Ohio 93 south from Akron. There are numerous parking spots and access roads. (Map B-67)*

About seven miles long, these irregularly shaped reservoirs are over 3,000 acres in area and are an excellent region to study waterfowl, shorebirds, and many landbirds.

Loons and grebes occur in spring and fall, along with Tundra Swans, Canada Geese, and good numbers of ducks. From April to October, Great Blue Herons, Great Egrets, Cattle Egrets, Green-backed Herons, and occasional Black-crowned Night-Herons can be found with a fair degree of certainty. Green-backed Herons are the first to depart, while a few Great Blue Herons linger into December or later during mild winters.

North of East Nimisila Road and east of Christman Road there is an open bog meadow where bitterns have been found, and Virginia Rails and Soras can be flushed out of the wet spots. In summer and early fall, this entire region should be checked for Marsh Wrens, the much rarer Sedge Wren, Savannah and Henslow's sparrows, and Bobolinks. Some of the plants found here in-

Bobolink

clude sphagnum, fringed gentian, shrubby cinquefoil, blazing star, and small orchids.

Ospreys are seen regularly each spring and fall; shorebirds in good numbers can be discovered where there are mudflats or shallow water from mid-July to mid-October.

North Chagrin Reservation

Take I-90 east of Cleveland and go south on Ohio 91, or, from the I-271 exit at Mayfield Heights, drive east a short distance to Route 91 (SOM Center Road) and drive north several miles. Park entrances will be on the right. (Map B–68)

This large tract of wooded hills along the Chagrin River constitutes the northeast link of Cleveland's Emerald Necklace. The 1,719-acre park contains wildflower and nature trails that meander through the beech-maple climax forest and hemlocks along the deeper ravines. Sunset Pond has an aerating system that keeps some of the water open for ducks and geese all winter.

Canada Geese, American Black Ducks, Mallards, and a few American Wigeons frequently overwinter. Some of the resident birds are the Red-shouldered and Red-tailed hawks, Ruffed Grouse, Barred Owl, Red-bellied, Downy, Hairy, and Pileated woodpeckers, Blue Jay, American Crow, Black-capped Chickadee, Tufted Titmouse, White-breasted Nuthatch, Northern Cardinal, and Song Sparrow.

Summer visitors and nesting birds are Least Bittern (has nested), Great Egret, Black-crowned Night-Heron, Canada Goose, Mallard, Sharp-shinned Hawk (has nested), Red-tailed Hawk, American Kestrel, Virginia Rail (nesting record at the Forest Lane Pond), American Woodcock, Yellow-billed and Black-billed cuckoos, Chimney Swift, Ruby-throated Hummingbird, Belted Kingfisher, Northern Flicker, Eastern Wood-Pewee, Acadian Flycatcher, Eastern Phoebe, Great Crested Flycatcher, Eastern Kingbird, Purple Martin, and Tree, Northern Rough-winged, and Barn swallows.

Also the Carolina (erratic), House, and Sedge wrens, Eastern Bluebird (cyclic), Veery, Wood Thrush, American Robin, Gray Catbird, Brown Thrasher, Cedar Waxwing, Yellow-throated, Warbling, and Red-eyed vireos, Yellow and probably Chestnut-sided warblers, Black-throated Green and Cerulean warblers, American Redstart, Ovenbird, Louisiana Waterthrush, Common Yellowthroat, Hooded Warbler, Scarlet Tanager, Northern Cardinal, Rose-breasted Grosbeak, Indigo Bunting, Rufous-sided Towhee, Chipping, Field, and Song sparrows, and Northern Oriole.

During the spring migration, birds pour through the reservation and a large list of species can be compiled in a single morning.

Lark Sparrow

Special regional insert

OAK OPENINGS (MAP A–69)
[Irwin Prairie, Secor Park, Oak Openings Park, Maumee State Forest, and Toledo Express Airport]

The Oak Openings of Lucas, Fulton, and Henry counties of northwest Ohio is one of Ohio's most unique natural assets. A wonderful diversity of landscape—broad sand dunes, open oak woods, swamp forest, alder bogs, wet and dry prairies—all contribute to making the area a naturalist's paradise. During the first part of the century, much of the wetlands were drained, forests were cut and grasslands burned. Although much reduced in size, small pockets of valuable habitat have been saved, and other areas are returning to their original state.

Oak Openings Metropolitan Park contains Ohio's only moving or "living" sand dunes. Nature hikes are a regular part of the park program during the warmer months.

The open oak woods on the dunes consist of black and white oaks with a forest floor of bracken fern, huckleberry and blueberry bushes, wintergreen, wild indigo, lupine, goldenrods and asters. Within the swamp forests, situated among the dunes, are pin oaks, elms, soft maples, wild cherries, tupelos, aspens, and poplars. Beneath these trees are buttonbush, blackberry tangles, spicebush, wild spirea, spikenard, bedstraw, and royal, cinnamon, and sensitive ferns. Wildflowers include: blazing star, wild phlox, lance-leafed and bird's-foot violets, and wild lily-of-the-valley.

The bogs provide the proper habitat for willows, alders, elderberry, and wild spirea. Large trees are few in number, but the undergrowth is almost impenetrable, consisting of wild raspberry, skunk cabbage, marsh marigold, jewelweed, boneset, prairie nettle, goldenrods, and a variety of other plants. When rainfall is normal, the scattered remnants of wet prairie retain water until midsummer. According to Lou Campbell in his *Birds of the Toledo Area,* the dominant plants are blue joint-grass, slough-grass, clumps of willows, cornel, buttonbush, nine-bark, and aspens. For the herpetologist-birder, locations like Irwin Prairie are excellent for hearing frogs and toads in the springtime. At the end of the boardwalk east of Irwin Road, the chorus of spring peepers and common tree frogs can be deafening, especially on warm, showery nights in mid-May. The data for the following five accounts, supplied by Tom Kemp, provide an excellent birding guide to the most productive areas in the region.

Irwin Prairie   *Drive west from Toledo on Ohio 2 to*
Crissey Road. Continue north on Crissey to
Bancroft. Turn west on Bancroft and
proceed to the parking lot, about 0.25
mile past Irwin Road on the south side.
The boardwalk through the prairie
begins here.

The boardwalk winds through second growth woodland and brush before it comes out onto the prairie near Irwin Road. American and Least bitterns once nested here and are still found infrequently. Cooper's and Broad-winged hawks are possible nearby nesters. Five species of rails have been found here: Virginia Rail and Sora are fairly common; King Rails have nested occasionally; Yellow Rails have been found several times in the spring; and the rare Black Rail has been recorded at least once.

Irwin Prairie is a good place to watch the courtship flights of Common Snipe and American Woodcocks, especially in March and April. Eastern Screech-Owls and Great Horned and Barred owls are resident in wooded areas. Another nice feature is the presence of both Alder and Willow flycatchers and the opportunity to compare their calls in May and June. Sedge and Marsh wrens can occasionally be seen or heard from the boardwalk, and Veeries are common in the wet woods surrounding the prairie. White-eyed Vireos nest, and Bell's Vireo, although quite rare, has been known to nest. Listen for the husky phrases of their song that Roger Tory Peterson describes as *cheedle cheedle chee? cheedle cheedle chew!* About eight species of warblers have been known to nest in the area, including Blue-winged Warblers, Yellow-breasted Chats, and, very rarely, Golden-winged and Mourning warblers. LeConte's Sparrows and Western Meadowlarks are rare visitors and should always be kept in mind.

Secor Park

Just across Bancroft Road from Irwin Prairie is Secor Park. Access is from Bancroft on the south, Central Avenue (Rte. 20) on the north, or Wolfinger Road on the east.

This fine tract of mature forest attracts nesting birds rarely found elsewhere in the Toledo area. A checklist of such species would include Acadian Flycatchers, Yellow-throated Vireos, Cerulean Warblers, American Redstarts, Ovenbirds, Northern Waterthrush (rare), Kentucky and Hooded warblers, Scarlet Tanagers, and Rose-breasted Grosbeaks.

Oak Openings Park

Follow Ohio 2 west from Toledo to Girdham Road. Proceed south on Girdham and you will soon reach the park.

This 4,000-acre tract of oak forest, pine plantation, swamp forest, and open fields is home to many of the Oak Openings' rarest breeding birds. Barred Owls can often be found just west of the Mallard Lake parking lot, and Red-shouldered Hawks should be looked for where the ravine crosses Oak Openings Parkway east of Wilkins Road. Broad-winged Hawks are fairly common nesting birds and can be found at a number of different localities.

The most exciting ornithological treasures, however, are the park's breeding songbirds. Nineteen warbler species (plus two warbler hybrids) and six vireo species have nested, and there are midsummer records for at least four additional warbler species. Hooded Warblers have nested near the Mallard Lake lodge, especially north of the lake and across the parkway southwest of the parking lot. Pine Warblers have also nested near the lodge and others may be heard singing along Wilkins Road north to the railroad tracks. Cerulean Warblers are sometimes found along the parkway just southwest of the lake. Red-breasted Nuthatches, Solitary Vireos, and Kentucky Warblers favor these same areas. In 1990, Golden-crowned Kinglets nested southeast of the junction of Reed and Wilkins roads, a first for Ohio.

From Wilkins Road and the railroad tracks, follow the trail to the southwest for possible Summer Tanagers, Ovenbirds, Louisiana Waterthrushes,

Kentucky, Mourning, Hooded, and Canada warblers. Chestnut-sided Warblers have been known to nest at the south end of the trail near Reed Road.

The dune/prairie habitat along Girdham Road south of the railroad tracks is probably the most reliable for Lark Sparrows. Near the dunes, listen for Prairie Warblers. Six sparrow species, Eastern Kingbirds, and Eastern Blue-birds frequent the fields near the junction of Reed and Girdham roads. Pine Warblers are often found in the pine stand across from the dunes and Blue-winged Warblers are fairly common in the area. A Blue Grosbeak was seen in 1989 and 1990. After dark, listen for Whip-poor-wills.

Another good area, one less visited, is located in the northwest corner of the park. From the intersection of Girdham and Sager roads, walk west along the horse trail until you come to the yellow marker designating the Boy Scout trail. Follow this trail and others nearby into an area of mature forest and a ravine where you can find Cerulean and Hooded warblers, Louisiana Water-thrushes, Acadian Flycatchers, and other forest-dwelling species.

There is always a chance of finding a Golden-winged Warbler by follow-ing Girdham Road south to the open area just north of the park maintenance buildings. Check singing birds carefully because typical Blue-wings sometimes deliver Golden-wing songs. Other places to explore include Monclova Road east and west of Girdham; a ravine near the junction of Reed and Jeffers roads, and south along Jeffers to a large open area on the west side of the road. Check for Blue-winged Warblers, Yellow-breasted Chats, and Lark Sparrows.

Maumee State Forest   *Directions to these scattered parcels of land on the western and southern edges of the Oak Openings are contained within the site descriptions.*

In Lucas County, check the wooded tract along Monroe Road between Reed Road and Ohio 64 for Chestnut-sided, Pine, Black-and-white, Kentucky, Mourning, and Hooded warblers. This is also a good Eastern Screech-Owl and Whip-poor-will spot. Where Wilkins Road intersects Ohio 64, walk through the pines and then along a ditch to the southwest. Look for Red-breasted Nut-hatches and Solitary Vireos.

An excellent section of forest is located farther west along Ohio 64 be-tween Jeffers and Monroe roads. Nesting Cooper's, Red-shouldered, and Broad-winged hawks can be found here along with Barred Owls and the possi-bility of Northern Saw-whet Owls. Passerines include Red-breasted Nut-hatches, Blue-winged, Chestnut-sided, and Pine warblers. Just west of this area across Monroe Road is a large field which attracted a pair of Blue Grosbeaks in 1988.

The best Fulton County areas can be found by driving west from Manore

Road on Archbold-Whitehouse Road (Fulton Co. Road C) to the intersection with County Road 2. There are three good wooded tracts to the northwest, northeast, and southwest of this corner. Veeries are common here and nesting warblers include Blue-winged, Chestnut-sided, Mourning, Hooded, and more. Red-breasted Nuthatches nest, and Solitary Vireos have been seen.

A fine area in Henry County is reached by driving south on County Road 2 to Henry County Road V (Neowash Road). Beginning at the Lucas-Henry County line, three large tracts run to the west and are bordered on the north by Neowash Road and on the south by Bailey Road (Henry County Road U). The wildest section is along County Road 2 south of Neowash Road. There is a small colony of Great Blue Herons in the swamp forest to the west, and Cooper's, Red-shouldered, and Broad-winged hawks nest in the vicinity.

A wet meadow farther south on County Road 2 is of special interest. Park at the south end of a line of cedars and walk west into the meadow. Birds to be found here include Common Snipe, Alder and Willow flycatchers, White-eyed Vireos, Blue-winged and Yellow warblers, Yellow-breasted Chats, and Swamp Sparrows.

Toledo Express Airport   *In Lucas County, 0.5 mile north of the*
                                           junction of U.S. 20 and Ohio 295.
                                           (Map A–88)

Good views can be obtained of the grassy areas along the runway for occasional Upland Sandpipers, Savannah and Grasshopper sparrows, and Bobolinks. Bell's Vireos have been found in the shrubby habitat at the bend in the road and Willow Flycatchers nest nearby. Orchard Orioles can be heard along this road, and Dickcissels are possible.

Schwamberger Prairie north of the airport can be reached from Old State Line Road. Look and listen for White-eyed Vireos, Blue-winged, Golden-winged, and Chestnut-sided warblers.

Winter Notes: Winter finches can be found throughout the Oak Openings. Evening Grosbeaks are fairly common and crossbills are occasional. Northern Goshawks are possible in late fall and winter. Black-capped Chickadees are abundant. An area to check for Long-eared and Northern Saw-whet owls is the line of cedars mentioned earlier along Henry County Road 2. Another place to look for these owls is in the cedars and white pines south of the Reed-Girdham Road intersection in Oak Openings Park.

End of regional insert

Old Woman Creek   *In Erie County, 2 miles east of Huron on*
                                                    U.S. 6. (Map A–70)

This 571-acre reserve contains a freshwater estuary and serves as a field laboratory and a place where students and the general public can enjoy a variety of
unique natural habitats: marshland, open water, a barrier sand beach, upland
forests, and old fields in early plant succession. Nearly 300 species of birds
have been seen in and around the reserve.

In season, there are lots of American Black Ducks and good numbers of
Wood Ducks, Blue-winged Teal, Northern Shovelers, Gadwall, and American
Wigeon. In rough weather, diving ducks avail themselves of the protected waters within the reserve. The Edward Walper Trail circles through a mile of
woods and diverse habitat. There is an observation deck overlooking the estuary and a Visitors Center with natural history exhibits, an aquarium, and
nature artwork.

Prolonged southerly winds sometimes push the waters of Lake Erie away
from the land and expose great habitat for shorebirds and additional feeding
areas for herons and their allies.

The reserve at Old Woman Creek is open daily from 8 A.M. to 5 P.M. The
Visitors Center is open Wednesday through Sunday, 1 to 5 P.M.

Oregon Power Plant   *Take Ohio 2 to Wynn Road east of Toledo*
Bay Shore Power Plant   *along the shore of Maumee Bay; proceed*
                                           north to Bay Shore Road, turn west and
                                        enter the parking lot just east of the power
                                                        plant. (Map A–71)

Most of this excellent birding area is off limits but some observations can be
made from outside the fence. Search the nearby shoreline; in late summer and
fall, this is a good place to find flocks of Black-bellied Plover, a few Sanderlings,
Ruddy Turnstones, and various peeps. The waters of the bay are visited by
impressive numbers of diving ducks—Ring-necked Duck, Canvasback, Lesser
Scaup, Ruddy Duck, and others—from October until ice forces them on their
way, usually in late December.

The entire area has a diversity of habitats, both natural and man-made,
and lies at a strategic confluence of migration routes. During the 1980s, considerable numbers of Ring-billed and some Herring gulls nested around several
large impoundments. American White Pelicans have been known to visit the
area.

Ottawa National Wildlife Refuge   *Located on Ohio 2 approximately midway between Toledo and Port Clinton and less than .5 mile west of Crane Creek State Park. (Map A-72)*

The Ottawa National Wildlife Refuge complex encompasses over 8,000 acres including an island and a series of marshes that hopscotch along the shores of Lake Erie from west of Port Clinton nearly to Toledo.

Eighty-six-acre West Sister Island, nine miles offshore, supports an important heron and egret rookery and has been designated a National Wildlife Area. Approximately 750 pairs of Great Egrets nest on the island, plus substantial numbers of Great Blue and Black-crowned Night-Herons, six to ten pairs of Snowy Egrets, and over 300 pairs of Double-crested Cormorants. Little Blue Herons and Cattle Egrets have nested in the past. Visitation is limited to authorized researchers.

The largest marsh, described here, abuts the Magee Marsh Wildlife Area and is headquarters for the entire Ottawa Complex. Little Cedar Point, née Cedar Point, the westernmost link in the system, is discussed above. The Navarre Marsh is jointly owned by the Toledo Edison and Cleveland Electric Illuminating companies and is the site of the Davis-Besse Nuclear Power Station. Darby Marsh, at this writing, is still being developed as a wildlife refuge.

The "backside" of the Ottawa Refuge, a productive birding area, is accessible from Veler Road, which is about five miles west of the headquarters building on Ohio 2. Directions are given later in this account.

An overflow channel parallels the right side of the entrance road to the headquarters building and parking lot of the main refuge, behind which is a wetland of grasses and sedges, a favorite feeding ground of geese and puddle ducks. Shorebirds also inhabit this fine environment; it is a good place to find Black-bellied Plovers, Semipalmated Plovers, Greater and Lesser yellowlegs, Solitary Sandpipers, a variety of peeps, Common Snipe, and an occasional Wilson's or Red-necked phalarope. In late summer and fall, look for Long-billed Dowitchers.

A few puddle ducks and occasional shorebirds can be found in the pond behind the headquarters building. Except in midwinter, Canada Geese will be everywhere and their clamorous honking will fill the air.

Most of the six miles of walking trails are atop dikes surrounding the large impoundments. Before investigating them, check the brushy area and woods immediately west of the parking lot for small landbirds.

March, April, and early May are the best months to see migrating hawks. Scan the sky every few minutes; use binoculars to look at, around, and under clouds where hawks might be riding the updrafts high overhead. This vicinity is one of the best in the state to find appreciable numbers of Sharp-shinned, Cooper's, and Red-shouldered hawks. In late April, May, and again in September, keep a sharp lookout for spiraling kettles of Broad-winged Hawks. Other raptors to look for are Northern Harrier, Red-tailed Hawk, American Kestrel, Merlin (rare), and Peregrine Falcon (rare). Bald Eagles nest on the refuge and one or two can usually be found year round. Small numbers of Ospreys are usually present during each migration, but seldom are more than one or two seen in a day. Rough-legged Hawks are uncommon winter residents and on the scarce side in migration.

The water level of the various impoundments varies from season to season. Water is regulated to achieve the growth of specific plant associations and to maintain proper soil-water combinations. By following the trail from the parking lot around the first impoundment, a loop of about two miles, most of the birds present can be observed. Heavy though they are to carry, a spotting scope on a tripod is almost a necessity.

Tundra Swans appear soon after the ice melts each spring. Through March, several thousand will probably be present throughout the region, although less than a hundred are apt to be on the impoundments. Also look for Wood Ducks, Green-winged Teal, American Black Ducks, Mallards, Northern Pintails, Blue-winged Teal, Northern Shovelers, Gadwalls, and American Wigeons. Along with the surface-feeding ducks there are usually a number of diving ducks. Look for Canvasbacks, Redheads, Ring-necks, Lesser Scaups, Buffleheads, Hooded and Common mergansers, and Ruddy Ducks. Other diving ducks can be seen on Maumee Bay to the west, Sandusky Bay to the east, on borrow pits, and frequently rafted up offshore.

In spring and fall, when a big migration is under way, small landbirds seek cover in marginal willows and shrubs and along the edges of the marsh. Such birds include Ruby-crowned Kinglets, Hermit Thrushes, Brown Thrashers, Yellow-rumped and Palm warblers. The small birds that pop up out of the grass and fly twenty or thirty yards only to disappear again are probably Savannah Sparrows. Listen for the metallic *chink* notes of Swamp Sparrows.

At the extreme north end of the dikes is a patch of flooded trees and tree-lined banks along a channel. These spots can be excellent for everything from Prothonotary Warblers and other songbirds to herons, Wood Ducks, Blue-winged Teal, Common Moorhens, American Coots, and Belted Kingfishers.

For shorebirds, the best time for a visit is May and again from mid-July to October. When water levels are ideal (shallow pools), impressive numbers of birds are often present. Species such as the Short-billed Dowitcher are common, and Dunlin (May and late September–October) at such times throng the mudflats. Other shorebirds regular in migration are the Semipalmated Plover, Greater and Lesser yellowlegs, Solitary, Spotted, Semipalmated, Least, and Pectoral sandpipers. Rarer species to look for include Black-bellied and Lesser Golden-Plover, Ruddy Turnstone, Red Knot, Sanderling, Western, White-rumped, Baird's, and Stilt sandpipers.

Ring-billed Gulls are ubiquitous. In August and September there are noticeable increases in Green-backed Herons. A few Cattle Egrets might be present. Caspian, Common, and Black terns are likely. By the end of the period, mixed flocks of Forster's and Common terns appear on the scene.

To get to the Veler Road section of the Ottawa Complex, take Ohio 2 five miles west, turn to the right, and proceed to the gate. Before starting out, please check the Ottawa headquarters for permission to enter the property. The large tract combines expanses of marsh, mudflats, meadows, and croplands. During the first half of the 1970s, this part of the refuge was extremely good for shorebirds and it is still an excellent place to visit for a variety of interesting species.

Beyond the gate, the road extends back into the marsh, in the process passing the site of an old farmhouse, orchard, and large fields. The first two locations are good for small flocks of migratory song birds in the spring and fall. Eastern Kingbirds, Willow Flycatchers, vireos, warblers, Indigo Buntings, Orchard Orioles, and Pine Siskins have been seen here. In March and April, it is a good place to find Rusty Blackbirds and an occasional Brewer's Blackbird.

The fields and fallow meadows along the road sometimes become slightly flooded; when this happens, look for plovers, yellowlegs, and other shorebirds.

This area is also a good habitat for Upland Sandpipers, Water Pipits, Dickcissels, Savannah and Grasshopper sparrows, Bobolinks, and Eastern Meadowlarks.

Look for Northern Harriers over the fields and marshes. Walk about a half mile and there might be flooded fields and flats on the right side of the road.

In addition to shorebirds, in season, the Veler Road location is a veritable spa for herons, egrets, geese, and surface-feeding ducks. Before leaving, scan the skyline to the east—chances are good that you will see a Bald Eagle perched in one of the distant trees.

A word of precaution: always bring extra clothing, especially jackets and sweaters—even if the weather is warm when you start out. Sudden changes in the weather and precipitous drops in temperature are commonplace along the lake.

In early days, the entire Ottawa complex was part of a 300,000-acre swamp that stretched from present-day Sandusky, Ohio, to Detroit, Michigan. Over the years, the formidable "Black Swamp" was drained until barely 15,000 acres of wetland remained. Since 1961, the federal government has saved more than 8,000 acres of these marshes. Ottawa, Little Cedar Point, and West Sister Island are the only national wildlife refuges in Ohio.

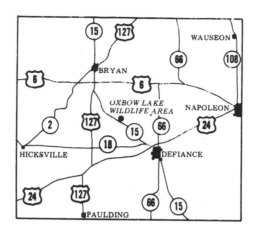

Oxbow Lake Wildlife Area

On Ohio 15 8 miles northwest of Defiance. (Map A-73)

A sizeable lake, two ponds, a bit of marsh, woods, fields, and farmland grace this attractive state wildlife area. Look for Pied-billed Grebes in the spring and fall; an occasional Great Blue or Green-backed heron, Wood Ducks, Blue-winged Teals, Ring-necked Pheasants, American Coots, American Woodcocks, and, sometimes, a Sora Rail in the marshy places.

Other species to look for include Red-headed Woodpeckers, Willow Flycatchers, Tree, Northern Rough-winged, and Barn swallows, Eastern Bluebirds, Gray Catbirds, Northern Mockingbirds, Brown Thrashers, Blue-winged, Yellow, and Cerulean warblers, Common Yellowthroats, Vesper, Savannah, and Song sparrows, and Northern Orioles.

Paulding Ponds

On Paulding County Road 107 on the southern edge of Paulding near the fairgrounds. (Map A-74)

In early spring, after the water is free of ice, these three ponds attract American Black Ducks, Mallards, Blue-winged Teals (April-May), Northern Shovelers, Gadwalls, American Wigeons, and occasional Redheads, Ring-necked Ducks, Buffleheads, and Hooded Mergansers. Greater and Lesser yellowlegs and Solitary and Spotted sandpipers sometimes find spots to feed along the pond's edges. All the swallow species can be seen during the spring migration.

Pearson Metropolitan Park   *On Ohio 2, 2 miles east of the Toledo-*
Detroit Expressway in Toledo.
(Map A–75)

Three miles of hiking trails wander through woods and past several ponds. In addition, there are all kinds of recreational activities such as picnicking, horseback riding, and pedal boating.

This is a fairly good place to look for migrating landbirds in late April and throughout the month of May. On mornings after a really heavy migration, the trees will be full of flycatchers, thrushes, vireos, warblers, tanagers, grosbeaks, and orioles. A few Broad-winged Hawks can be flushed out of the trees from April 20 to May 10. Wood Ducks are sometimes found on the ponds, and a pair of Belted Kingfishers is frequently present.

Nesting birds include the Red-headed Woodpecker, Northern Flicker, Eastern Wood-Pewee, Barn Swallow, Black-capped Chickadee, White-breasted Nuthatch, House Wren, Wood Thrush, Gray Catbird, Brown Thrasher, Red-eyed Vireo, Cerulean Warbler, Common Yellowthroat, Northern Oriole, Scarlet Tanager, Rose-breasted Grosbeak, and Indigo Bunting.

Pickerel Creek Wildlife Area   *In Sandusky County, the Wildlife Area lies*
between the south shore of Sandusky Bay
and Route 6. Access is gained along the
north side of Ohio Route 6 from Riley
Township Road 256 and Townsend
Township Road 280. Parking lots and
access roads are situated throughout the
area. (Map A–76)

The ODNR Division of Wildlife acquired this 2,106-acre tract in 1987 and manages it primarily as a public hunting (by permit) and fishing area. Birders are welcome except during the hunting season. The northern portion lies in the center of some of the best remaining wetland habitat along Sandusky Bay. It was once an extensive wet prairie; wild rice and other waterfowl foods grew in abundance.

Today slightly over 40% of the area is open land with the remainder in woods, brush, and flooded marsh units. During the spring and fall waterfowl migrations, Canada Geese and hundreds of dabbling ducks congregate here, and there is always a chance of seeing a small flock of Tundra Swans. The cattails and aquatic plants come alive with the peeping notes of teal, the plaintive whistled *whee whew* calls of American Wigeon, and the quacking of American Black Ducks and Mallards.

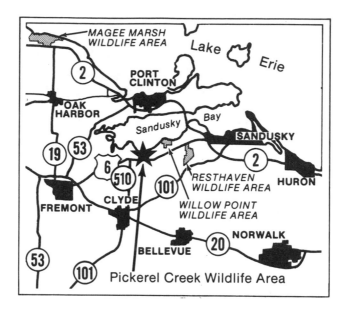

Other frequently seen species include American and Least bitterns, Great Egrets, Green-backed Herons, Black-crowned Night-Herons, Hooded Mergansers and small numbers of other diving ducks, Ospreys, Northern Harriers, Ring-necked Pheasants, Virginia and Sora rails, Common Moorhens, American Coots, Solitary Sandpipers, American Woodcocks, and occasional other shorebirds.

A large colony of the rare eastern prairie fringed orchid grows here. Apparently limited to Ohio, Michigan, Wisconsin, Indiana, Illinois, Maine, and Virginia, this is one of only 54 locations in the United States where the threatened species has been found.

Pipe Creek Wildlife Area

*Take Ohio 250, 4, or 6 into Sandusky,
following directions to the Cedar Point
causeway. Before reaching the causeway,
turn right (east) at the McDonald's
restaurant and proceed to the Sandusky
Water Plant. A small parking lot is
located east of the Water Plant.
(Map A–77)*

Formally known as the Sandusky Big Island wetland, the Pipe Creek Wildlife Area contains four pie-shaped units totaling 100 acres. It is home to the largest colony of Common Terns in the state, a species designated as endangered in

Ohio. No two days are alike during the spring and fall migrations. Because each unit is managed for different wetland types, there is a nice diversity of bird life. Common Loons, Double-crested Cormorants, bitterns and herons, dabbling and diving ducks, Ospreys, Bald Eagles, Northern Harriers, American Coots, Common Moorhens, shorebirds, and marsh songbirds can be found, in season, in various locations. Walking trails start at the parking lot. Each unit is surrounded by dikes, which are accessible year-round except during the waterfowl hunting season. Some units and dikes may also be off limits during the breeding season of the terns, depending on the location of the colony.

Climb the observation tower in the eastern unit to get a good view of the marsh and adjacent Sandusky Bay. In the central two units, depending on water levels, look for shorebirds. Breeding waterfowl include Canada Goose, American Black Duck, Mallard, and Blue-winged Teal. Great Black-backed Gulls are common in the winter.

Pymatuning State Park

Take either U.S. 6 or Ohio 7 to this large park, which is east of Andover. Many good observation points are located in Pennsylvania and can be reached by continuing north and then east on U.S. 6 to Linesville. (Map B-78)

This state park is a tract of 8,919 acres along the shores of the 17,000-acre reservoir. The surrounding land is quite flat, with swamp forests in the low areas, and beech-maple woods on higher ground. The reservoir is shallow and has 21 low islands, in addition to several extensive mudflats. The islands are covered with trees, underbrush, and marshy spots; many inlets and bays occur along the shore.

Waterfowl that breed around the reservoir include Canada Goose, Wood Duck, American Black Duck, Mallard, Blue-winged Teal, Northern Shoveler, Gadwall, and Hooded Merganser. Spring migration for waterbirds peaks between mid-March and mid-April; the major fall migration is between mid-October and the first of December. Substantial numbers of all the surface-feeding and diving ducks occur, including rarities such as the Eurasian Wigeon, Greater Scaup, Oldsquaw, and all three scoters.

The list of birds that nest or summer in the region is impressive and includes the Pied-billed Grebe, American and Least bitterns, Great Blue Heron, Great and Cattle egrets, Green-backed Heron, the waterfowl mentioned above, Bald Eagle, Northern Harrier, Red-tailed Hawk, American Kestrel, Ring-necked Pheasant, King Rail, Virginia Rail, Sora, Common Moorhen, American Coot, Killdeer, Spotted and Upland sandpipers, Ring-billed and Herring gulls, Caspian, Common, and Black terns, Mourning Dove, Yellow-billed and

Black-billed cuckoos, Eastern Screech-Owl, Great Horned and Barred owls, Common Nighthawk, Chimney Swift, Ruby-throated Hummingbird, and Belted Kingfisher.

Other summering birds are Downy and Hairy woodpeckers, Northern Flicker, Pileated Woodpecker, Eastern Wood-Pewee, Acadian, Willow, and Great Crested flycatchers, Eastern Kingbird, Horned Lark, Purple Martin, Tree, Northern Rough-winged, Cliff, and Barn swallows, Black-capped Chickadee, Tufted Titmouse, White-breasted Nuthatch, House, Sedge, and Marsh wrens, Eastern Bluebird, Gray Catbird, Brown Thrasher, Cedar Waxwing, Yellow-throated, Warbling, and Red-eyed vireos, Blue-winged, Yellow, and Cerulean warblers, American Redstart, Common Yellowthroat, Scarlet Tanager, Northern Cardinal, Indigo Bunting, Rufous-sided Towhee, Chipping, Field, Vesper, Savannah, Grasshopper, Henslow's, and Song sparrows, and Northern Oriole.

Birds frequently seen during the winter months are the Canada Goose, American Black Duck, Mallard, Common Goldeneye, Bald Eagle, Northern Harrier, Red-tailed and Rough-legged hawks, most of the woodpeckers, Horned Lark, Black-capped Chickadee, Tufted Titmouse, Red- and White-breasted nuthatches, Brown Creeper, Golden-crowned Kinglet, Eastern Bluebird, Cedar Waxwing, American Tree, Song, Swamp, and White-throated sparrows, Dark-eyed Junco, Red and White-winged crossbills, Common Redpoll (erratic), and Evening Grosbeak.

River Park   *On Hiram-Rapids Road 3 miles south of Burton in Geauga County. (Map B-79)*

Located along the upper reaches of the Cuyahoga River, this 50-acre spot includes an interesting marsh with deeper pools that attract migratory waterfowl in spring and fall. Congregations of swifts and swallows skim the water on cool days in the spring, and Hermit Thrushes and Rusty Blackbirds are present until early May. American and Least bitterns occur rarely; Wood Ducks, Soras, and American Coots more commonly. In areas of deadwood, Tree Swallows and Prothonotary Warblers nest; Marsh Wrens are sometimes found in the cattails, and Willow Flycatchers in the willow and alder scrub.

Rocky River Reservation   *Take U.S. 20 in Cleveland to Ohio 252, go south on 252 to Cedar Point Road, then east for .25 mile to the parking lot. (Map B–80)*

This 5,614-acre tract, which runs north and south along the Rocky River on the western limits of Cleveland and Lakewood, is an excellent place to find a variety of birds at all seasons of the year. Within the park are remnant Indian fortifications, small ponds, a lagoon, wooded hills and valleys, a picturesque river, and a mill with a mill race. Nature trails, special wildflower trails, the services of a resident naturalist, and a pleasant picnic area are all available.

Nesting and summering birds found here are quite similar to those listed in the accounts on North Chagrin Reservation and Hinkley Reservation.

Some of the more unusual birds that have been found here are: nesting Yellow-crowned Night-Herons, Brewster's and Lawrence's warblers (hybrids), Yellow-throated Warbler, Bohemian Waxwing, Blue Grosbeak, LeConte's Sparrow, and Red Crossbill. In late April and early May, Broad-winged Hawks are frequently seen overhead, plus smaller numbers of other raptors including Northern Harrier and Sharp-shinned, Cooper's, Red-shouldered, Red-tailed, and Rough-legged (uncommon) hawks. An occasional Osprey can be seen soaring over on a good migration day.

Sand Run Metropolitan Park　　*In northwest Akron, take I-77 to Route*
Seiberling Nature Center　　　*18, then go east for 2.3 miles to Smith*
　　　　　　　　　　　　　　　　Road. Proceed east on Smith Road for
　　　　　　　　　　　　　　　　1.5 miles to the entrance. (Map B–81)

This 987-acre park is steeped in Indian history; the fortifications and villages of many tribes and nations once dotted the promontories and terraces along the Cuyahoga River valley. The Seiberling Nature Center is located within the park, and there are picturesque trails through the woods and up to high bluffs.

Nowadays, Turkey Vultures soar overhead, Sharp-shinned Hawks sit quietly on the inside branches of large trees, and the reverberating yelps of Pileated Woodpeckers ring through the less frequented areas of forest. Veeries and Wood Thrushes sing duets of silvery music. Very little has changed from earlier years. Yellow-billed and Black-billed cuckoos are both known to nest here. All of Ohio's breeding woodpeckers are represented, and the roster of breeding flycatchers includes Eastern Wood-Pewee, Acadian, Willow (in the bottomlands), and Least (rare) flycatchers, Eastern Phoebe, Great Crested Flycatcher, and Eastern Kingbird.

Nesting warblers include the Blue-winged, Yellow, Chestnut-sided, Cerulean, American Redstart, Ovenbird, Louisiana Waterthrush, Common Yellowthroat, Hooded Warbler, and Yellow-breasted Chat.

Secrest Arboretum　　　　　*In Wooster, take Ohio 83 about a mile*
　　　　　　　　　　　　　　　south of town and turn east on County
　　　　　　　　　　　　　　　Road 359. (Map B–82)

Part of the nearly 2,000-acre Ohio Agricultural Research and Development Center, the arboretum has over 1,800 species and cultivated varieties of trees

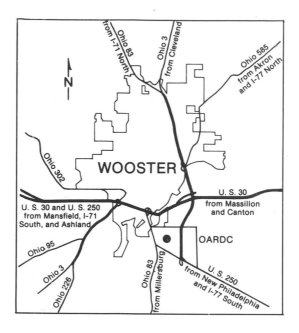

and shrubs in a natural setting. Walnut Hollow features over 150 kinds of azaleas and rhododendron plantings. Trails through the mixed hardwood forest allow visitors to enjoy a host of wildflowers, ferns, mosses, and birds. Other highlights include twisted silver fir trees, young bristlecone pines, dawn redwoods, and well over 100 varieties of flowering crabapple trees. Hundreds of different kinds of roses are displayed in an old-fashioned garden, and nearby is a collection of more than 100 kinds of holly.

Spring and summer birds that can be seen in this pleasant environment are the Eastern Kingbird, Barn Swallow, Carolina Chickadee, House Wren, Gray Catbird, and Cedar Waxwing. Listen for the songs of Red-eyed Vireos, Yellow Warblers, Common Yellowthroats, and Northern Orioles. Northern Cardinals, Indigo Buntings, Chipping and Song sparrows, and American Goldfinches are common summer residents.

Seiberling Nature Center   *See Sand Run Metropolitan Park.*

Sheldon Marsh State Nature   *Take U.S. 6 in Erie County 1.5 miles*
Preserve   *west of Huron and 0.5 mile west of the*
                                    intersection of Rye Beach Road. (Map A–83)

Over 450 acres of relatively undisturbed forest, marsh, and Lake Erie shoreline are protected in this attractive preserve, sandwiched between a golf course, hayfields, and a nearby motel. The area's diverse habitat attracts an excellent array of birdlife.

Visitors cannot drive past the parking lot inside the entrance, but a mile-long wheelchair-accessible road goes to the barrier beach past old fields, plantings of ornamental trees and multiflora rose, a creek estuary, and through a mature hardwood forest. Partway out, an observation platform, also accessible to wheelchairs, overlooks the eastern end of an extensive marsh with isolated stands of cattails and large patches of spatterdock. Mudflats attractive to shore-birds are sometimes exposed here, usually when southerly winds blow the water lakeward. On the inland side of an off-limits NASA building at the road's end, a path leads to a mile of sand spit, which offers views of the marsh to the south through openings in a formidable wall of phragmites and willows.

It is the last landfall for northbound migrants and the first for southbound ones, so the trees and brushy areas attract hordes of landbirds, especially in late April and May. Thirty-seven species of warblers have been seen here, including the hybrid Brewster's and Lawrence's.

Early in the day, in order to take advantage of the available light, birders do best by walking out along the old "government road" (reached by a trail at the southeast corner of the parking lot or via the Old Field Trail), which meets the main road halfway out. Within the "Y" where the roads meet is a brushy—sometimes flooded—area where skulkers such as Mourning and Connecticut warblers are most often found during migration.

Connecticut (front) and Mourning Warblers

Some of the interesting nesting birds include: Green-backed Heron, Canada Goose, Wood Duck, Blue-winged Teal (probable), Hooded Merganser (probable), Red-tailed Hawk, Sora, Common Moorhen, Spotted Sandpiper, American Woodcock, Black-billed Cuckoo, Ovenbird, Common Yellowthroat, Scarlet Tanager, Rufous-sided Towhee, and Swamp Sparrow.

Several cattail marshes between the golf course and the preserve are good places to look for rails and Swamp Sparrows. Prothonotary Warblers nest here and also around the estuary. Gulls—Bonaparte's, Ring-billed, Herring, and Great Black-backed—and terns—Caspian, Common, Forster's, and Black—are often seen in flight over the lake and marsh areas, or loafing at the tip of the spit. A few gulls nest on the spit, so visitors should take care not to disturb them. A dozen rarer gull species have been seen here or nearby.

On the beach and mudflats—and in the marsh—spring and fall shorebird migrants sometimes occur in large numbers for so small an area. Species routinely seen include Black-bellied and Semipalmated plovers, both yellowlegs, Solitary and Spotted sandpipers, Ruddy Turnstones, Sanderlings, Semipalmated, Least, and Pectoral sandpipers, Dunlins, Short-billed Dowitchers, and Common Snipe. Seen less often but always possible are Willets and Red Knots, Western, White-rumped, Baird's, and Stilt sandpipers, and Wilson's and Red-necked phalaropes. Red Phalaropes are occasionally found, mostly during the colder months. Piping Plovers, Whimbrels, Hudsonian and Marbled godwits, and Ruffs have been recorded. A Spotted Redshank was once seen in the area.

In the spring, look to the sky for migrating raptors. In winter, Eastern Screech-Owls and Great Horned Owls are found in the woods, Long-eared Owls in conifers, Short-eared Owls in the fields, and in midwinter there is always a good chance of spotting a Snowy Owl, especially near the lakeshore. Some years, cold weather also brings Snow Buntings to the beach, erratic winter finches, the possibility of a Northern Shrike and, on red-letter days, a Glaucous or Thayer's gull. From October through April, a variety of waterfowl can be seen, including all of the common dabblers and divers, plus random occurrences of Oldsquaws and scoters.

The preserve and its environs have produced other rarities, e.g., Brown Pelican, Yellow Rail, Heermann's Gull, Harris' and LeConte's sparrows. The preserve is open daily from 8 A.M. to dusk. A brochure with a map and a checklist is available near the parking lot.

South Bass Island

Take the ferry boat from Port Clinton, Lakeside, or Sandusky. (Map A–84)

Located several miles north of Catawba, this island is 3.5 miles long and 1.5 miles wide with a low, slightly rolling terrain which consists of cultivated vineyards, old fields, and numerous patches of woods and brushy tangles. The village of Put-in-Bay is on the island, as is the Franz Theodore Stone

Laboratory, a biological research station operated by The Ohio State University. The most prominent landmark, visible for miles around, is Perry's Victory and International Peace Monument. Over the years, many migrating birds have been killed on windy nights when eddies of air slammed them into this edifice.

The best birding is around the middle of May, especially during inclement weather. At such times, large numbers of transient landbirds seek refuge on the island. One of the best places to find these concentrations is the wooded area along the western shoreline, between the southern tip of the island and Peach Point, which juts northward toward Middle Bass Island.

The first spring migrants reach the island in early March, and include Killdeers, Mourning Doves, Eastern Meadowlarks, Purple Finches, and some of the sparrows. Between the middle of March and the first of April, Common Loons can often be seen offshore, along with Horned Grebes, Double-crested Cormorants, and Red-breasted Mergansers. A variety of other ducks frequent the harbor, along with Ring-billed, Herring, and newly arrived Bonaparte's gulls. By April 1, Belted Kingfishers, Eastern Phoebes, Cedar Waxwings, and Rufous-sided Towhees are in evidence.

Warblers reach the island about May 3, but the really big waves occur May 10–20. The raptor migration extends through April into the first part of May, when Sharp-shinned, Cooper's, Red-shouldered, Broad-winged, and Red-tailed hawks fly over, sometimes in large numbers. The fall migration of hawks is never as good, although a flight of Rough-legged Hawks sometimes passes high over the island about mid-October.

Migrating shorebirds appear on the reefs and mudflats around the island in July. The species seen most often are Semipalmated Plover, Greater and Lesser yellowlegs, Solitary and Spotted sandpipers, Ruddy Turnstone, Sanderling, Semipalmated and Least sandpipers. A few Short-billed Dowitchers can be found during the season and, occasionally, a Red Knot.

Summer residents and visitors include Great Blue Herons, Great Egrets, Green-backed Herons, Black-crowned Night-Herons, Wood Ducks, American Black Ducks, Mallards, Killdeers, Spotted Sandpipers, American Woodcocks, Ring-billed and Herring gulls, Common and Black terns, Yellow-billed and Black-billed cuckoos, Chimney Swifts, Ruby-throated Hummingbirds, Belted Kingfishers, Downy Woodpeckers, Northern Flickers, Eastern Wood-Pewees, Willow Flycatchers (uncommon), Great Crested Flycatchers, Eastern Kingbirds, Purple Martins, Tree, Northern Rough-winged, and Barn swallows, American Crows, occasional Carolina Wrens, House Wrens, American Robins, Gray Catbirds, Brown Thrashers, Cedar Waxwings, Red-eyed Vireos, Yellow Warblers, American Redstarts (uncommon), Common Yellowthroats, Yellow-breasted Chats, Northern Cardinals, Indigo Buntings, Rufous-sided Towhees, Savannah, Grasshopper, Chipping, Field, and Song sparrows, Eastern Meadowlarks, Orchard and Northern orioles.

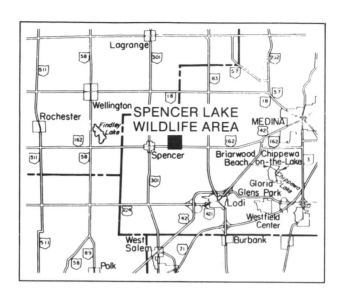

Spencer Lake Wildlife Area

Take Ohio 162 in Medina County; about 2 miles east of Spencer, turn north on the access road. (Map B–85)

A 70-acre lake is situated in this 595-acre wooded park, which includes stands of beech-maple and oak-hickory forest. There are grassy fields where one should look for Horned Larks and Savannah Sparrows, and pockets of marsh vegetation around the lake where a few Mallards and Blue-winged Teals nest.

In spring and fall, Water Pipits can sometimes be found in the fields and near the water's edge, Ospreys investigate the lake, and small numbers of grebes and ducks stop over.

**Springville Marsh
State Nature Area**

Take U.S. 23 north of Carey to Township Road 24; turn west and cross the railroad tracks. (Map A–86)

This 200-acre marsh is one of the largest remnants of wetland in the interior of northwestern Ohio. Birds to look for during the warm months are the Green-backed Heron, Wood Duck, Mallard, Cooper's Hawk, Ring-necked Pheasant, Sora, Killdeer, Yellow-billed Cuckoo, Belted Kingfisher, Willow Flycatcher, Eastern Kingbird, Marsh Wren, Warbling Vireo, Yellow Warbler, Common Yellowthroat, and Northern Oriole.

Small numbers of surface-feeding ducks stop here in migration (nine Fulvous Tree Ducks were spotted in April of 1975). A pond with mudflats is close to the road, and in the spring, summer, and fall it frequently attracts Semipalmated Plovers, Greater and Lesser yellowlegs, Solitary and Spotted sandpipers, Semipalmated, Least, and Pectoral sandpipers, Dunlins, Short-billed Dowitchers, and Common Snipe.

Stebbins' Gulch   *See Holden Arboretum.*

Tinkers Creek Nature Preserve   *Take I-480 to the Twinsburg-Aurora exit.*
and State Park   *The park and preserve are 4 miles*
                                                southwest of Aurora, 1.5 miles west of
                                                Hudson-Aurora Road on Davis Road.
                                                (Map B–87)

The 1,086-acre state park combines upland woods, fields, and marsh. About 500 acres of marsh and a number of spring-fed ponds constitute the nature preserve. All of this provides a nice habitat mix, and a morning's birding can yield everything from Veeries, Cerulean and Hooded warblers, and Louisiana Waterthrushes to American Bitterns, Great Egrets, rails, and good numbers of waterfowl. Brown Creepers and Prothonotary Warblers have nested.

Van Buren State Park   *Take I-75 in Hancock County about 7*
                                                miles north of Findlay and drive east on
                                                Ohio 613 for 1 mile. (Map A–89)

Grassland and patches of beech-maple woods create a nice setting for the 70-acre lake located here. Small numbers of ducks, geese, and gulls can be seen in early April and late fall. A few of the summer birds are Red-headed Woodpecker, Great Crested Flycatcher, Horned Lark, Barn Swallow, Tufted Titmouse, Eastern Bluebird, Cedar Waxwing, Red-eyed Vireo, Northern Oriole and, some years, Summer Tanager.

Virginia Kendall Metropolitan   *Take Ohio 8 north from Akron, or south*
Park   *from I-80 (Ohio Turnpike Gate 12); turn*
                                                west on Ohio 359. (Map B–90)

This large park (2,039 acres) brings together beech-maple and oak-hickory woods, hemlock-lined rugged ravines, a 12-acre lake, fields, meadows, and marsh. Over 12 miles of delightful trails wind through the various habitats.

    Lookout points on some of the higher cliffs are frequently occupied by birders in spring and fall scanning the skies for birds of prey. Turkey Vultures follow the flight line, as do modest numbers of Sharp-shinned, Cooper's, and Red-tailed Hawks, a few Red-shouldered Hawks, kettles of Broad-wings, an occasional Rough-legged Hawk, a few Ospreys and Northern Harriers, and even a Peregrine Falcon on a red-letter day—and American Kestrels, of course. Sometimes even a Northern Goshawk is seen in late fall or winter.

On some May mornings, the areas around the lake, wooded edges, and groves of trees are alive with transient warblers and other landbirds. After mid-May, this is a good place to find Olive-sided Flycatchers (perched on dead branches atop tall trees), Yellow-bellied Flycatchers, Gray-cheeked Thrushes, Philadelphia Vireos, and Bay-breasted, Blackpoll, Wilson's, and Canada warblers.

Red Crossbills, White-winged Crossbills, Common Redpolls, Pine Siskins, and Evening Grosbeaks are sometimes seen in the winter.

Northern Shrike

Waite Hill   *Take I-90 east of Cleveland to Ohio 306;*
drive south about 1.5 mile, then turn
right into any one of several streets and
proceed through the scenic neighborhood.
(Map B-91)

Waite Hill is a wooded, park-like residential area where Annette Flanigan made a bit of ornithological history before retiring and moving to Florida. On some days during the spring and fall migrations, she would mist-net and band as many as 15 warbler species in a single day. Some of her outstanding banding records and observations follow.

On 8 August 1974, a Yellow-bellied Flycatcher was banded, and two days later it was seen with another bird of the same species; undoubtedly early migrants. A Black-backed Woodpecker was seen on 7 January 1959. Thirty Bohemian Waxwings were observed in nearby Kirtland Hills on 2 January 1963, and one was seen at Waite Hill on 27 March 1966. A Boreal Chickadee was netted, banded, and photographed on 23 December 1972. Northern Shrikes have been seen several times. A very late Hermit Thrush was banded on 3 June 1974, and a Swainson's Thrush on 10 August 1974. An extremely young Swainson's Thrush was banded on 2 August 1976.

A late Red-eyed Vireo was banded on 2 November 1975, a late Warbling Vireo on 15 October 1973. Early Tennessee Warblers were banded 12 August 1975, a Cape May Warbler on 18 August 1970, and a Yellow-rumped Warbler on 13 August 1975. A very late Lincoln's Sparrow was banded on 5 June 1975.

There have been many sightings of Tundra Swans flying over. Other records include Cattle Egret, Sandhill Crane, Northern Saw-whet Owl, Sharp-tailed Sparrow, the Gambel's race of White-crowned Sparrow, and White-winged Crossbills.

West Branch State Park   *On Ohio 5 in Portage County about 6*
miles east of Ravenna. (Map B-92)

Michael J. Kirwin Lake, a 2,650-acre reservoir, was formed by building a long earthen dam across a tributary of the Mahoning River. The rolling terrain combines old fields and beech-maple woods.

The lake is visited by transient waterbirds in migration and into the winter—until freeze-up. Common Loons, Pied-billed and Horned grebes, Double-crested Cormorants, Tundra Swans, Canada Geese, and most duck species can be found from March through April, and again from October into December. Marshy edges here and there attract American Coots and a few rails and moorhens.

In summer, listen for the rattling songs of Marsh Wrens. Prairie Warblers and Yellow-breasted Chats have been reported nesting. Late-summer Bobolinks sometimes gather in fallow fields and, through September, stands of giant ragweed should be searched for migrant *Parulidae* such as Nashville, Yellow, Magnolia, Blackpoll, Bay-breasted, Palm, and more rarely, Connecticut warblers. Shorebirds sometimes occur along Ohio 14 and Knapp Road. During the cold months, Bald Eagles have been spotted, and Northern Harriers, Rough-legged Hawks, and Short-eared Owls are possible.

White City Park   *Take I-90 east from downtown Cleveland; exit north onto 136th Street, turn east on Ohio 283 (Lake Shore Boulevard), then turn left on the road just before the intersection with East 140th Street. This will be a short distance east of the Easterly Sewage Treatment Plant. (Map B–93)*

Formerly an excellent spot to find rare shorebirds during the summer and fall months—offshore waterbirds during the fall, winter, and spring, and multitudes of gulls from late fall to early spring. Permission is now required to enter the property, and the area is seldom birded.

Rarities that have been found here included Laughing, Franklin's, Little, and Sabine's gulls, Black-legged Kittiwakes, Piping Plover, American Avocet, Willet, Whimbrel, Hudsonian Godwit, Red Knot, Purple, Stilt, and Buff-breasted sandpipers, Long-billed Dowitcher, and Red Phalarope.

Woodlawn Cemetery   *Located in west Toledo, most easily reached from westbound I-475. Take the Central Avenue/Jackson Road exit, then turn south on Jackson Road. Turn left (or east) on Central Avenue and proceed to the first light. Turn left and enter the cemetery. (Map A–94)*

Large numbers of conifers and other seed-bearing trees make this an attractive place for winter finches. Pine Siskins are usually present and Common Redpolls often occur. Both crossbills are sometimes seen during irruption years and Pine Grosbeaks are possible. Large numbers of fruiting trees have been known to attract Bohemian Waxwings.

The cemetery is an excellent place to look for warblers and other spring migrants. Sharp-shinned Hawks sometimes inhabit mature hemlock trees and Cooper's Hawks are known to nest. From March through the first part of May,

Common Redpolls

a scarch of yew plantings and other dense conifers will frequently turn up at least one Saw-Whet Owl.

Summer residents include Great Horned Owl, Red-headed, Downy, and Hairy woodpeckers, Eastern Wood-Pewee, Great Crested Flycatcher, Black-capped Chickadee, Tufted Titmouse, White-breasted Nuthatch, House Wren, Wood Thrush, Gray Catbird, Brown Thrasher, Cedar Waxwing, Red-eyed Vireo, Northern Cardinal, Rose-breasted Grosbeak, Chipping and Song sparrows, Northern Oriole, House Finch, and American Goldfinch.

PART II

The West-Central Counties

ONCE FOREST LAND broken only by occasional swaths of prairie, marsh, and a few large swamps—and traversed by clear rivers and streams—the counties of central and western Ohio are now predominantly farmland dotted with small towns and the urban-industrial sprawl of larger cities. Yet, in this drastically altered environment, there still exist a significant number of natural areas—forests and ungrazed woodlots, remnant bogs, lakes, and tree-lined rivers—many of them wisely set aside as parks and nature preserves. In this century, numerous reservoirs and thousands of farm ponds—not to speak of such specialized environments as sewerage treatment ponds, golf courses, airports, quarries, and landfills—have further altered the landscape. In spite of all these changes, each spring and fall millions of bird migrants of several hundred species pass through our state to and from their breeding grounds. About one-third of these nest in the west-central region.

Part II describes sites in 22 counties. The westernmost counties of the region and birding sites therein, shown on Map C, are Auglaize, Champaign, Clark, Darke, Greene, Hardin, Mercer, Miami, Logan, Montgomery, Preble, and Shelby. The central counties, shown on Map D, are Delaware, Fayette, Franklin, Knox, Licking, Madison, Marion, Morrow, Pickaway, and Union. Descriptions of, and directions to, the sites are presented in alphabetical order.

Alum Creek Reservoir

Take Ohio 23 north from Columbus to Lewis Center Road and follow it east to the dam. To reach the upper part of the reservoir, take Ohio 42 east from Delaware. (Map D-1)

This sizeable reservoir was first fully filled in 1975. The surrounding land is maintained for recreational purposes by the Ohio Department of Natural Resources. Less than a mile from the dam on the west side of the reservoir is a woods that extends along both sides of Lewis Center Road. Along the wooded edges, look for migrant songbirds in the spring and fall. In late spring and summer, the sloping field that leads to the water's edge is excellent for such erratics as Dickcissel and Henslow's Sparrow and, more commonly, Horned Larks, Savannah and Grasshopper sparrows, Bobolinks, and Eastern Meadowlarks.

A long man-made beach, accessible from Lewis Center Road, stretches northward along the shore and is a good place to look for Water Pipits, Ruddy

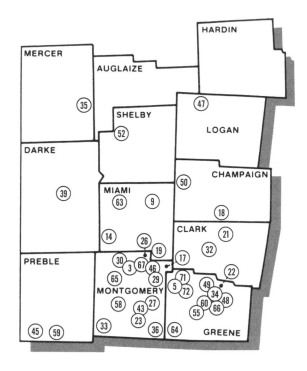

MAP C

3 Aullwood Audubon Center
5 Beaver Creek Wetlands
9 Big Woods Reserve
14 Bruckner Nature Center
17 Carriage Hill Farm and Reserve
18 Cedar Bog State Memorial
19 Charleston Falls Preserve
21 Clarence J. Brown Reservoir/Buck Creek
   State Park
22 Clifton Gorge
23 Cox Arboretum
26 Dayton International Airport
27 Dayton River Corridor
29 Eastwood Reserve
30 Englewood Reserve
32 George Rogers Clark State Park
33 Germantown Reserve
34 Glen Helen Nature Preserve
35 Grand Lake St. Marys
36 Grant Park/Sugar Valley Park
39 Greenville City Park

43 Hills and Dales Park/Calvary and
   Woodland cemeteries
45 Hueston Woods State Park
46 Huffman Reserve
47 Indian Lake
48 Indian Mound Reserve
49 John Bryan State Park
50 Kiser Lake State Park
52 Lake Loramie State Park
55 Narrows Reserve, Little Miami River
58 Possum Creek Farm and Reserve
59 Rush Run State Wildlife Area
60 Sara Lee Arnovitz Nature Preserve
63 Stillwater Prairie Reserve
64 Sugarcreek Reserve
65 Sycamore State Park
66 Tawawa Forest
67 Taylorsville Reserve
71 Wright-Patterson Air Force Base
72 Wright State University Woods

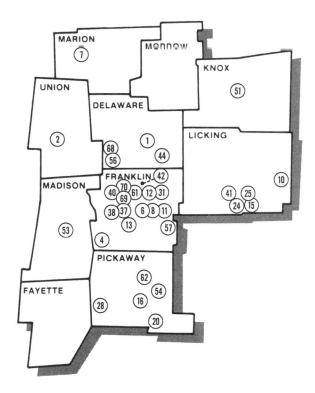

MAP D

Turnstones, Sanderlings, and a scattering of other shorebirds in the spring and during the early morning in late summer. Scan the water for loons, grebes, gulls, terns, and ducks in spring and fall.

Africa Road parallels the east side of the reservoir where the boat ramp areas are the best places for observing the water. The majority of waterfowl, including large numbers of American Coots, concentrate around inlets on the western shore. During the summer, fallow fields along Africa Road sometimes attract Sedge Wrens, Dickcissels, and Bobolinks.

A circuit of the upper end of the reservoir is possible by taking Old State Road north from Ohio 42, turning east on Ohio 521 for a short distance, then returning south along Hogback Road, which offers some scenic views of the upper reservoir and good birding in surrounding woods and fields.

American Legion Memorial Park   *Located off U.S. 33 on the northwest edge*
of Marysville. (Map D–2)

This is a pleasant spot to visit in April and May to look for warblers and other arboreal migrants. Trails wander through groves of large deciduous trees with an understory sprinkled with wildflowers and along a tree-lined stream.

Aullwood Audubon Center   *Located north of Dayton near the city of*
and Farm   *Englewood, in Montgomery County. From*
I-70, exit at Ohio 48, proceed north to
Englewood Dam and turn east across the
dam, then right to the Center. From I-75,
exit at U.S. 40, drive through Vandalia,
past Frederick Road to first road on the
left, turn left to the Center on Aullwood
Road. To get to the farm, take Frederick
Road south from U.S. 40. (Map C–3)

In 1957 Mrs. John W. Aull gave her 200-acre farm to the National Audubon Society to be used as an outdoor education center. It is now one of Audubon's regional nature centers as well as a working farm.

Varied habitats include a prairie, numerous wooded areas, streams, pine plantations, farm fields, marshy areas, and two ponds. Several hiking trails wind through the area. Almost 200 species of birds have been recorded since the center was established. Of these, 81 have nested or were observed during the nesting season. The area is also a refuge for foxes, raccoons, skunks, opossums, and many smaller mammals. Fish, frogs, and turtles inhabit the freshwater ponds and streams. There is a splendid variety of native trees and wildflowers, as well as big bluestem and Indian grasses towering 10 feet high.

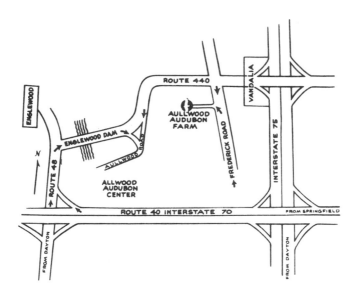

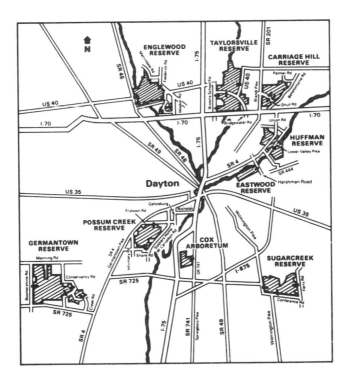

Dayton Area

The two small ponds and bordering marshes attract Great Blue and Green-backed herons, Wood Ducks, Mallards, Ospreys, and American Coots. Raptors include Cooper's Hawk, Eastern Screech-Owl, Great Horned and Barred owls. Many migrants pass through Aullwood in both the spring and fall season. Rare species include Yellow-bellied Flycatcher and Golden-winged, Connecticut, and Mourning warblers. Fox and Lincoln's sparrows are found in dense cover at these times. Ovenbirds have nested here.

Winter birding at Aullwood is best around the nature center where well-stocked feeders sometimes attract Purple Finches, Pine Siskins, and, during incursion years, Evening Grosbeaks. Rarities have included a wide variety of birds including Golden Eagle and Brewster's Warbler.

Nearby are two other good birding sites, Aullwood Garden (a part of Englewood Reserve) and the Dayton International Airport.

Battelle-Darby Creek Metropolitan Park

Drive west of Columbus on U.S. 40 to Darby Creek Drive (5.3 miles west of I-270); turn south and proceed for 3 miles. (Map D–4)

This attractive natural area expansion program now includes 3,115 acres of oak-hickory woodlands and habitat-rich bottomlands bordering two creeks. The bluffs overlooking Darby Creek are known for their prairie wildflowers.

Beginning at the parking lot, several trails lead into the woods, follow ravines, and emerge at the creek. The trails to the north eventually come out onto the higher bluffs; there is also one trail that follows the creek. In the spring and fall, many landbird species can be found here, and because of the diversity of habitat, a surprising number of waterfowl, shorebirds, and marsh inhabitants have been recorded.

Great Blue Herons and Green-backed Herons are often seen along the creek, and American Bitterns, Great Egrets, and Black-crowned and Yellow-crowned night-herons have been seen on occasion. Waterfowl that have been observed include the Canada Goose, Wood Duck, Mallard, Northern Pintail, Blue-winged Teal, American Wigeon, Canvasback, Redhead, and Hooded Merganser.

Turkey Vultures are frequently seen soaring over the scenic valley, and there is even one record of a stray Black Vulture. Small numbers of hawks and Ospreys follow the creek valley in their migrations.

In March and April, American Woodcocks perform, and after the sun goes down Eastern Screech-Owls and Great Horned and Barred owls have all been observed and presumably nest.

Other birds seen regularly during the breeding season are Yellow-billed

Cuckoos, Ruby-throated Hummingbirds, Belted Kingfishers, all of the Ohio-nesting woodpeckers, Eastern Wood-Pewee, Acadian and Willow flycatchers, and Eastern Phoebe.

Northern Rough-winged and Barn swallows skim over the fields and along the creek; Carolina Chickadees, Tufted Titmice, and White-breasted Nuthatches are commonly found in the woods; and House Wrens, Blue-gray Gnatcatchers, Gray Catbirds, Northern Mockingbirds, and Brown Thrashers can be found along the edges. Wood Thrushes, Yellow-throated Vireos, Cerulean Warblers, Ovenbirds, and Scarlet Tanagers can be found, or at least heard, in the deep woods. One or two pairs of Louisiana Waterthrushes nest along the deep ravines.

To get to the Little Darby Creek section of the park, continue south on Darby Creek Drive to Alkire Road, proceed west (right) a short distance to Gardner Road and turn north (right) to the parking area.

Beaver Creek Wetlands   *Located in Greene County east of Beaver Valley Road. Current access is limited to stream crossings along New Germany-Trebein and Fairground roads. Take U.S. 35 east from Dayton to Factory Road, north to Dayton-Xenia Road, east to Beaver Valley Road. (Map C–5)*

The Beaver Creek Wetlands form a narrow corridor of almost 1,000 acres along Big Beaver Creek from Fairborn to the Little Miami River. The area is one of the last remaining wetlands in the state of Ohio that is just as it was at the turn of the 19th century. It contains both rare plants and a variety of animals, including beavers which are again building dams along the creek. The wetland is also ideal habitat for the rare and localized Baltimore Checkerspot butterfly. The butterfly larvae feed on turtlehead, a flowering plant found in abundance along the creek. Acquisition of lands along the ten-mile corridor is currently underway (more than 40% has been preserved), and plans are being developed for a system of trails with strategically placed boardwalks and observation platforms. Currently, access is limited. Permission must be obtained to visit areas where the existing paved roads traverse the marsh.

Over 100 species of birds have been sighted in the wetlands. Species include Great Egret, Black-crowned and Yellow-crowned night-herons, Osprey, Bald Eagle, Northern Harrier, Red-shouldered Hawk, Yellow, King, Virginia, and Sora rails. Nesting species include Great Blue Heron, Canada Goose, Wood Duck, Mallard, Blue-winged Teal, Red-tailed Hawk, Great Horned Owl, Belted Kingfisher, Willow Flycatcher, Tree and Barn swallows, and Eastern

Black-crowned and Yellow-crowned Night-Herons

Bluebird. The Ohio Division of Wildlife, the Ohio Nature Conservancy, the Dayton Audubon Society, and the Greene County Park District are working with the Beaver Creek Wetlands Association in developing plans to preserve this remarkable area.

Bexley City Park

Take Nelson Road in Columbus north from East Broad Street and turn right at Clifton Avenue. If the park entrance is closed, continue to Parkview Avenue, turn left and enter the driveway just north of the large mansion that is located on the grounds. There is a parking lot at the end of the driveway. (Map D–6)

Located on the banks of Alum Creek, this is a pleasant place to hike any time of the year. Trails lead along the creek and through the woods. A colorful array of summering birds can be found—from Great Crested Flycatchers and Wood Thrushes to Indigo Buntings and Northern Orioles. The trail along the creek and the trees and shrubs around the parking lot can be excellent for migrating warblers and other landbirds.

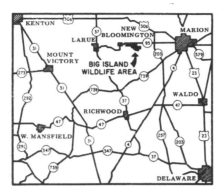

Big Island Wildlife Area

From the center of Marion drive west on Ohio 95 about 7 miles; turn left (south) on Espyville Road (T-84) and proceed 0.5 mile. Other entry points are along La Rue-Prospect Road (C-37), a right turn 1.4 miles south of Ohio 95. (Map D–7)

Although this 1,923-acre tract, the site of a primeval wet prairie, has been managed by the Ohio Department of Natural Resources mostly for fishing and hunting, it is nevertheless a splendid place for finding a wide variety of interesting birds. Three diked impoundments contain 382 acres of ponds, cattail marsh, and scattered rushes surrounded by forests, wet meadows, successional fields, croplands, and riparian woodlands along the Scioto River. All of these habitats may be reached on foot from surrounding roads at a dozen or so unmarked entries which can be spotted by their gravel surfaces.

Two trails are usually mowed through fields west of the impoundments from graveled entries on the north side of La Rue-Prospect Road. A rookery of herons and egrets is located in the big woodlot beyond the westernmost impoundment. Between the cattail marsh and the railroad tracks to the north are 400 acres of wetlands with prairie plants, including some small sedge meadows. As part of an ongoing program to enhance shorebird habitat, the water in the impoundments is drawn down in late summer and early fall to create mudflats. Current plans call for an observation blind to enhance close-up viewing.

Waterfowl are a prime attraction in season with all of the common dabbling ducks well represented, while smaller numbers of diving ducks stop over to feed and rest. From the middle of March through April, there are usually good numbers of Redheads, Ring-necked Ducks, and Lesser Scaups present, and smaller gatherings of Canvasbacks, Buffleheads, Hooded Mergansers, and

Ruddy Ducks. Other waterbirds encountered during migrations include: Horned Grebes, Tundra Swans, Snow Geese, all of the commonly encountered shorebirds, and Ohio's four expected tern species. Ospreys are frequent spring and fall visitors.

Northern Harriers, Rough-legged Hawks, and Short-eared Owls are usually encountered during the winter months. Other owls—Eastern Screech-Owl, Great Horned, Barred, and occasional Long-eared and Northern Saw-whet owls—are sometimes found in the woods adjacent to the impoundments.

Summer residents include Pied-billed Grebe, Least Bittern, Green-backed Heron, Canada Goose, Wood Duck, Blue-winged Teal, Virginia and Sora rails, Common Moorhen, American Coot, Spotted Sandpiper, Belted Kingfisher, Red-headed Woodpecker, Willow Flycatcher, Marsh Wren, Blue-winged Warbler, Yellow Warbler, Savannah and Swamp sparrows, and Orchard Oriole.

Casual nesting species or rare summer visitors include American Bittern, Great Egret, Black-crowned Night-Heron, Green-winged Teal, American Black Duck, Northern Pintail, Northern Shoveler, Gadwall, American Wigeon, Redhead, Ruddy Duck, and King Rail.

Rare migrants or vagrants that have been recorded in the area include Eared Grebe, Snowy Egret, Little Blue Heron, Cattle Egret, Greater White-fronted Goose, Greater Scaup, Merlin, Peregrine Falcon, Yellow and Black rails, Sandhill Crane, Willet, Whimbrel, Buff-breasted Sandpiper, LeConte's and Sharp-tailed sparrows, Western Meadowlark, and Yellow-headed Blackbird. During winter months, look for Lapland Longspurs and Snow Buntings associating with flocks of Horned Larks in surrounding fields.

Big Walnut Park   *From I-70 in Columbus, exit at Hamilton Road, North; continue on Hamilton Road to Livingston. Drive east on Livingston about 1.5 miles. (Map D–8)*

This Columbus park features a mature river bottom forest of sycamores, cottonwoods, and sugar maples which run in a narrow strip along the creek between Livingston Avenue and East Main Street. There is also a small pond, parkland, brush, and weed fields.

In late April and most of May, this is a fine place to find migratory landbirds in good numbers. Green-backed Herons, Wood Ducks, Greater and Lesser yellowlegs, Solitary and Spotted sandpipers occur along the creek. In late April and mid-September, look for kettles of Broad-winged Hawks. Resident birds are similar to those described for Blacklick Woods Metropolitan Park. Stephen W. Kress compiled a list of 120 species of birds in this park, including 32 species of warblers.

Big Woods Reserve   *East of Piqua, in Miami County. From*
I-75, take U.S. 36 east 3.2 miles, right
1 mile on Union-Helby Road, then 0.5
mile on Statler Road to Garbry's Big
Woods Sanctuary. To reach reserve
entrance, continue east on Statler Road,
then right on Casstown-Sidney Road.
(Map C–9)

This 272-acre reserve includes the 150-acre Garbry's Big Woods Sanctuary containing outstanding plant and animal habitats typical of those which existed in Ohio prior to settlement. The largest stand of upland woodland in Miami County, the area is primarily undisturbed wet beech-maple forest. A 42-inch-wide, all-weather boardwalk, which accommodates wheelchairs nicely, meanders for nearly 0.7 mile through the forest. The sanctuary is noted for its outstanding spring wildflower displays. Picnic areas, trails, and a fishing pond complete the reserve.

Look for woodland birds such as Cooper's and Red-tailed hawks, Great Horned Owl, Red-headed, Red-bellied, Downy, Hairy, and Pileated woodpeckers, Eastern Wood-Pewee, White-breasted Nuthatch, Wood Thrush, Ovenbird, and Yellow-breasted Chat. Migrant Wood Ducks and Osprey sometimes visit the reserve. Northern Bobwhites nest in adjacent fields, and Northern Harriers are often seen soaring just above the grass. This is a fine place in April and May to witness the migration of warblers and other songbirds.

Black Hand Gorge State Nature   *From Newark take Ohio 16 east to Ohio*
Preserve   *146, then south to County Road 273.*
Continue south a short distance to the
entrance near the village of Toboso.
(Map D–10)

About 300 million years ago Ohio was covered by an inland sea. Sand and rock eroding from the mountains of Pennsylvania formed a vast delta that eventually became what is known as Black Hand sandstone, after the large black hand drawn by Indians on the walls of this deep gorge cut by the Licking River. It is thought the hand pointed the way to the flint deposits of nearby Flint Ridge. Picturesque trails developed by the Ohio Department of Natural Resources lead to the gorge.

Oak, hickory, Virginia pine, and mountain laurel abound on the hillsides, where birds like Red-bellied and Pileated woodpeckers, Acadian Flycatcher, Ovenbird, and Kentucky and Hooded warblers nest. In the floodplain, sycamores, cottonwoods, and box elders provide habitat for Eastern Kingbirds, Cedar Waxwings, Warbling Vireos, Indigo Buntings, and Northern Orioles. In spring, troupes of warblers, vireos, tanagers, and grosbeaks sometimes fill the treetops with color and song.

Buttonbush Trail is a good location for Yellow-billed Cuckoos. Yellow-throated Warblers nest near the railroad trestle.

Blacklick Woods Metropolitan Park

Take I-70 in Columbus to the north exit at Brice Road. Proceed north on Brice Road to Livingston Avenue and turn east. The park is about 1 mile distant. (Map D-11)

The forest areas of this large park are laced with paths that wind through lowlands of swamp forest with white oak, pin oak, bur oak, and silver maple trees. Typical trees of the higher ground include beech, sugar maple, white ash, black cherry, hickory, white oak, and red elm.

Between the several parking lots, there are groves of trees, playgrounds, and expanses of grassy parkland. Vantage points for birding are the clearing around the Beech-Maple Lodge, the nearby parking spaces and small pond, clearings within the woods, and an old roadway between the woods and the golf course. In spring and summer, scan the golf course for Killdeer, Upland Sandpipers, Purple Martins, and Barn Swallows. Overhead, look for Red-shouldered and Red-tailed hawks and American Kestrels.

Frequently seen April and early May migrants include the Yellow-bellied Sapsucker, Eastern Phoebe, Red-breasted Nuthatch, Winter Wren, Brown Thrasher, Hermit Thrush, Eastern Bluebird, Blue-gray Gnatcatcher, Golden-crowned and Ruby-crowned kinglets, Solitary Vireo, Blue-winged, Orange-crowned, Yellow-rumped, Pine, Palm, and Black-and-white warblers, Louisiana Waterthrush, Rufous-sided Towhee, Chipping, Field, Fox, Song, Swamp, White-throated, and White-crowned sparrows, Rusty Blackbird, and Purple Finch.

Some representative nesting birds to look for are Wood Duck, Red-shouldered and Red-tailed hawks, American Kestrel, Yellow-billed and, more rarely, Black-billed cuckoos, Red-headed, Red-bellied, and Pileated woodpeckers, Eastern Wood-Pewee, Acadian Flycatcher, Eastern Phoebe, Great Crested Flycatcher, Eastern Kingbird, Blue-gray Gnatcatcher, Eastern Bluebird, Wood Thrush, Northern Mockingbird, Brown Thrasher, Cedar Waxwing, Red-eyed Vireo, Yellow Warbler, American Redstart (uncommon), Common Yellowthroat, Yellow-breasted Chat, Northern Oriole, and Scarlet Tanager.

Eastern Screech-Owl and Great Horned and Barred owls are year-round residents in the deeper woods; American Woodcock perform their courtship flights each spring over the fields east of the Interpretive Center.

Red-shouldered Hawk

The Interpretive Center is located within the Walter A. Tucker Nature Preserve at the end of the main driveway. The Center has one-way windows for viewing bird feeders and a sizeable pond. In late afternoon, white-tailed deer frequently feed close to the windows.

Blendon Woods Metropolitan Park

From I-270 in Columbus, exit east onto Ohio 161 and proceed 1 mile. An alternate route is to take Sunbury Road north from Columbus and turn right at Ohio 161. (Map D–12)

In addition to extensive wooded ravines and uplands, this splendid park embraces the 118-acre Walden Wildlife Refuge with its 11-acre Thoreau Pond and elevated observation shelters equipped with spotting scopes for viewing waterfowl. The pond is kept free of ice during the coldest winters by an underwater aerating system; ducks and geese are attracted by the grain put out for them. The refuge is open year-round.

A new nature interpretive center with a "window on wildlife" was recently completed and, as at all the Columbus and Franklin County Metro Parks, many of the facilities have now been made handicapped-accessible. There are miles of hiking trails and bird walks and other nature activities are scheduled on a regular basis.

Waterbirds frequently seen at Thoreau Pond in season include: Pied-billed and Horned grebes, Great Blue Heron, Green-backed Heron, Canada Goose, Wood Duck, Green-winged Teal, American Black Duck, Mallard, Northern Pintail, Blue-winged Teal, Northern Shoveler, Gadwall, American Wigeon, Canvasback, Redhead, Ring-necked Duck, Lesser Scaup, Common Goldeneye, Bufflehead, Hooded and Common mergansers, and Ruddy Duck. Less common species have included the Double-crested Cormorant, American Bittern, Great Egret, Tundra Swan, Snow Goose, Greater Scaup, Oldsquaw, and Black Scoter. Ospreys, gulls, and terns occasionally investigate the pond. On one occasion, a Bald Eagle stopped by.

Migrants at Blendon Woods are essentially the same as those described for Green Lawn Cemetery. An impressive list of nesting birds includes the Green-backed Heron, Canada Goose, Wood Duck, Mallard, Red-shouldered, Broad-winged, and Red-tailed hawks, Spotted Sandpiper, American Woodcock, Eastern Screech-Owl, Great Horned and Barred owls, Ruby-throated Hummingbird, all of the summering woodpeckers, Eastern Wood-Pewee, Acadian and Willow flycatchers, Eastern Phoebe, Great Crested Flycatcher, Eastern Kingbird, Carolina and House wrens, Blue-gray Gnatcatcher, Eastern Bluebird, Wood Thrush, Cedar Waxwing, White-eyed, Yellow-throated, and Red-eyed vireos, Blue-winged, Yellow, and Cerulean warblers, Ovenbird, Louisiana Waterthrush, Kentucky Warbler, Common Yellowthroat, Yellow-breasted Chat, Summer and Scarlet tanagers, Rose-breasted Grosbeak, Rufous-sided Towhee, and Northern Oriole.

Bolton Field Airport

Drive west on West Broad Street in Columbus to Norton Road, which is on the eastern edge of New Rome. Proceed south on Norton Road for 3 miles, or exit I-270 at Georgesville Road and proceed south to Norton Road. (Map D-13)

Lots of grassland and a number of low wet spots attract migrating shorebirds, especially in the spring if there has been ample rain. The best area is along the entrance driveway leading to the administration building. Migrants include Kill-deer, Greater and Lesser yellowlegs, Solitary and Upland sandpipers, various peeps, including occasional large flocks of Pectoral Sandpipers, and Common Snipe. Some years flocks of Lesser Golden-Plovers stop over for short visits.

Several pairs of Upland Sandpipers usually stay to nest, along with Horned Larks, Savannah and Grasshopper sparrows, and Eastern Meadow-larks. Johnson Road, bordering the south edge of the airport, is worth checking for all the above species, plus Snow Buntings and Lapland Longspurs in winter.

Brukner Nature Center   *In Miami County, west of Troy. From*
                                  Dayton take I-75 north to Ohio 55. West
                                     on Ohio 55 and then Horseshoe Bend
                                     Road to the entrance. (Map C-14)

Over 170 species of birds have been seen near this nature center and well over 100 species are seen there each year. Riparian habitat along the Stillwater River, designated a state scenic river, with woods, meadows, and two small ponds, may be reached from the nature center. In addition to a sizeable area of riparian woods, much of the 165-acre preserve is upland woods, both beech-maple and hickory-oak. There is also an area of mature red and white pines, which has attracted a number of winter finches.

Watching the nature center feeders from an enclosed observation platform and viewing rooms is an excellent way to observe wintering finches. Some years the feeders host Purple Finches, Common Redpolls, Pine Siskins, and Evening Grosbeaks. Red Crossbills are rare visitors, and Red-breasted Nut-hatches feed alongside the more common Carolina Chickadees, Tufted Tit-mice, White-breasted Nuthatches, Dark-eyed Juncos, and House Finches. Black-capped Chickadees are seen during years of incursion. Also visit the display of native Ohio wildlife at the center.

Representative birds in the surrounding woodlands include: Eastern Screech-Owl, Great Horned and Barred owls, and Red-bellied, Downy, Hairy, and Pileated woodpeckers. Carolina Wrens are present year-round; House Wrens are summer residents. Migrant Winter Wrens are spotted along em-bankments and in dense undergrowth. Several species of warblers nest, includ-ing Yellow, Cerulean, American Redstart (rare), Kentucky, and Common Yellowthroat.

The nature center is a good place to look for migrant passerines during the spring migration. On a good day, it is possible to find more than 25 species of warblers passing through the grounds. Wood Ducks and a few other water-fowl sometimes drop into the small ponds. Unusual birds seen in the area have included Osprey, Northern Goshawk, Lesser Golden-Plover, Snowy Owl, Con-necticut and Mourning warblers, and White-winged Crossbill.

Prothonotary Warbler

Buckeye Lake   *Take I-70 about 20 miles east*
of Columbus and go south for
1 mile on Ohio 79.
(Map D-15)

This 3,300-acre impoundment is surrounded by remnant woods, fallow and cultivated fields, resort and year-round housing, and several small towns and villages. Waterfowl that visit the lake are substantially less numerous than they were before 1960; however, nearly all species of ducks that occur in Ohio may be found on the lake in spring and fall. The largest concentrations are usually found in March when there is a minimum of boating and no hunting: fairly large assemblages of dabbling ducks occur—Green-winged Teals, American Black Ducks, Mallards, Northern Pintails, Northern Shovelers, Gadwalls, American Wigeons, and, toward the end of the month, newly arrived Wood Ducks and Blue-winged Teals—with rafts of bay ducks such as Canvasbacks, Redheads, Ring-necked Ducks, and Lesser Scaups, along with Common Goldeneyes, Buffleheads, all three merganser species, and Ruddy Ducks. Common Loons, Pied-billed and Horned grebes, and Double-crested Cormorants are usually present by late March, along with considerable numbers of Ring-billed and Herring gulls and occasional flocks of dainty Bonaparte's Gulls. Most waterbirds prefer the deeper middle and western parts of the lake. For a complete ornithological history of the entire area, refer to *The Birds of Buckeye Lake,* by Milton B. Trautman (Ann Arbor: University of Michigan Press, 1940).

Calamus Marsh   *On Ohio 104 about 0.7 mile south of*
Ohio 22 west of Circleville. (Map D–16)

This rather small marsh lies along an abandoned railroad spur and is densely vegetated with calamus, cattails, and sedges with relatively few patches of open water. According to the late Edward S. Thomas, Calamus Marsh has been well known to local ornithologists for more than 100 years.

During the spring and fall, small flocks of puddle ducks can be found feeding and resting in the marsh. These include Green-winged Teal, American Black Ducks, Mallards, Northern Pintails, Blue-winged Teal, Northern Shovelers, and American Wigeon. Wood Ducks nest in the vicinity. Sometimes a few bay or diving ducks can be found, such as Redheads, Ring-necked Ducks, and Hooded Mergansers.

Pied-billed Grebes are regular visitors, and probably a few pairs nest. The same is true of the American Bittern, Virginia and Sora rails, Common Moorhens, and American Coots. Early in the spring, look for Rufous-sided Towhees, Fox and Swamp sparrows, and Rusty Blackbirds. Later, during the spring migration, hike back along the railroad tracks to turn up migrant landbirds and—possibly—a pair of nesting Prothonotary Warblers.

Summer birds include the Great Blue and Green-backed herons, Turkey Vulture, American Kestrel, Killdeer, Mourning Dove, Chimney Swift, Belted Kingfisher, Red-headed and Downy woodpeckers, Northern Flicker, Eastern Wood-Pewee, Eastern Kingbird, Barn Swallow, Blue Jay, American Crow, House and Marsh wrens, American Robin, Gray Catbird, Cedar Waxwing, Warbling and Red-eyed vireos, Yellow Warbler, Common Yellowthroat, Yellow-breasted Chat, Summer Tanager, Northern Cardinal, Indigo Bunting, Field and Song sparrows, Red-winged Blackbird, Eastern Meadowlark, and Northern Oriole.

Carriage Hill Farm and Reserve   *North of Dayton in northeast Montgomery*
County and southeast Miami County. Take
I-75 north from Dayton, east on I-70 to
Ohio 201. North to Shull Road and then
east to parking lots. (Map C–17)

Nearly 1,000 acres in size, this reserve consists of woodlands and meadows interspersed with small streams, three small ponds, and a 14-acre lake with a boardwalk through a shallow marshy area at the west end. In addition, there is a working historical farm complete with barn, animals, blacksmithing, woodworking, and a country store, all maintained to represent rural life in the 1880s. There are nearly five miles of hiking trails, bridle trails, and picnicking facilities. Cross-country skiing is allowed when conditions are favorable.

The woodlands and brushy fields and meadows are home to American Woodcocks, Eastern Screech-Owls, Great Horned Owls, Carolina Wrens, Eastern Bluebirds, Common Yellowthroats, Yellow-breasted Chats, Rufous-sided Towhees, Field Sparrows, and Orchard and Northern orioles. Migrant waterfowl sometimes stop briefly on the lake.

Feeders are maintained behind the country store and attract common woodland birds such as Red-bellied Woodpecker, Carolina Chickadee, Tufted Titmouse, White-breasted Nuthatch, Northern Cardinal, and Dark-eyed Junco. Birds occasionally seen include Long-eared and Saw-whet owls, Sedge Wren, and American Pipit. Both Chestnut-sided Warblers and Henslow's Sparrows have occasionally nested.

Part of a nine-reserve system, Carriage Hill is managed by the Park District of Dayton-Montgomery County.

Cedar Bog State Memorial

Drive 9.5 miles north of Springfield into Champaign County on Ohio 68 to Woodburn Road and turn left. Or, from Urbana drive 3.5 miles south on Ohio 68 to Woodburn Road. (Map C–18)

Cedar Bog, a 50-acre remnant of what once was a marl swamp of over 7,000 acres, was created by limestone glacial deposits, surface water, and ground water saturation. About 150 acres have been added to the preserve in order to provide a protective buffer zone.

This remnant of the last ice age is the only place in Ohio where arborvitae trees occur in a bog, and it also boasts a white cedar forest of excellent quality. Cool alkaline spring water oozes to the surface, enabling many plants which bordered the glaciers as recently as 10,000 years ago to survive in this remaining northern microclimate.

Among the plants found at Cedar Bog are the dwarf birch, lady's slipper orchid, marsh marigold, large-flowered trillium, fringed gentian, grass-pink orchid, sundew, grass-of-Parnassus, Jack-in-the-pulpit, large-flowered bellwort, drooping trillium, bishop's cap, two-leaf Solomon's plume, yellow lady's slipper, shrubby cinquefoil, and poison sumac.

Cedar Run, a constantly flowing stream with practically no seasonal fluctuation in temperature or volume, provides cool waters that contain brook trout and the spotted turtle with its bright yellow polka dots. The Massasauga, or swamp rattlesnake, is another reptile that distinguished the bog. Several rare butterflies dependent on this unique habitat are the Milbert's Tortoiseshell, the Silvery Checkerspot, and the Swamp Metalmark.

Wood Ducks and Mallards probably nest nearby. Turkey Vultures, Red-

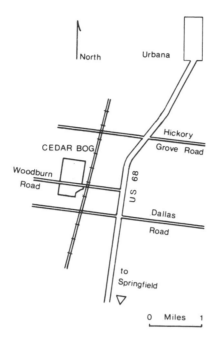

tailed Hawks, and American Kestrels are commonly seen. Killdeers nest, as do occasional American Woodcocks. American Bitterns, Virginia and Sora rails are sometimes seen during migrations.

Other birds that summer or nest in the area include Mourning Dove, Yellow-billed Cuckoo, Barred Owl, Chimney Swift, Ruby-throated Humming-bird, Belted Kingfisher, Red-headed, Red-bellied, Downy, and Hairy wood-peckers, Northern Flicker, Eastern Wood-Pewee, Acadian Flycatcher, Eastern Phoebe, Great Crested Flycatcher, Eastern Kingbird, Horned Lark, Barn Swal-low, Blue Jay, American Crow, Carolina Chickadee, Tufted Titmouse, White-breasted Nuthatch, Carolina and House wrens, Blue-gray Gnatcatcher, Wood Thrush, American Robin, Gray Catbird, Cedar Waxwing, European Starling, White-eyed and Red-eyed vireos, Blue-winged and Yellow warblers, Common Yellowthroat, Yellow-breasted Chat, Northern Cardinal, Indigo Bunting, Field and Song sparrows, Red-winged Blackbird, Eastern Meadowlark, Common Grackle, Brown-headed Cowbird, Northern Oriole, and American Goldfinch.

The bog is open from April through October Wednesday through Sun-day. Tours are conducted on Saturday and Sunday at 1 and 3 P.M. During the winter months the bog is open by reservation only. Cedar Bog is administered jointly by the Ohio Historical Society and the Ohio Department of Natural Resources.

Charleston Falls Preserve

North of Dayton, in southeast Miami County. From I-75 take Engle Road exit west, north on Engle Road 0.6 mile, right on Old Springfield Road (becomes Ross Road) 3.4 miles to park entrance.
(Map C-19)

Named after the nearby community of West Charleston, this 169-acre park preserves a 37-foot "miniature Niagara" waterfall along spring-fed Charleston Creek as it drops toward the Great Miami River a mile to the west. Uncommon plants line the limestone faces of the accompanying gorge. Over 2.5 miles of hiking trails wind through diverse habitats and varied landscapes including an upland woods, a tall grass prairie, thorny-scrub habitat, an area of conifers, a pond, and several fields. Evidence of Native American presence in the form of burial mounds, fire pits, and artifacts can be seen near the falls. A boardwalk viewing area with a limestone cave nearby, a prairie observation tower, and a small picnic area complete the facilities of this relatively undisturbed preserve.

Northern Bobwhite and American Woodcock nest. The abundance of thickets and brush offers good habitat for many sparrow species. The woods near Charleston Falls and along the creek is home to a pair of Pileated Woodpeckers, in addition to Yellow-throated Warblers and Louisiana Waterthrushes. Yellow Warblers and Common Yellowthroats are also easily found on the preserve. The woods can be excellent for migrants. Long-eared and Northern Saw-whet owls have been found in the conifers. The preserve is managed by the Miami County Park District and is just north of Taylorsville Reserve and several miles east of Dayton International Airport.

Charlie's Pond

Take Ohio 23 south from Circleville for 4.3 miles and turn west at Radcliff Road. Proceed another mile to the slough.
(Map D-20)

Sometimes called Upper Davenport, the area is located in the Scioto bottomlands and has attracted a surprising number of birds considering its small size. Although there is more water on the north side of the road, don't ignore the opposite side which is boggy and contains tangles of underbrush. An occasional heron or egret is found at the pond, in addition to migrating bitterns, puddle ducks, rails, and shorebirds. A few Common Snipes can usually be flushed up from wet spots along the edges in the spring and during the fall migration. Bands of swallows frequently feed over the pond, Swamp Sparrows can be found in the brush in April and May and again from September until early winter, and Water Pipits sometimes linger in the vicinity.

After checking out the pond, continue west on Radcliff Road; turn north on River Road and drive a mile or so to its end. Watch for Red-tailed Hawks and American Kestrels anytime, and Northern Harriers and Rough-legged Hawks from November to April. A Golden Eagle and a Merlin have been reported here in the past. The wide, gently rolling fields also attract shorebirds, especially during the spring months when the ground has been plowed and sky ponds appear after heavy rains. At such times, the chances of seeing flocks of Lesser Golden-Plover and Pectoral Sandpipers are particularly good.

Horned Larks are common, and from the end of January through June this is a fine place to see the males perform their courtship (or territorial) flight songs. Snow Buntings and, more rarely, Lapland Longspurs can be found in flocks of Horned Larks during winter months. Smith's Longspurs have been recorded in the area several times. Spring and summer birds include the Upland Sandpiper, Eastern Kingbird, Barn Swallow, Eastern Bluebird, Loggerhead Shrike (rare), Dickcissel (erratic), Grasshopper, Field, Vesper, and Song sparrows, Red-winged Blackbird, Eastern Meadowlark, and American Goldfinch.

Clarence J. Brown Reservoir and Buck Creek State Park

Northeast of Springfield, in Clark County. From the east, exit from I-70 north of Springfield onto Ohio 40, proceed west 2.4 miles, then right onto Bird Road and continue 1.7 miles to the park entrance. From the west, take I-70 to U.S. 68. North on U.S. 68 to Ohio 334 to Ohio 4, south to Croft Road, left to the park. (Map C-21)

This attractive park offers birders a variety of habitats to investigate: a 2,100-acre deep-water lake, shallow inlets, seasonal mudflats, patches of woods, extensive grasslands, fishing ponds, a picturesque wooded creek, numerous brushy areas, and fallow fields in the surrounding countryside. Facilities include a beach complex, picnic areas, cabins, campground, and marina.

The boat ramp, parking areas, and Robert Eastman Road near the entrance are good observation spots for waterbirds. While cruising the roads that circle the reservoir, look for Great Blue and Green-backed herons, Belted Kingfishers, raptors of half a dozen species including Northern Harrier, Rough-legged Hawk, and Short-eared Owl, found over grasslands and open fields, and a wide variety of other birds. Ospreys and Bald Eagles are sometimes spotted. Horned Larks are year-round residents in the grassy areas of the park.

Waterfowl are prevalent, sometimes in large numbers, in March and early April and again from late October until freeze-up, including a number of unusual visitors such as Tundra Swans, Greater White-fronted Goose, Oldsquaw, Black and Surf scoters. Common Loons and Pied-billed and Horned grebes are frequent fall and early winter visitors. Unusual species include Red-throated Loon and Red-necked Grebe. Eared Grebes have been found with increased regularity in the fall near the dam. Shorebirds are present in late July, August, and September, when water levels are down. Marsh Wrens (and occasional Sedge Wrens) are found at the north end of the lake.

Both the beach area at the south end of the lake near the dam and seasonal mudflats at the north end are worth checking, particularly when the lake is lowered in the fall. Regular species include Black-bellied Plover, Semipalmated Plover, Killdeer, Greater and Lesser yellowlegs, Spotted, Semipalmated, and Least sandpipers, Dunlin, and Common Snipe. Numerous rare shorebirds have been attracted to the area including Willet, Upland Sandpiper, Hudsonian Godwit, Ruddy Turnstone, Red Knot, Western, White-rumped, Baird's, and Buff-breasted sandpipers, and Wilson's Phalarope.

The beach area at times attracts large numbers of gulls and terns, including Bonaparte's, Ring-billed, and Herring Gulls, and occasional Caspian Terns. Rare gulls have included Laughing (late summer) and Franklin's gulls (regular in fall) and Black-legged Kittiwake.

Great and Snowy egrets, Little Blue Herons, and other wading birds are occasional visitors. Other rarities have included American White Pelican, Golden Eagle, Merlin, Peregrine Falcon, King Rail, Loggerhead Shrike, Bell's Vireo, and Brewer's Blackbird.

Southwest of the dam along Croft Road is **Old Reid Park**. Although it is a hangout for a large flock of domestic geese and ducks, wild ducks sometimes stop to see what's going on. Ducks that have been found here include Redhead, Oldsquaw, and Common Goldeneye.

Northeast of the lake is an agricultural area of long-grass fields. During late May and early June, this has been a consistently good location for Dickcissels, a number of sparrows including Vesper, Savannah, Grasshopper, and rarely, Henslow's, and Bobolinks. To get there, go south from the park entrance on Buck Creek Lane to Old Columbus Road, then east to Grant Road, north 1.5 miles to Yeazell Road, 1 mile east to Hodge Road, then back to the north end of the lake on Catawba Road.

Clifton Gorge (John L. Rich State Nature Preserve)

Follow Ohio 343 east of Yellow Springs in Greene County to the town of Clifton. Parking is 0.25 mile west of Clifton on the south side of Ohio 343. Alternatively, turn south on Ohio 370 and proceed to John Bryan State Park where hiking trails paralleling the Little Miami River lead to the gorge. (C–22)

Hemlocks, yews, and mountain maples inhabit the steep slopes of this gorge through which the Little Miami River flows. Hiking trails skirt the north side of the gorge and pass through fine habitat for the Barred Owl, Eastern Wood-Pewee, Acadian Flycatcher, Wood Thrush, Yellow-throated Vireo, Black-and-white Warbler (rare), Louisiana Waterthrush, Scarlet Tanager, and Rufous-sided Towhee. The 263-acre preserve is managed by the Ohio Department of Natural Resources. For other birds of the area, see Glen Helen account.

Cox Arboretum

On Ohio 741 1 mile north of Ohio 725 in south Dayton, Montgomery County. (Map C–23)

Shade trees, rock, herb, and shrub gardens, a conifer hillside, greenhouses, arboretum center with horticulture library and gift shop, and natural areas—a pond, a seral (succession) meadow, a stream, and woods—make up this outstanding 160-acre area managed by the Park District of Dayton-Montgomery County. In late April and May, warblers and other migrants are seen and heard in many parts of the arboretum—over 70 species have been seen in the woods alone. The entire area provides excellent opportunities to learn about some of the basic songs of breeding birds in May and June. Listen for the songs of House Wrens, Wood Thrushes, Gray Catbirds, Red-eyed Vireos, Yellow Warblers, Common Yellowthroats, Indigo Buntings, Chipping, Field, and Song sparrows, and Northern Orioles. During the months of March and April it is also an excellent locale to listen for and watch American Woodcocks.

Cranberry Bog Nature Preserve

Take I-70 east from Columbus to Ohio 79; proceed south about .5 mile, turn left and follow the road to Hunt's Landing. (Map D–24)

This nine-acre floating island composed entirely of sphagnum moss and other compacted vegetation is just off the north shore of Buckeye Lake. Wave action from storms, wind, and power boats has drastically reduced the size of the bog. Plants found here in addition to cranberry include poison sumac, pitcher plant, swamp pink orchid, and rose pogonia.

Under the hot sun of late summer, chunks and matted pieces of partly submerged bog float to the surface of the water, especially near the east end of the island. This provides favorable habitat for migrating shorebirds which can be observed close at hand from a boat. Among them look for Black-bellied Plover, Lesser Golden-Plover, and Semipalmated Plover, Greater and Lesser yellowlegs, Solitary, Spotted, Semipalmated, Western, White-rumped, Baird's, and Pectoral sandpipers, Dunlin later in the season, Stilt and Buff-breasted sandpipers, Short-billed Dowitcher, Wilson's and Red-necked phalaropes.

During the late spring and summer, there is a good chance of seeing wading birds such as the American Bittern and Great Blue and Green-backed herons. Wood Ducks can usually be seen around the island along with Belted Kingfishers, Purple Martins, and Northern Rough-winged, Bank, and Barn swallows. On the island itself, look for Carolina Chickadees, House Wrens, Cedar Waxwings, Prothonotary and Yellow warblers, Common Yellowthroats, Song Sparrows, and Red-winged Blackbirds.

Because the ecology of the island is very fragile, access is limited. Written permission for visitations may be obtained from the Division of Natural Areas and Preserves, Ohio Department of Natural Resources, Fountain Square, Columbus, Ohio 43224. For most birding activities, a trip around the island by boat is entirely adequate.

Darby Creek Metropolitan Park   *See Battelle-Darby Creek Metropolitan Park.*

Dawes Arboretum   *Take I-70 east from Columbus to Ohio 13 and drive north a short distance past U.S. 40. (Map D-25)*

Over 2,500 different woody plants grow in this botanist's and naturalist's wonderland. Winding drives and trails traverse an area that contains a five-acre lake, a cypress swamp, pine plantings, native and exotic trees, including the rare Franklinia discovered in the 1700s by William Bartram in Georgia, streams that meander through woods and meadows, a Japanese garden, administrative buildings, a greenhouse—and a good sample of seasonal birds.

Late April and May are especially recommended since this is a fine place to witness the parade of warblers and other songbirds passing through the state at that time. Nesting birds are typical of central Ohio. Descriptive literature can be obtained by writing: The Dawes Arboretum, Rte. 5, Newark, Ohio 43055.

Dayton International Airport   *In Vandalia, north Montgomery County.*
From downtown Dayton, take I-75 north,
then west on I-70 to the first exit, north
on Airport Access Road to the main
terminal. (Map C–26)

The grassy areas surrounding this international airport are attractive during the summer months to a sizeable population of Upland Sandpipers. From May to August it is possible to find the sandpipers feeding alongside the runways, especially at the east end of the airport. Take the Engle Road exit off I-75 (second exit north of I-70) west to North Dixie Road, then turn right to small aircraft terminal and Stevens Aviation.

Snowy Owls and Snow Buntings have been found here in winter. Other unusual species have included Peregrine Falcon, Lesser Golden-Plover (in surrounding fields), Northern and Loggerhead shrikes, Savannah and Grasshopper sparrows, and Bobolinks.

Dayton River Corridor   *In Montgomery County, from downtown*
Dayton, north and south along the Great
Miami and Stillwater rivers.
(Map C–27)

The Dayton River Corridor runs both north and south from downtown Dayton for about 26 miles through the county, from Wegerzyn Garden Center and Island Park in north Dayton to Rice Field in Miamisburg. Over the entire distance there is a paved bikeway along the Great Miami and Stillwater rivers which provides access to look for migratory waterfowl, shorebirds, gulls, and terns.

The rivers have long ago been dammed and channeled to prevent a repeat of the 1913 flood, which devastated downtown Dayton under 10 feet of muddy water. However, depending on water levels, gravel bars are often still present. During exceptionally cold weather, almost all lakes, reservoirs, streams, and rivers in the area freeze up except for a segment of the Great Miami River just south of downtown Dayton which is kept open by a large power plant.

During the summer months, Yellow-crowned Night-Herons regularly nest to the west of the downtown area along Wolf Creek. They are usually easiest to spot near dusk at the mouth of Wolf Creek where it joins the Great Miami River. To get there, take Third Street west from downtown across the Great Miami River, then north on Edwin C. Moses Boulevard across Wolf Creek to Riverview Park. It is probably best to bird this area with several companions.

The area just north and south of the U.S. 35 bridge can be particularly good for wintering waterfowl, especially during cold spells, when the water is kept open by a large power plant. From downtown Dayton, take Third Street to South Perry and Longworth Streets south to Washington Street, then west to either East Miami Boulevard (also known as Veteran's Parkway) on the east side of the river or Edwin C. Moses Boulevard on the west side. The Stewart Street bridge farther south allows return access. Species found here include Green-winged Teal, American Black Duck, Mallard, Gadwall, American Wigeon, Redhead, Greater (rare) and Lesser scaup, Common Goldeneye, Common Merganser, and Killdeer. This area is near Calvary and Woodland cemeteries and Hills and Dales Park.

Bends in the river to the north of the Moraine Air Park in the city of Moraine and in the West Carrollton area can be of interest. The West Carrollton exit off I-75 (Central Avenue) provides access to the east side of the river all the way to Miamisburg.

Rarities found along the corridor have included Red-necked Grebe, Eared Grebe, Tundra and Mute swans, Oldsquaw, White-winged Scoter, Bald Eagle, Piping Plover, Willet, Black-legged Kittiwake, and Short-eared Owl. When the river level is down during corridor maintenance, dam construction, or drought, exposed mudflats attract a variety of shorebirds. The area is administered by the Dayton-Montgomery County Park District, the Miami Conservancy District, and the River Corridor Committee.

Deer Creek State Park   *Take I-71 southwest from Columbus about*
                                             16 miles to the Mt. Sterling exit; follow
                                             Ohio 56 into Mt. Sterling to the junction
                                             with Ohio 207, turn east on 207 and
                                             proceed 5 miles to the lake. (Map D–28)

This 1,277-acre lake is located amid parkland totaling over 7,000 acres. Most parts of the lake are easily reached by a network of all-weather access roads. Shorebirds can be found in spring in wet meadows, on the sand beach near the dam and on muddy points of land. In late summer, mudflats appear first in inlets and at the upper end, which can be reached from Ohio 207. Trails through a marsh and a meadow are located near the park office near Dawson Yankeetown Road.

Common Loons, Horned Grebes, Canada Geese, and rafts of ducks are common sights in March and November; Tundra Swans and Double-crested Cormorants are sometimes seen. Great Blue Herons are present most of the year; Green-backed Herons can be found during the warm months and, rarely, an American Bittern is discovered hiding in grassy margins or marshy areas. Notable landbirds that have been seen in the vicinity include the Bald Eagle, Rough-legged Hawk, Great Horned and Barred owls, Whip-poor-will, Pileated

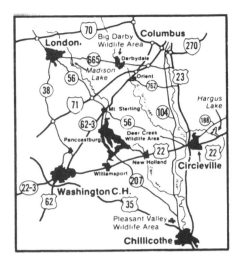

Woodpecker, Willow Flycatcher, Cliff Swallow, Loggerhead Shrike, Mourning Warbler, Summer Tanager, and Henslow's Sparrow.

Edward S. Thomas Nature Preserve
See Sharon Woods Metropolitan Park.

Eastwood Reserve
Just northeast of Dayton, in Montgomery County. From downtown Dayton, take Ohio 4/69 northeast to Harshman Road exit, then right to the park entrances.
(Map C–29)

This newest reserve (one of nine) in the Park District of Dayton-Montgomery County includes 185-acre Eastwood Lake and a couple of smaller lakes situated along the Mad River just downstream from Huffman Reserve and Wright-Patterson Air Force Base. A two-mile-long nature and hiking trail starts at adjacent Eastwood Park (part of the reserve), on the south side of the Mad River, and winds through a newly established meadow. In addition to boat racing and shows, water skiing, sailing, and fishing, there are picnic tables and shelters.

Species often seen here include Common Loon, Pied-billed and Horned grebes, Double-crested Cormorant, Black-crowned Night-Heron, and many migrating waterfowl, including diving ducks such as Canvasback, Redhead, Greater (rare) and Lesser scaup, and Ruddy Ducks. Ospreys occur in the spring and fall. Spotted Sandpipers are sometimes seen around the lake edges, and Bonaparte's Gulls stop by during migration. Many swallows, including Purple Martin and Cliff, can be seen swooping over the lake.

Unusual or rare birds that have been seen here include Red-throated Loon, Western, Red-necked and Eared grebes, Surf and White-winged scoters, Harlequin Duck, Oldsquaw, Willet, Ruddy Turnstone, Western Sandpiper, Laughing Gull, Black-legged Kittiwake, Caspian, Forster's, and Black terns, and Snowy Owl.

Englewood Reserve   *Northwest of Dayton, in Montgomery County. From I-70, north of Dayton, exit at Ohio 48 and go north to U.S. 40; turn right and drive east across the dam and turn left into the reserve entrance. (Map C-30)*

A lake with a waterfowl sanctuary, hiking and bridle trails, picnicking sites, Aullwood Garden, canoeing, ice skating, fishing, and birding are some of the year-round attractions found on this 1,500-acre reserve. There are also fields and meadows, woods, including a remnant swamp forest complete with board-walk, the Stillwater River, plantings of pines and shrubs, three waterfalls, and increasing areas of marsh—all of which attract a wide variety of birds. Over 200 species are seen annually, and about 90% of all the species occurring in west-central Ohio have been seen here, making this park a consistently good locale for rarities away from Lake Erie.

Migrant waterbirds include Double-crested Cormorant, Green-winged Teal, Mallard, Northern Pintail, Blue-winged Teal, Northern Shoveler, American Wigeon, Lesser Scaup, and Common Goldeneye. More unusual species include Greater Scaup and Canvasback. Wood Ducks and Mallards remain to breed. Depending on water levels, a number of shorebirds may also be found, including Semipalmated Plovers, Greater and Lesser yellowlegs, Spotted, Semipalmated, Least, and Pectoral sandpipers. Solitary Sandpipers are often found in the marshy area at the north end of the lake.

Breeding species include Great Blue Heron, Cooper's Hawk, Eastern Screech-Owl, Great Horned and Barred owls, Red-headed and Red-bellied woodpeckers, Eastern Wood-Pewee, Acadian and Willow flycatchers, Eastern Kingbird, White-eyed, Yellow-throated, Warbling, and Red-eyed vireos, Blue-winged, Yellow, Yellow-throated, Cerulean, Prothonotary, and Kentucky warblers, Yellow-breasted Chat, Summer and Scarlet tanagers, Rufous-sided Towhee, Orchard (decreasing) and Northern orioles. American Woodcocks put on their dramatic evening shows in March and April. Pileated Woodpeckers are often sighted, and Warbling Vireos are a sure thing in the cottonwoods along the river.

Migrants include Bonaparte's, Ring-billed, and Herring gulls, Caspian, Common, Forster's, and Black terns, Olive-sided Flycatcher, Purple Martin (sometimes large numbers in the fall), other swallows, and, at times, many warblers. Golden-winged, Connecticut, and Mourning warblers are sometimes discovered. In winter, Yellow-rumped Warblers are frequently present, Pine Siskins are somewhat less regular, and Common Redpolls have appeared irregularly. Long-eared and Saw-whet owls are known to frequent the pine plantation northeast of the lake near Patty Falls.

Rarities and less common species have included American Bittern, Great and Snowy Egret, White Ibis, Little Blue Heron, Tundra Swan, Surf Scoter, Northern Goshawk, Sandhill Crane, Piping Plover, American Avocet, Willet, Red Knot, Sanderling, Western, White-rumped, Baird's, and Stilt sandpipers, Wilson's and Red-necked phalarope, Henslow's Sparrow, and Bobolink.

Along Aullwood Road just south of Aullwood Audubon Center is **Aullwood Garden,** a 32-acre country garden and home donated by Mrs. John Aull. This special garden is well worth a visit for its abundant floral display, towering trees, and serenity. Many of the birds are the same as those seen at Aullwood Audubon Center. The Englewood Reserve is one of nine "Green Mansions" operated by the Park District of Dayton-Montgomery County and is across the highway from the Aullwood Audubon Center. Also nearby are the Dayton International Airport and Taylorsville Reserve.

Gahanna Woods Park and State Nature Preserve

Take Ohio 16 east from Columbus and turn left on Ohio 317; proceed to Taylor Station Road and turn right. (Map D–31)

In addition to 50 acres of woods and swamp forest, there are adjoining acres of fields, hedgerows, thickets, and groves of trees. The woods are composed of mature beech, maple, cherry, and ash, while other portions contain predominantly swamp forest species such as pin oak and silver maple.

During the spring migration, this is an excellent area in which to find a host of landbirds, including Connecticut and Mourning warblers during the last two-thirds of May.

George Rogers Clark State Park

East of Springfield, in Clark County. Exit from I-70 3 miles west of Springfield, or take U.S. 40 to Ohio 369 and drive south to the park entrance. (Map C–32)

A seven-acre lake, groves of trees, an oak-maple forest, and open grasslands attract numerous migrants in the spring and fall. In late April and May, the

park is a good place to find many species of warblers, vireos, and other passerine birds. Small numbers of waterbirds stop briefly on the lake.

Germantown Reserve

*Located about 15 miles southwest
of Dayton in Montgomery County.
From Dayton, take Ohio 4 southwest
about 10 miles; go west on Ohio 725
through Germantown for several miles.
Go right on Conservancy Road, across
the dam to the entrance. To reach the
nature center follow Ohio 725 past
Conservancy Road to Boomershine
Road, right about 1 mile to the
entrance. (Map C–33)*

An old earthen flood-control dam is at the east end of this 1,600-acre site,
which includes a large tract of giant beech and maple trees covering ravines
and hollows, a bass stream with floodplain riparian forest, picnicking sites, and
land in various stages of plant progression, including a remnant bluestem grass
prairie, and a prairie seed nursery. The western section of the park includes
open grassy fields, and a sizeable stand of eastern red cedars provides cover in
a northern portion. There is an underground nature center, complete with
active feeders. The center is wheelchair accessible. Over ten miles of trails,
some quite rugged, provide access to most sections of the park with its spectacular scenery and rich bird life.

Breeding species include Wood Duck, Sharp-shinned and Red-tailed
hawks, American Woodcock, Eastern Screech-Owl, Great Horned and Barred
owls, Whip-poor-will, Pileated Woodpecker, Eastern Wood-Pewee, Eastern
Bluebird, Brown Thrasher, Yellow-throated and Red-eyed vireos. Nesting warblers are the Blue-winged, Northern Parula, Yellow, Yellow-throated, Prairie,
Cerulean, American Redstart (rare), Worm-eating (rare), Ovenbird, Louisiana
Waterthrush, Kentucky, and Hooded (best locale in Miami Valley). Summer
Tanagers are rare; Scarlet Tanagers are fairly common. Grasshopper and Hen-
slow's sparrows are casual nesters.

Red-breasted Nuthatches, Purple Finches, and Pine Siskins occur in winter. Rare and uncommon birds have included Bald Eagle, Merlin, Sandhill
Crane, Upland Sandpiper, Long-eared, Short-eared, and Northern Saw-whet
owls, Loggerhead Shrike, the hybrid Brewster's Warbler, and Bobolink.

Germantown Reserve is the largest of nine "Green Mansions" operated
by the Park District of Dayton-Montgomery County.

Glen Helen Nature Preserve

In Greene County, about 7 miles north of Xenia. Take U.S. 68 to Yellow Springs, and go south on Corry Street at the north edge of town to the main entrance and Visitors Center. To reach the raptor center, follow Ohio 343 east to the entrance. (Map C–34)

Scenic and geologically valuable, this 960-acre tract embraces a steep-sided valley, good hiking trails, and a lovely cascade. There is forest, farmland, and prairie, all in various stages of succession, as well as a Hopewell burial mound, and the Yellow Spring, with its iron-laden orange water. The preserve is part of Antioch College and includes a visitors and nature center, raptor rehabilitation center, and a 100-acre study-forest managed by Yellow Springs High School. Much of the wooded area is resplendent with wildflowers in the spring. Hardwood trees include chinquapin, white and bur oaks, sugar maple, basswood, and black walnut. The understory is composed largely of redbud and spicebush.

Nesting in the woods are such birds as Cooper's, Red-shouldered, and Red-tailed hawks, Eastern Screech-Owl, Great Horned and Barred owls, Pileated Woodpecker, Eastern Wood-Pewee, Acadian Flycatcher, Great Crested Flycatcher, Blue-gray Gnatcatcher, Wood Thrush, Red-eyed Vireo, Cerulean Warbler, Ovenbird, Louisiana Waterthrush, Scarlet Tanager, and Rufous-sided Towhee.

Other birds nesting in clearings and along wooded edges are the American Woodcock, Yellow-billed Cuckoo, Belted Kingfisher, Eastern Kingbird, Carolina and House wrens, Eastern Bluebird, Gray Catbird, Northern Mockingbird, Brown Thrasher, Yellow-throated and Warbling vireos, Blue-winged, Yellow, and Yellow-throated warblers, Common Yellowthroat, Yellow-breasted Chat, Summer Tanager, Indigo Bunting, Chipping, Field, and Song sparrows, Northern Oriole, and American Goldfinch.

Grand Lake St. Marys

Located in Auglaize and Mercer counties. Take I-75 to Wapakoneta, exit west onto U.S. 33, proceed to St. Marys. To reach the State Fish Farm, take Ohio 703/364 1 mile west of town and turn south on Ohio 364. To get to the Mercer County Waterfowl Refuge, continue south on Ohio 364, then turn west onto Ohio 219 and follow it to the southwest shore and the village of Montezuma. Take Ohio 703 northwest to the refuge. (Map C–35)

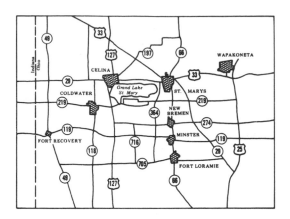

Sometimes known as Lake St. Marys, this is the largest body of water wholly within the state of Ohio. The lake covers approximately 13,500 acres and was created over a century ago by the construction of two earthen dams for a feeder reservoir to the Miami-Erie Canal System. Hundreds of Double-crested Cormorants nested at that time in tree snags along the south shore, and flocks of American White Pelicans were sometimes present in late summer. Toward the end of the last century, the lake was dotted with oil wells and the water level was lowered by a severe drought; surrounding land was cleared, intensive agriculture begun, and most of the timber was cleared from the exposed lake bed. Several areas along the lake are part of the Grand Lake St. Marys State Park, which is 13,920 acres in size including the 13,500 acres of the lake. The Mercer County Waterfowl Management Area and Refuge contains 1,408 acres and is located three miles south of Celina. The State Fish Farm is located along the east side of the lake.

Mercer County Waterfowl Refuge is an excellent area to observe geese and ducks each spring and fall; the State Fish Farm attracts shorebirds and waterfowl. Water circulates ice-free in some of these ponds, and the discharge of warm water at the power plant in Celina provides wintering fish-eating waterbirds with an abundance of small shad. Winter winds and wave action usually create ribbons of open water elsewhere on the lake in all but the coldest weather. Species seen with a fair degree of regularity from October through April are the Common Loon, Pied-billed and Horned grebes, Double-crested Cormorant, Green-winged Teal, American Black Duck, Mallard, Blue-winged Teal, American Wigeon, Canvasback, Redhead, Ring-necked Duck, Lesser Scaup, Common Goldeneye, Bufflehead, and all three mergansers.

Some of the scarcer waterbirds recorded around the lake include the Red-throated Loon, Red-necked Grebe, American White Pelican, Mute Swan, Brant, Greater White-fronted Goose, Snow Goose, Cinnamon Teal, Eurasian Wigeon, Greater Scaup, Oldsquaw, and Black, Surf, and White-winged scoters.

A decline in aquatic vegetation has reduced the numbers of marsh-inhabiting birds in recent years and almost eliminated bitterns and rails as breeding species. Great Blue Herons are common and nest in a rookery about four miles to the south, and a scattering of Green-backed Herons nest in wooded spots around the margins of the lake. Infrequent waders and marsh-loving visitors have included the American and Least bitterns, Great and Snowy egrets, Little Blue Heron, and Cattle Egret, Black-crowned Night-Heron, Glossy Ibis, Sandhill Crane, King, Virginia, Sora, Yellow, and Black rails, Common Moorhen, and Marsh Wren. American Coots are common migrants, but rare nesting birds.

The **State Fish Farm** on Ohio 364 south of Villanova is the choice location to find migrant waterfowl and shorebirds from April to June and July to November. Late summer and fall draining and cleaning of the ponds creates ideal mudflat habitat for migrating shorebirds, and the system of roadways and dikes allow close access to the birds. The best way to bird the area is to drive the paved and gravel roads, using your car as a blind. Regular migrants include Black-bellied and Semipalmated plovers, Greater and Lesser yellowlegs, Solitary, Spotted, Semipalmated, Western, Least, White-rumped, Baird's, Pectoral, and Stilt sandpipers, as well as Ruddy Turnstone, Sanderling, Dunlin, both dowitchers, and Common Snipe. Killdeers are often abundant. Rare birds seen at this locality have included Brant, Lesser Golden-Plover, Piping Plover, American Avocet, Black-necked Stilt, Willet, Upland Sandpiper, Whimbrel, Hudsonian and Marbled godwits, Red Knot, Purple and Buff-breasted sandpipers, and all three phalaropes.

The following gulls have been recorded at the lake: Laughing, Franklin's, Bonaparte's, Ring-billed, Herring, Iceland, Glaucous, Great Black-backed, and Sabine's. Tern species seen here are the Caspian, Common, Forster's, and Black.

Watch for migrant Merlins and Peregrine Falcons, which occasionally visit the fish farm and pursue shorebirds. This is also a good area for American Pipits, and there is always a chance of finding a Yellow-headed or Brewer's blackbird.

A diversity of habitat exists around the shores of the lake—cultivated and fallow fields, wet meadows, drainage ditches, tree- and brush-lined creeks, hedgerows, patches of woods, forests, orchards, cemeteries, and small towns. **Kessler's Woods** is located northeast of the lake; **Elm Grove Cemetery** is off Greenville Road at the east end of the lake; **Liette-Wealock Woods** is to the east of Route 364 at the southeast corner of the lake; the state park headquarters is on Route 29 just west of Villanova; and many good observation points for viewing the lake—and varied land habitats—can be reached along the south side of the lake from Route 703. Some of these latter locations include Windy Point Road (leading to a section of the State Park), Karafit and Cottonwood roads, Club Island Road, and Behm Road.

Some other breeding birds of interest are the American Woodcock, Red-headed Woodpecker, Willow Flycatcher, all of the swallows with the possible

First-year Iceland (front) and Glaucous gulls

exception of Cliff (seen regularly during migration), Yellow-throated Vireo, Yellow and Cerulean warblers, Ovenbird, Yellow-breasted Chat, Scarlet Tanager, and Orchard and Northern orioles. In open fields, especially those planted in alfalfa and clover, look for Dickcissels, Vesper, Savannah, and Grasshopper sparrows, and Bobolinks.

Grant Park   *In Washington Township and Centerville,*
Sugar Valley Park   *southwest Montgomery County. Grant Park can*
                             be reached by taking Alex Bell Road 0.5 mile
                             east from the I-675 and Ohio 48 interchange,
                             south on Paragon Road to Normandy Ridge
                             Road, then right to the parking lot beside
                             Normandy School. To reach Sugar Valley Park,
                             take Ohio 48 south from downtown Centerville
                             1 mile, turn east on Spring Valley Pike for 2
                             miles, then turn north on Rooks Mill Lane
                             for 0.5 mile. Park along the road at the
                             stream crossing. (Map C–36)

Grant and Sugar Valley parks are the largest nature parks of the Centerville-Washington Park District in the south Dayton metropolitan area. Both parks provide miles of streamside hiking through areas of woodlands and open meadows as well as limited picnicking facilities.

Grant Park, 183 acres in size, surrounds Holes Creek and is crossed by a pedestrian bridge which gives access, even at times of high water, to the principal central areas of the park. Mature and second-growth forest, riparian habitat, and grassy meadows assure that a variety of woodland birds can be found on any visit. Near the main entrance lies the Grant Nature Center.

Sugar Valley Park is 173 acres in size and lies along Sugar Creek, a tributary of the Little Miami River, a National Scenic River. Preserved primarily as a nature park, the area is also rich in historical value. It contains the best preserved millrace and site of a sawmill operated in the early 1800s, in addition to the well that served a pioneer log cabin. Many species of trees grow in the park, including large stands of mature oak, beech, maple, hickory, and sycamore. Fossils are abundant in the streambeds.

Both of these parks are fine places to observe spring migrants and, to a lesser degree, birds migrating south in the fall. Some of the breeding specialties are Yellow-billed Cuckoo, Acadian Flycatcher, Eastern Kingbird, Wood Thrush, Yellow-throated, Cerulean, and Kentucky warblers, Ovenbird, and Scarlet Tanager. Unusual migrants have included Golden-winged and Connecticut warblers and Lincoln's Sparrow.

Greenlawn Avenue Dam, Reservoir and Bike Path

Take I-71 south of downtown Columbus to the Greenlawn Avenue exit and drive east about 1 mile. Just before reaching the bridge, turn north into the deadend street paralleling the Scioto River. Or from South High Street, drive west on Whittier Street to the small park and boat ramp. (Map D-37)

On the west side of the river, the bike path passes under the bridge and continues south of Greenlawn Avenue to Frank Road. From mid-April through May, many migrant birds that follow the river can be seen to advantage. Yellow-bellied Sapsuckers, Northern Flickers, Winter Wrens, Ruby-crowned Kinglets, Hermit Thrushes, flocks of American Robins, Brown Thrashers, Yellow-rumped Warblers, Rufous-sided Towhees, Dark-eyed Juncos, and bands of sparrows give way to flycatchers, vireos, warblers of many species, tanagers, and grosbeaks as the spring progresses.

By the end of April, House Wrens appear and seem to be everywhere along the path. This is also one of the best places around Columbus to look for the first returning Yellow Warblers. Listen for the *skeow* call of recently arrived Green-backed Herons along the riverbank, and overhead watch for diurnal migrants such as Chimney Swifts, Barn Swallows, and mixed flocks of blackbirds. There is also always a chance of seeing a few Black-crowned Night-Herons or an Osprey along this stretch of the river.

By the first of May, there will be an abundance of Common Yellowthroats, Indigo Buntings, and many other migrating songbirds. The bike path is especially good for Yellow-billed Cuckoos, Veeries, Swainson's and Wood thrushes, Ovenbirds, Scarlet Tanagers, Rose-breasted Grosbeaks, and large numbers of transient Indigo Buntings. Warbling Vireos and Northern Orioles show up early in May and stay to nest in the cottonwoods above the dam. The rapids below the dam should be scanned for Yellow-crowned Night Herons, a few shorebirds—most likely Greater or Lesser yellowlegs—and Belted Kingfishers.

The reservoir behind the dam attracts waterbirds in the fall, during open winters, and in early spring. American Black Ducks, Mallards, Blue-winged Teals, and American Wigeons appear by mid September. Later in the season, and again in early spring, look for Pied-billed and Horned grebes, Canvasbacks, Redheads, Ring-necked Ducks, Lesser Scaups, Common Goldeneyes, Buffleheads, and any of the three merganser species. Flocks of Ring-billed Gulls and occasional Bonaparte's Gulls are seen in spring and fall, and a few Herring Gulls join wintering Ring-bills during the colder months.

Some of the more unusual birds that have been seen here include Double-crested Cormorant, Little Blue Heron, Cattle Egret, Tundra Swan, Eurasian Wigeon, Greater Scaup, Oldsquaw, White-winged Scoter, Merlin, American Avocet, Hudsonian and Marbled godwits, Franklin's Gull, Great Black-backed Gull, Snowy Owl, and Lark Bunting.

Green Lawn Cemetery   *Take I-71 south of downtown Columbus to the Greenlawn Avenue exit and drive west on Greenlawn Avenue for 0.7 mile to the entrance. (Map D–38)*

On a good day in late April or early May, an observer may record 60–80 species of birds in two or three hours in this wooded, park-like cemetery. On arriving, park outside the gate and investigate the nearby bushes, trees, and the wooded ravine behind the administration building. In March and April, the ravine is an excellent place to find American Woodcock (a pair or two sometimes nest), Louisiana Waterthrush, Rufous-sided Towhee, Fox Sparrow, and Rusty Blackbird.

Go around the south gatepost and shrubbery to the small woods nearby and walk along its western edge. Look for Killdeers, Northern Flickers, and large flocks of American Robins during March and April in the adjoining field.

Follow the woods around its perimeter, paying special attention to the surrounding brushy slopes and scrub trees. These are good places to find Con-

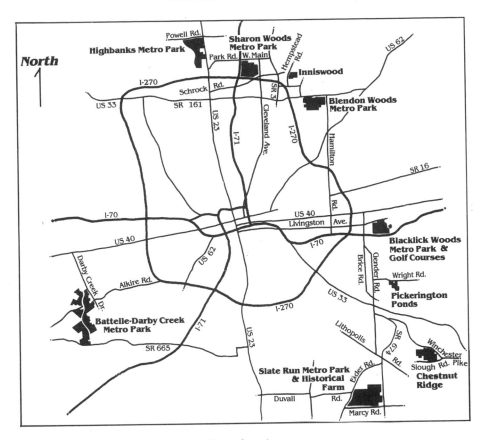

Columbus Area

necticut and Mourning warblers, Yellow-breasted Chats, Wilson's and Canada warblers, and Lincoln's Sparrows in May.

Among the nesting birds are the American Kestrel, Yellow-billed Cuckoo, Eastern Wood-Pewee, Willow Flycatcher, Carolina Chickadee, Carolina and House wrens, Gray Catbird, Brown Thrasher, Cedar Waxwing, Red-eyed Vireo, Yellow Warbler, Common Yellowthroat, Indigo Bunting, Chipping, Field, and Song sparrows, Northern Oriole, and American Goldfinch.

The most popular birding spot at Green Lawn is the site of what was once a small quarry and is now called the "pit." Surrounded by trees and bushes, this pleasant pond is near the center of the cemetery. To get there, drive through the entrance, follow the red center stripe to the first road past Section 85, turn right and park near the sculpture of Emil Ambos, the fisherman. The grave of humorist James Thurber is a few steps farther west in the Fisher family plot. The pit is beyond the shrubbery on the north side of the road.

Waterbirds—Pied-billed Grebes, Wood Ducks, Mallards, Blue-winged Teals, Hooded Mergansers, Black-crowned and Yellow-crowned night-herons, American Coots, Solitary and Spotted sandpipers, and Belted Kingfishers—are also seen from time to time.

The grove of trees just east of the tangle deserves close scrutiny. Flocks of Pine Siskins and Purple Finches are frequently found in the treetops associating with American Goldfinches. Rose-breasted Grosbeaks—sometimes a dozen or more in a single tree—are quite common by May 5. These are also good warbler trees, and sometimes a northward-bound Evening Grosbeak puts in an appearance.

In March and April, look in yew plantings for Northern Saw-whet Owls. Great Horned Owls nest in tree cavities and usually fledge their young by May 1. Scan the skies for migrating Broad-winged Hawks in late April and early May. Other raptors—most often Sharp-shinned, Cooper's, and Red-tailed hawks and American Kestrels—also fly over, usually in small numbers. Hawk flights usually occur between 9 A.M. and 2 P.M.

Another good spot at Green Lawn is an old iron bridge spanning a shallow ravine. To get there from the west end of the pit, drive or walk south to the first roadway to the right and proceed west for about 100 yards. Near the bridge in April, look for Yellow-bellied Sapsuckers, Winter Wrens, Hermit Thrushes, Hooded Warblers, Rufous-sided Towhees, and Fox Sparrows. Later in the season, along the gentle slopes of the ravine, there are apt to be Veeries, Gray-cheeked, Swainson's, and Wood thrushes, American Redstarts, Ovenbirds, and Kentucky and Canada warblers. Before leaving the ravine, check the large larch tree just beyond the Smith monument for a Cooper's Hawk nest. The grove of maple and sweet gum trees up over the south slope frequently yields an abundance of thrushes, assorted warblers, Purple Finches, and Pine Siskins.

A long, low wooded ridge extends much of the length of Green Lawn from near the bridge all the way to the north boundary of the cemetery. It can be easily reached from the pit by walking a short distance westward. Large oaks are interspersed among many other kinds of trees, all of which attract good numbers of migrants. The oaks have the added advantage of being late leafers, thus offering easy viewing until the middle of May.

The spring migration usually peaks in central Ohio between May 7 and 12, although there is some yearly variation. Additional large numbers of birds continue to migrate through the area as late as May 25.

Rare birds at Green Lawn have included Mississippi Kite, Chuck-will's-widow, Bell's Vireo, Kirtland's and Swainson's warblers, Blue Grosbeak, and Harris' Sparrow.

Greenville City Park

Located in the city of Greenville, Darke County, near Greenville High School along Harmon and Park Drives. From the downtown traffic circle, take East Main Street (Ohio 121) 10 blocks, then turn left onto Park Street. (Map C–39)

The Altar of Peace, commemorating treaties between Anthony Wayne and a consortium of Indian tribes, is located here along with a replica of a stockade, a stream, a woodland, a cemetery, lakes, and ponds. There are plenty of picnic tables and shelters as well as facilities for sports such as baseball diamonds, basketball and tennis courts, a swimming pool, Marling Band Shell and Harmon Field Stadium. From mid-March through May, this is a good place to witness the progress of landbird migration and to observe occasional migrant waterfowl.

Griggs Dam

Follow Ohio 33 northwest from downtown Columbus and turn left 1.1 mile past Lane Avenue into the park entrance. Turn left again, then take the unimproved road to the right. (Map D–40)

From April to mid-September scan the rapids below the dam for Yellow-crowned Night-Herons. One or two pairs of these prehistoric-looking waders nest in trees along the shore or in nearby ravines. The river below the dam remains free of ice except in the coldest weather. A few waterfowl take advantage of the open water and they can be observed from the road that goes through the campground. Most numerous are Mallards, but they are sometimes joined by Pied-billed Grebes, Green-winged Teals, American Black Ducks, American Wigeons, Common Goldeneyes, and Hooded Mergansers. After returning to near the entrance, take the drive to the right, which follows the Scioto River for several miles above the dam. In the spring, modest numbers of ducks including Canvasbacks, Redheads, Ring-necked Ducks, and Lesser Scaups can be found strung out along the river.

About two miles north of Ohio 161, at the Franklin-Delaware county line, there is a pulloff on the left side of the road. This is a pleasant spot from which to bird right out of the car window. During the cold months, it is possible to see Common Goldeneyes shooting the rapid currents of the river. In summer, a sizeable roost of Turkey Vultures may be observed in nearby trees.

Hebron State Fish Hatchery

Take I-70 about 30 miles east of Columbus. Exit at Ohio 37, turn south, and proceed for approximately 1 mile. Go left on Ohio 79 1.3 miles, then turn left again and drive along the old canal for another mile to the entrance and parking lot. (Map D-41)

Constructed in 1938 with WPA funds, the Hebron Hatchery produced its first crop of fish in 1941. It became a state facility in 1982. Bluegill sunfish, walleyes, saugeyes, hybrid striped bass, and channel catfish are propagated for stocking in lakes and reservoirs all over Ohio.

The grounds include about 75 acres of woods, fields, and marsh habitat, in addition to 63 ponds which cover about 69 acres. Nature trails connect the ponds and woods; other miles can be logged by walking the pond dikes looking for shorebirds. Wooded stream banks, remnant swamp forest, and wet meadows provide an abundance of plant life. Elm, ash, and soft maples in wet places give way to beech, sugar maple, white oak, pin oak, and honey locust on high ground.

The first ponds to investigate are immediately south of the parking lot, with another a short distance to the northeast. After checking these for shorebirds, walk east behind the nearby houses. Over 30 ponds are in this area: at any given time some are full, some are half empty, and some are drained. After working these, cross the walkway and turn your attention to the numerous ponds located south of the wooded stream.

Shorebirds are the *pièces de résistance* at the hatchery and, like all good things, they can't always be counted on unless conditions are exactly right. The perfect habitat for sandpipers and plovers is a recently drained pond with a few pools of shallow water or seepage to keep the bottom damp. May is the big shorebird month in spring. Southbound migrants reappear by the middle of July. The movement peaks from late August through the first part of September but continues well into October. Rare shorebird species that have been recorded are Piping Plover, American Avocet, Willet, Hudsonian and Marbled godwits, Red Knot, Western, White-rumped, and Baird's sandpipers, Stilt and Buff-breasted sandpipers, Ruff, Long-billed Dowitcher, and all three phalaropes.

Other rare and unusual species have included Western Grebe, Little Blue Heron, Cattle Egret, Yellow-crowned Night-Heron, Glossy Ibis, Tundra and Mute swans, Snow Goose, King Eider, Oldsquaw, Black, Surf, and White-winged scoters, Yellow Rail, King Rail, Purple Gallinule, Little Tern, Forster's Tern, five species of owls including the Snowy and Short-eared, Bewick's Wren, Sedge Wren, Loggerhead Shrike, Prothonotary Warbler, Lapland Longspur, Snow Bunting, Common Redpoll, and Evening Grosbeak,

Big Woods, a fine swamp forest, can be viewed from the southernmost dikes of the Hebron Fish Hatchery. Its large trees, woodland pools, and dense thickets and tangles are sometimes alive with small landbird migrants in late April and May and again in the fall.

Highbanks Metropolitan Park   *Take U.S. 23 north of Columbus to the park entrance which is 2.7 miles north of I-270. (Map D–42)*

This 1,055-acre park is remarkable for its scenery, archaeological features (prehistoric Indian earthworks), and birds. Trails lead through a medley of habitats, including rugged wooded ravines, open fields, brush, forest edges, parkland, and wooded riverbanks.

Counted among the breeding birds are Green-backed Herons, Wood Ducks, Mallards, Spotted Sandpipers, Belted Kingfishers, Northern Rough-winged Swallows, Cedar Waxwings, Warbling Vireos, and Northern Orioles nesting along the river. Fallow fields with occasional bushes and grassland are preferred by Killdeers, Eastern Kingbirds, Northern Mockingbirds, Field Sparrows, and Eastern Meadowlarks. Wooded edges and thickets attract American Woodcocks, Yellow-billed and, occasionally, Black-billed cuckoos, Ruby-throated Hummingbirds, House Wrens, Blue-gray Gnatcatchers, Gray Catbirds, Brown Thrashers, Blue-winged Warblers, Yellow Warblers, Common Yellowthroats, Yellow-breasted Chats, Northern Cardinals, Indigo Buntings, and Chipping Sparrows.

Hills and Dales Park
Calvary and Woodland
Cemeteries

In south Dayton, Montgomery County. From downtown Dayton, go south on Ludlow Street to South Patterson Boulevard. After passing the Carillon bell tower, take the Schantz Avenue exit. Immediately turn right onto South Patterson and proceed 1.5 miles to the Patterson Memorial Statue. (Map C–43)

Located in the city of Kettering, this 500-acre suburban park can be a productive birding locale due to its variety of habitats: woodlands with small winding streams, open grassy areas and overgrown upland meadow, swamp meadow, and edge habitat associated with an adjacent golf course. There are also a number of picnic shelters available.

To reach the swamp meadow, the most consistently good birding area in the park, go 0.3 mile beyond the Patterson Statue where two roads fork off to the left. Take the right-hand fork (Park Road) and cross a stone bridge. Park in the pulloff immediately past the bridge, or near the picnic areas along the left-hand fork. The swamp meadow is a short distance down the old service road. This is a good place for migrant warblers and other passerines.

Cross Patterson Road and climb the hill to the edge of the golf course. Walk north along the golf course edge toward the statue and you will find an area with conifers. Winter birds found here include Red-breasted Nuthatch, Brown Creeper, Ruby- and Golden-crowned kinglets, Purple Finch, and Pine Siskin. East of the Patterson Statue, through a gate and down a service road, American Woodcocks perform their early spring nuptials over an upland meadow. Unusual species found in the park include Worm-eating Warbler, Sharp-tailed Sparrow, and Red Crossbill.

A short distance to the west is **Calvary Cemetery**, perched on a hill overlooking the Great Miami River Valley. A good mix of deciduous and coniferous trees, shrubs and brushy edges makes good winter habitat for such diverse species as Sharp-shinned Hawk, Pileated Woodpecker, Rusty Blackbird, Purple Finch, and Pine Siskin. Snow Buntings have been seen in adjoining fields. The cemetery entrance is just south of Carillon Historical Park, off Patterson Boulevard.

Woodland Cemetery is another nearby area worth checking during migration. This historic hilltop cemetery affords a fine view of the city of Dayton and bisects Stewart Street adjacent to the University of Dayton. Go east on Stewart Street where it intersects with Patterson Boulevard to Brown Street, then north on Brown to Woodland Avenue and the cemetery entrance.

Hoover Reservoir

*Take Ohio 161 or I-270 north of
Columbus to Sunbury Road, then proceed
north through the village of Central
College to the dam. (Map D–44)*

The flooding of the Hoover Reservoir basin in 1956 attracted large numbers of waterbirds to central Ohio for the first time in memory. The first two years an estimated 30,000 ducks were present at one time at the peaks of spring migration. Even though silting and deoxidation of the water has drastically reduced those high numbers of birds, the reservoir still can be exceptionally good at times.

The park area below the dam, including the overflow basin, rapids, willow thickets, and a tree-lined drainage ditch, is always productive and should be checked out before proceeding north on Sunbury Road. Along the way there are several pulloffs and boat ramp areas from which to scan the water for Common Loons, Pied-billed and Horned grebes, and small rafts of ducks from late October to mid-April. In the spring and fall, American Coots feed along the shore and on the grassy banks.

Continue north along Sunbury Road and turn off onto the second gravel road just above the Smothers Road bridge. In late summer and fall, when the water is low, this is a good place to find small numbers of shorebirds, including the possibility of Buff-breasted Sandpipers. Ring-billed Gulls seen during the summer are non-breeding birds; occasional Common and Black terns are early southbound migrants.

Inniswood Metro Park is not far from Hoover Dam. In Westerville, take Schrock Road to Hemstead Road and turn right. This 91-acre site includes the beautiful home of the late Grace and Mary Innis, beautiful gardens, spacious lawns, and a handicapped-accessible boardwalk that loops through a mature woodland.

Hoover Nature Preserve

*Take Ohio 161 or I-270 to Sunbury
Road. Proceed north to the intersection
with Big Walnut Road.*

The Hoover Nature Preserve was created in 1988 and covers an area which begins at the intersection of Sunbury and Big Walnut roads and continues along both the east and west shores of Hoover Reservoir.

There are numerous areas to explore at the preserve. On Big Walnut Road just west of Sunbury Road there is a large natural wetland tract. Adjacent to this area is Mudhen Pond, a man-made wetland enhancement project.

The preliminary design of the enhancement area includes an upstream wetland basin, a permanently inundated shallow water habitat, and a series of deeper channels to attract wading birds and waterfowl. The project includes a parking area and observation points for viewing the wetlands. A Great Blue Heron rookery is nearby. Great Blue Herons, Great Egrets, Green-backed Herons, puddle ducks, Soras, Marsh Wrens, and Swamp Sparrows inhabit the area.

Another good birding spot is in the vicinity of the Oxbow Road boat ramp. Take Big Walnut Road west to Tussic Road, turn north on Tussic and continue to Oxbow. Here there are several excellent observation points for viewing the reservoir. Loons, grebes, swans, geese, and ducks can be seen during migration. Interesting and rare species spotted here have included American White Pelican, Snow Geese, Brant, Eurasian Wigeon, Oldsquaw, all three scoters, and Sabine's Gull.

From the Oxbow Road area drive north on Old Route 3-C to Weise, Plum, or Dustin roads. These roads provide access to the northwest shore of the reservoir and its extensive late summer and fall mudflats. When the water level is down the flats attract a good variety of migrating shorebirds including Black-bellied Plover, Lesser Golden-Plover, an occasional American Avocet or Willet, numerous Greater and Lesser yellowlegs, and sometimes a thought-provoking assortment of peeps.

In the fall, the area attracts impressive numbers of Great Blue Herons, smaller numbers of Great Egrets, Green-backed Herons, occasional Little Blue Herons, and Black-crowned Night-Herons. Species which nest in the area include Wood Duck, Spotted Sandpiper, Ruby-throated Hummingbird, Carolina and House wrens, Gray Catbird, Northern Mockingbird, Brown Thrasher, White-eyed Vireo, Prothonotary, Blue-winged, and Yellow warblers, Yellow-breasted Chat, Indigo Bunting, and Northern Oriole.

Dustin Road abuts the Blackhawk Golf Club. Park along the edge of the road and scan the small inlet below. In the spring and summer Prothonotary Warblers nest along the water's edge. There is a small bay at Dustin Road that attracts ducks in the spring and, when the water level is low, a few shorebirds, herons and egrets. Where the road turns sharply left, there is an old unused road to the right. Follow it to reach the edge of Little Walnut Creek, then walk along the trail which follows the creek. Yellow-billed and Black-billed Cuckoos, Eastern Screech-Owls, Pileated Woodpeckers, Prothonotary Warblers, and Rose-breasted Grosbeaks are found here.

The preserve includes an area just south of Galena. Turn into the road next to the Galena Municipal Building. The entrance to an old road that goes back into this area starts in back of the business center. Follow this old roadbed on foot as it parallels Big Walnut Creek to its end at the reservoir's edge. When the water is low and mudflats are exposed you can walk far out to a point that offers a great view of feeding shorebirds and protruding snags that provide resting places for Double-crested Cormorants, gulls, and terns.

The east side of the preserve along Sunbury Road contains an 89-acre narrow strip of land combining a habitat mix of open fields, small ponds, and woodland that attracts hawks, pheasant, bobwhite, Tree Swallows, bluebirds, finches, warblers, assorted sparrows, and Bobolinks.

A bit farther south, an unrepaired old road near the Eastside Yacht Club meanders northward along the east shore of the reservoir until it reaches the foundations of a bygone bridge. In the spring, the trees along this road are sometimes good for migrant warblers, vireos, and orioles of both species. A number of vantage points provide views of Pelican Island and the upper end of the reservoir. During open winters, search the waters offshore for loons, grebes, diving and dabbling ducks. Ospreys patrol the shores in spring and fall and Double-crested Cormorants are being seen almost year-round.

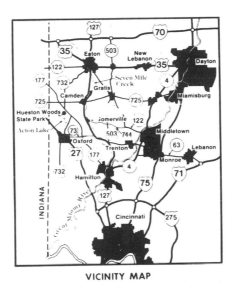

VICINITY MAP

Hueston Woods State Park

North of Oxford, in southern Preble County just off Ohio 177. Part of the park lies in Butler County. From Oxford, take Ohio 732 north about 5 miles to the main entrance. (Map C–45)

A 3,584-acre tract of forest—much of it virgin woodland—and 625-acre Acton Lake complement recreational areas, a modern guest lodge, cabins, boating and fishing facilities, an 18-hole championship golf course, a nature and raptor rehabilitation center, and miles of trails for hiking and horseback riding. Sledding, skating, ice fishing, ice boating, and cross-country skiing are available during the winter months. Originally, this area was a Council Site for the Western Ohio Indian tribes. The Hueston Woods State Nature Preserve, an area of 200 acres of virgin Ohio forest, is located on the south shore of the lake.

Acton Lake induces modest numbers of waterbirds to feed and rest during spring and fall migrations, including the Common Loon, Horned Grebe, occasional herons and egrets, scatterings of puddle ducks, and rafts of diving ducks. A few shorebirds are sometimes found in inlets and along muddy edges.

A few of the representative summering birds are the Black Vulture, Cooper's, Red-shouldered, and Red-tailed hawks, Yellow-billed Cuckoo, Eastern Screech-Owl, Great Horned and Barred owls, Red-headed, Red-bellied, Downy, and Hairy woodpeckers, Northern Flicker, Pileated Woodpecker, Acadian Flycatcher, Carolina Wren, Blue-gray Gnatcatcher, Eastern Bluebird, Cedar Waxwing, Yellow-throated Vireo, Yellow, Pine, and Cerulean warblers, Ovenbird, Common Yellowthroat, Yellow-breasted Chat, Summer and Scarlet tanagers, and Rufous-sided Towhees. Winter species may include finches as well as Red-breasted Nuthatch and Evening Grosbeak.

Rare species have included Tundra Swan, Greater White-fronted Goose, and Lapland Longspurs.

Huffman Reserve

Located in Greene County astride Ohio 4 a short distance northeast of Dayton. Enter on the east side of the highway off Lower Valley Pike. (Map C–46)

A 30-acre lake with boating (trolling motors only) and sailing, woods with hiking trails, parkland with extensive picnicking opportunities, bits of prairie remnant, and the Mad River provide the setting for this 282-acre Park District of Dayton-Montgomery County Reserve. Huffman Dam is part of a system of five earthen flood control dams managed by the Miami Conservancy District. The reserve is situated near Wright-Patterson Air Force Base, the Wright Memorial, and just upstream from Eastwood Reserve.

The lake attracts good numbers of transient waterbirds and shorebirds—Double-crested Cormorants, Great Blue and Green-backed herons, Canada Geese, Northern Pintails, Blue-winged Teals, Northern Shovelers, Gadwalls, Redheads, Lesser Scaups, Buffleheads, Hooded and Red-breasted mergansers, and Ruddy Ducks—during their migrations. Shorebirds, including Greater and Lesser yellowlegs, Solitary, Spotted, and Pectoral sandpipers are found on sandbars in the Mad River. Ospreys sometimes fish in the lake.

Resident nesting birds include Red-tailed Hawks, Eastern Screech-Owls, Great Horned Owls, Yellow-billed Cuckoos, Red-headed Woodpeckers, Great Crested Flycatchers, Eastern Bluebirds, Warbling Vireos, Yellow Warblers, Common Yellowthroats, Indigo Buntings, Chipping Sparrows, and Northern Orioles. Prothonotary Warblers have been found along the Mad River. Many other passerines pass through the area during migration.

Indian Lake   *Located adjacent to U.S. 33 in Logan County. The state park is off Ohio 273. (Map C–47)*

Patches of woods on the northwest shore, a few marshy inlets, fallow and cultivated fields, and widespread development surround this 6,448-acre man-made lake. Although less productive for waterfowl than in the first half of the century, considerable numbers of ducks and geese still stop briefly in spring and again in fall until freeze-up. Ohio 368 at the east end of the lake connects several offshore islands and provides a number of good observation points.

Spring shorebirds occur in wet fields, sky ponds, and along muddy edges; in fall they are dispersed around the lake, mainly in bays and inlets with mud-flats. In late spring and early summer, birds of the open fields include American Kestrel, Killdeer, Barn Swallow, Eastern Kingbird, Horned Lark, Savannah (scarce), Grasshopper, and Field sparrows, Bobolink, and Eastern Meadowlark.

Indian Mound Reserve   *Located in Greene County midway between Xenia and Cedarville. Take U.S. 42 northeast from Xenia to several parking lots. (Map C–48)*

This diverse area of 165 acres lies along Massie Creek and includes meadows, woods, Cedar Cliff Falls, and Massie Creek gorge. Earthworks by both the Adena and Hopewell Native American cultures have been preserved here, in addition to a dam built by early settlers to power a mill and two old mill sites. Along the trails are white cedars and yews, primitive liverworts, many ferns, and, often, beautiful wildflower displays. Along the north side of the gorge, the trail is often at treetop level, and a large stand of conifers may produce an owl or two.

Pileated Woodpeckers, Eastern Phoebes, thrushes of several species, many migrant warblers, Scarlet Tanagers, and sparrows including American Tree, Chipping, and Field are to be expected in this beautiful park. The area is managed by the Greene County Park District.

John Bryan State Park   *Located in Greene County. Take Ohio*
343 about 2 miles east of Yellow Springs;
turn south on Ohio 370 and proceed to
the park entrance. (Map C–49)

This forested valley and ravine is situated between Glen Helen Nature Reserve and Clifton Gorge. Grist mills and an old homestead are added historical attractions. Picnicking and camping offer other incentives to enjoy this pleasant state park. Scenic trails with huge fallen rocks and tall cedars follow the Little Miami River upstream to Clifton Gorge. The state park area sometimes has a large roost of Turkey Vultures. The riverbanks are an excellent place to look for Louisiana Waterthrushes. See the Glen Helen account for birds typical of the region.

John L. Rich State Nature   *See Clifton Gorge.*
Preserve

Kiser Lake State Park   *In northwest Champaign County. Take*
U.S. 36 west from Urbana to the
intersection of Ohio 235; turn north and
drive about 5 miles to the entrance.
(Map C–50)

The park encompasses 864 acres of forest and parkland, a shallow springfed lake, and bordering marshland. North of the campground, an amphitheater and nature center are the focal points for park activities, which include a summer nature program. Motor boats are not permitted on the lake.

This is a pleasant and relaxing spot for birding and hiking any time of the year. During the spring months, a host of warblers and other arboreal species can be found in the woods and fields around the lake. Nesting birds include Yellow-billed Cuckoo, Red-headed Woodpecker, Eastern Wood-Pewee, Barn Swallow, Carolina Chickadee, Gray Catbird, Red-eyed Vireo, Common Yellowthroat, Indigo Bunting, Field Sparrow, Song Sparrow, and Northern Oriole. Ospreys have been seen during the past few years, and nesting platforms are planned in the near future.

This is an excellent lake for waterfowl when the ice breaks up in early spring. Common Loons, Pied-billed and Horned grebes, Canada Geese, Wood Ducks, American Black Ducks, Mallards, Northern Pintails, American Wigeons, Canvasbacks, Redheads, Ring-necked Ducks, Lesser Scaups, Common Goldeneyes, Buffleheads, all three mergansers, and Ruddy Ducks can be expected. Waterfowl rarities have included Oldsquaw and Greater Scaup.

Knox Woods Nature Preserve   *Located in Knox County 3 miles northeast*
                                          of Mt. Vernon on the south side of U.S.
                                          36, east of the former Knox County
                                          Children's Home. (Map D–51)

This 30-acre tract of near-virgin mixed deciduous trees contains fine examples of black, red, white, and scarlet oak, sugar maple, shagbark hickory, black walnut, and American beech. Wildflowers include Jack-in-the-pulpit, hepatica, bloodroot, and large-flowered trillium. A trail circles through the woods, providing access to spring nesting territories of such birds as the Barred Owl, Red-headed Woodpecker, Great Crested Flycatcher, Carolina Chickadee, Wood Thrush, Yellow-throated Vireo, Cerulean Warbler, Scarlet Tanager, and Rose-breasted Grosbeak.

Lake Loramie State Park   *In Shelby County, located on Ohio 362*
                                          between Fort Loramie and Minster.
                                          (Map C–52)

Surrounded by farm fields, woods, and parkland, the 825-acre lake attracts grebes, ducks, and occasional flocks of Ring-billed Gulls in the spring and fall. Paths wind through wildflower-dotted woods on the south shore.

Lake St. Marys   *See Grand Lake St. Marys.*

Madison Lake State Park   *In Madison County on Ohio 665 about 5*
                                          miles east of London. (Map D–53)

Small numbers of waterfowl—American Wigeons, Redheads, Ring-necked Ducks, and Lesser Scaups—stop in spring and fall at this 100-acre impoundment. Horned Larks and Vesper Sparrows nest in surrounding fields. In the mid-20th century, the introduced Gray Partridge flourished in the region.

A. W. Marion State Park   *In Pickaway County, take either U.S. 22*
                                          or Ohio 188 about 5 miles east of
                                          Circleville and turn off onto the marked
                                          roads. (Map D–54)

Rolling parkland, beech-maple forests, and a 145-acre lake are featured at this attractive park. The lake is visited briefly in March and April and again in late October and November by migrant flocks of American Wigeons, Redheads, Ring-necked Ducks, Lesser Scaups, and their allies. A trail starting at the campground circles through fields and woods from which seasonal birdlife can be observed.

Narrows Reserve, Little Miami River

Located in western Greene County, west of Xenia. From Xenia, go west on U.S. 35 about 4 miles to Factory Road, then south 1.2 miles to the park entrance across Indian Ripple Road. (Map C–55)

The Narrows Reserve is a natural area dedicated to the preservation, study, and enjoyment of the river valley's natural features. The reserve lies along the Little Miami River, Ohio's first national and state scenic river. Managed by the Greene County Park District, this 162-acre park includes picnic tables, a canoe launch, river research and interpretive facilities, and 3.5 miles of hiking trails. The area is divided into upper, middle, and lower narrows and includes riparian forest with giant sycamores, a large woodlot with ancient oak trees, a meadow, and a spring. The upper trails are good places to look for owls and deer near dusk. At the Interpretive Center, feeders are actively maintained with an indoor observation room providing excellent opportunities to observe common woodland birds.

Breeding birds include Great Blue and Green-backed herons, Wood Duck, Red-tailed Hawk, Spotted Sandpiper, American Woodcock, Barred Owl, Red-headed, Red-bellied, Downy, Hairy, and Pileated woodpeckers, Belted Kingfisher, Yellow-billed Cuckoo, Wood Thrush, Yellow-throated, Warbling, and Red-eyed vireos, Northern Parula, Yellow-throated, Cerulean, and Prothonotary warblers, Louisiana Waterthrush, Kentucky Warbler, Indigo Bunting, Orchard Oriole, and American Goldfinch.

In the spring and fall, additional warblers are often seen including Tennessee, Nashville, Chestnut-sided, Magnolia, Cape May, Yellow-rumped, Black-throated Green, Blackburnian, Palm, Bay-breasted, Black-and-white, and American Redstart. Rare species have included Peregrine Falcon and Connecticut Warbler.

Northmoor Park

See Whetstone Park.

O'Shaughnessy Reservoir

Drive north of Columbus on Ohio 257 approximately 12 miles. (Map D–56)

Before the Hoover, Delaware, and Alum Creek dams were built, O'Shaughnessy Reservoir and Buckeye Lake were the principal places to look for waterfowl in central Ohio. With the advent of the newer and larger reservoirs, O'Shaughnessy doesn't receive the attention it once did, but it is still worth visiting.

Late summer mudflats are good for Great Blue Herons, increased numbers of Green-backed Herons, and a scattering of shorebirds. Yellow-crowned Night-Herons nest along the tree-lined shores of the river below the dam.

Just north of the Columbus Zoo, there is a lagoon that is difficult to observe from the road, but can be seen from inside the zoo. From October to April, wild Canada Geese join the zoo flock. An occasional Snow Goose (usually the blue phase) or Richardson's Goose (the small race of the Canada) can also be discovered. For the next six miles there are numerous pulloffs for observing any waterbirds that might be present. Many ducks hug the far shore, so use of a spotting scope is advised.

Pickerington Pond Metro Park Nature Preserve (Wright Road Pond)

On the east side of Columbus, exit I-70 south onto Brice Road; bear left onto Gender Road, then after several miles east onto Wright Road for about 2 miles to Bowen Road. (Map D-57)

This pond, marsh, and woodland were saved from the maw of encroaching development through the efforts of the Nature Conservancy. It is an excellent place to look for birds from March through May and during the extended fall migration from late July all the way to December. Good views of the pond can be obtained from either Wright or Bowen road.

Puddle ducks favor the far shore and sometimes feed in numbers on green duckweed at the east end of the pond, while diving birds are more apt to be in the center. Marshy areas and much of the lake can best be observed from recently relocated Bowen Road.

Waterbirds seen with a fair degree of frequency include the Common Loon, Pied-billed and Horned grebes, Tundra Swan, Canada Goose, Bonaparte's and Ring-billed gulls and Caspian, Common, and Black terns. Modest numbers of puddle and diving ducks are usually present during migration, especially in March and April. Transient Ospreys sometimes remain for a day or two, and Double-crested Cormorants have been seen more frequently in recent years.

Grassy edges and mudflats yield Great Blue and Green-backed herons, an occasional Great Egret, and shorebirds—Semipalmated Plovers, Greater and Lesser yellowlegs, Solitary, Spotted, Semipalmated, Least, and Pectoral sandpipers, Dunlins, and Common Snipes—in small numbers and when conditions are right.

Large numbers of Chimney Swifts, Purple Martins, Tree, Northern Rough-winged, Bank, and Barn swallows, and, infrequently, a few Cliff Swallows converge on the pond on cool days in April and May. In early spring and autumn, look for Water Pipits and newly arrived Yellow-rumped and Palm warblers. Noteworthy species that have nested include the Pied-billed Grebe, Green-backed Heron, Canada Goose (many), Blue-winged Teal, Sora, American Coot, and Marsh Wren.

Rare species seen in migration include Least Bittern, Little Blue Heron, Tricolored Heron, Cattle Egret, Glossy Ibis, Mute Swan, Snow Goose, Eurasian Wigeon, Greater Scaup, Surf Scoter, Virginia Rail, a possible Spotted Redshank, Red Knot, and Franklin's Gull.

Improvements recently completed or slated for the near future include parking areas, trails through an abutting woods, and a viewing deck and blind. Many of the facilities will be handicapped-accessible.

Possum Creek Farm and Reserve

Located southwest of Dayton in Montgomery County. From downtown Dayton take U.S. 35 west to Ohio 4 (Germantown Pike), proceed south about 4 miles, then go east on Frytown Road to the entrance. (Map C–58)

Four small ponds and a lake are set amid woods, old fields, and patches of marsh at this 518-acre Park District of Dayton-Montgomery County reserve. Picnic shelters, hiking and bridle trails, and group camping are available. Winter sports such as cross-country skiing and ice skating are permitted when conditions allow. Several tall grass prairie areas were planted by the Park District in 1980 and now are a major feature of this park. Possum Creek Farm is at the southern edge of the park and features a farmhouse, barnyard, farm equipment, and animals, all typical of the 1950s. Beyond the barn are an orchard, a farm pond, pastures, and a trail leading to a woods, a stream, and a small marsh. The entrance is off Shank Road on the southern edge of the reserve.

In early spring and fall, a variety of waterfowl—Wood Ducks, Mallards, Blue-winged Teals, American Wigeons, and Ring-necked Ducks—can be seen on the lake and ponds. Great Blue and Green-backed herons are present during the warm months, and Ospreys are sometimes spotted as they investigate the ponds. Wet spots and marshland attract Greater and Lesser yellowlegs, Solitary and Spotted sandpipers, and small peeps such as Semipalmated and Least sandpipers.

Counted among the breeding birds are American Woodcock, Willow Flycatcher, Eastern Kingbird, Barn Swallow, Carolina Wren, Eastern Bluebird, Warbling Vireo, Field Sparrow, and Northern Oriole. The tall grass prairie has attracted Sedge Wrens, which are most often seen in late summer. Rarities have included Merlin, Peregrine Falcon, and Yellow Rail.

Rush Run State Wildlife Area

*In southern Preble County 5 miles
southeast of Camden on Northern Road.
Take Ohio 725 east from Camden 2
miles, south on Old Trace Road 3 miles,
right on Northern Road 1 mile. The
headquarters is along Northern Road and
the lake is 0.75 mile north on Pogue-
Frazee Road. (Map C–59)*

This enjoyable spot combines a 1,183-acre tract of oak-hickory-beech woods, brushy patches, several small ponds, and a 54-acre lake. The diversity of habitat attracts a wide variety of birds at all times of the year.

Species commonly seen in summer include Green-backed Heron, Wood Duck, Mallard, Turkey Vulture, Red-tailed Hawk, Ring-necked Pheasant, Killdeer, Spotted Sandpiper, American Woodcock, Yellow-billed Cuckoo, Belted Kingfisher, Red-headed Woodpecker, Acadian Flycatcher, Eastern Kingbird, Purple Martins, Northern Rough-winged and Barn swallows, House Wrens, Eastern Bluebirds, Wood Thrushes, Gray Catbirds, Brown Thrashers, Yellow and Cerulean warblers, Common Yellowthroats, Indigo Buntings, Rufous-sided Towhees, Chipping, Field, and Song sparrows, Northern Orioles, and American Goldfinches. During the spring and fall, the lake and ponds attract Blue-winged Teals, Northern Shovelers, American Wigeons, Redheads, Ring-necked Ducks, Lesser Scaups, Soras in wet overgrown edges, American Coots, Greater and Lesser yellowlegs, Solitary Sandpipers, and occasional Common and Black terns.

After a heavy nocturnal migration during late April and the first two weeks in May, the wooded edges, groves of trees, and brushy areas are sometimes alive with a multitude of flycatchers, vireos, warblers, finches, and sparrows. Although hunting is allowed during the appropriate seasons, the hunting areas are well marked, and birders are welcome at any season.

**Sara Lee Arnovitz Nature
Preserve**

*In north Xenia, Greene County. Take U.S.
68 north, then turn right on Kinsey Road
to the preserve, just east of Xenia High
School. (Map C–60)*

Close to downtown Xenia, this nature preserve includes a wet meadow and marsh complete with a boardwalk, observation deck, and nature trails along Old Town Creek. Great Blue and Green-backed herons often feed here, and the rattle of Belted Kingfishers is a common sound. Eastern Screech-Owls and Great Horned and Barred owls vie for territories at night. During migration, all the species of warblers regularly seen in west-central Ohio have been found here. Other birds frequently encountered are Indigo Bunting, Rufous-sided Towhee, Swamp and Song sparrows, and American Goldfinch.

Sharon Woods Metropolitan Park

Drive north on Cleveland Avenue in Columbus after exiting from I-270 and go just past Schrock Road. (Map D–61)

The park embraces 760 wooded acres of oak, ash, sycamore, and maple trees, as well as recreational parkland and a small lake. The Edward S. Thomas Nature Preserve, a 320-acre tract of undisturbed woodland, is included within the park.

The 11-acre Schrock Lake attracts small numbers of waterbirds in the spring and fall including an occasional Common Loon, Pied-billed and Horned grebes, Wood Ducks, Mallards, Blue-winged Teals, Gadwalls, Redheads, Ring-necked Ducks, Lesser Scaups, Buffleheads, and Ruddy Ducks. A group of five Surf Scoters visited the lake one spring.

Horned Larks and Eastern Meadowlarks are found in the grassy fields. During migration periods, flocks of swallows fly over the lake, and good numbers of landbirds can be found along the edges of the woods. A representative sample of nesting birds includes Killdeer, American Woodcock, Red-headed and Red-bellied woodpeckers, Great Crested Flycatcher, Eastern Kingbird, Barn Swallow, House Wren, Blue-gray Gnatcatcher, Eastern Bluebird, Gray Catbird, Northern Mockingbird, Brown Thrasher, Cedar Waxwing, Red-eyed Vireo, Yellow Warbler, Common Yellowthroat, Northern Cardinal, Indigo Bunting, Rufous-sided Towhee, Chipping, Field, and Song sparrows, Northern Oriole, and American Goldfinch.

Stage's Pond State Nature Preserve

Take U.S. 23 south from Columbus about 14 miles beyond I-270; turn east onto Hagerty Road and drive 6 miles to the entrance and parking area. (Map D–62)

Stage's Pond is a glacial relict called a kettlehole, formed about 11,000 years ago by a huge chunk of Wisconsinan glacier ice. As the ice melted, deposits of glacial till gravitated into the kettlehole, which was a byproduct of the end moraine about three miles east of the pond.

The 45-acre pond is surrounded by over 70 acres of trees, grasses, and aquatic vegetation. Several hundred yards to the south, spring rains collect in a series of gentle depressions that often attract more waterbirds than the pond. An observation blind overlooks these sloughs and can be reached by following the trail due west of the parking lot bulletin board.

Soon after winter ice melts, a few ducks appear. Accompanying the first American Black Ducks and Mallards are Green-winged Teals, Northern Pintails, Northern Shovelers, Gadwalls, American Wigeons, Canvasbacks, Redheads, Ring-necked Ducks, and Lesser Scaups. By mid-March, Wood Ducks, Blue-winged Teals, and Hooded Mergansers are usually present, along with American Coots.

Great Blue and Green-backed herons are present during all the warm months, and other herons and egrets should be looked for during migration periods, including American and Least bitterns. Greater and Lesser yellowlegs, Solitary, Spotted, and Pectoral sandpipers and Common Snipes are commonly found in the spring. Northern Harriers are frequently found hunting over the sloughs and surrounding fields from November to April.

The main system of trails leads through a woods north of the parking lot and one trail descends into grassy bottomlands and follows the west shore of Stage's Pond. Tree Swallows nest in dead trees around the pond, Soras can be found in grassy spots during spring migration, and congregations of postbreeding season Wood Ducks are a common sight in late summer and fall.

In April, surrounding plowed fields and wet spots sometimes yield flocks of Lesser Golden-Plovers, occasional Upland Sandpipers, Pectoral Sandpipers, and Water Pipits.

Stillwater Prairie Reserve   *West of Piqua, in northwest Miami County. From I-75 take U.S. 36 west 1 mile to downtown Piqua, then follow Ohio 185 out of town and west 8.5 miles to the reserve. (Map C–63)*

Noted for its remnant prairie and wildflowers, this 217-acre reserve is set among rolling hills and meadows. Adjacent to the Stillwater River, the reserve contains several woodlands including a mature beech-maple woods, meadows, brushy fields, and two ponds, in addition to a relict native Ohio prairie. Columbine and harebells cling to fern-covered slopes. Two miles of trails provide ample access to riparian, woodland, and grassland habitats. A large deer herd is often seen at dawn or dusk. In addition to birding, recreational opportunities include picnicking, fishing, hiking, and cross-country skiing.

There is a large roost of Turkey Vultures and a feeding station is maintained for them. Representative nesting species include Great Blue and Green-backed herons, Wood Duck, Red-tailed Hawk, American Woodcock, Eastern Screech-Owl, Great Horned and Barred owls, Belted Kingfisher, Red-bellied, Downy, and Hairy woodpeckers, Northern Flicker, Pileated Woodpecker, Wood Thrush, Prairie Warbler, Common Yellowthroat, Yellow-breasted Chat,

Eastern Meadowlark, and Red-winged Blackbird. Winter brings a few Rough-legged Hawks to the meadows, and White-throated and White-crowned sparrows to the brushy edges along the woods. Occasional waterfowl drop into the ponds. The park is managed by the Miami County Park District.

Sugarcreek Reserve

Located southeast of Dayton. Take Wilmington Road south from I-675 at the Montgomery-Greene County line. After crossing Ohio 725, proceed on Wilmington Road until it intersects with Conference Road. The main parking lot is 0.25 mile east on Conference Road. (Map C-64)

Located just south of Bellbrook in the metro-Dayton area, this Park District of Dayton-Montgomery County reserve is a favorite with Dayton-area birders. The reserve consists of 596 acres of upland and riparian woodlands following beautiful Sugar Creek, which has created a deep ravine. There is a tall grass prairie which flowers in mid to late summer and provides abundant habitat for grass-loving species. Although much of the area was once farmland, a variety of natural habitats now exist as a result of succession and land management techniques.

Highlights of the park include the Three Sisters, three huge 550-year-old oak trees, and the Osage Orange Tunnel, a living tunnel created by the arching branches of old Osage orange trees. There is a horseback riding center, bridle trails, an archery center, and five miles of scenic hiking trails. Across Sugar Creek on the northeast side is Spring Lakes Park. The cattails and edge habitat are at times attractive to migrant warblers.

The park has attracted a large variety of these transients, including Golden-winged, Orange-crowned (rare), Chestnut-sided, Magnolia, Cape May, Blackburnian, Blackpoll, Bay-breasted, Canada, Connecticut, and Mourning. Northern Waterthrushes pass through the area and Louisiana Waterthrushes breed along the streams. The American Redstart is a rare nester. Savannah and Lincoln's sparrows are frequently seen during migration.

Other nesting birds include Red-tailed Hawk, Great Horned and Barred owls, Pileated Woodpecker, Yellow-billed Cuckoo, Willow Flycatcher, White-eyed Vireo, Northern Parula, Blue-winged, Yellow-throated, Cerulean, Kentucky, and Hooded warblers, Yellow-breasted Chat, Indigo Bunting, Rufous-sided Towhee, Field Sparrow, and American Goldfinch. Unusual species seen in the area include Double-crested Cormorant, Black Vulture, Red-shouldered Hawk, and Sandhill Crane.

Sugar Valley Park   *See Grant Park.*

Sycamore State Park   *Located in Montgomery County west of*
Trotwood. Take Wolf Creek Pike west from
Trotwood about 4 miles, turn right on
Providence Road, and proceed to the
entrance and parking areas. (Map C–65)

A new state park of 2,300 acres, this primarily flat area along the upper
reaches of Wolf Creek contains woods, meadows, pine stands, a couple of
ponds, a spring, and small creeks and streams. Giant sycamore trees provide
cover over the nature trail accessed from Wolf Creek Pike. Picnicking, horseback riding, fishing, sledding, ice skating, and snowmobiling as well as hiking
and birding are some of the many activities available. In addition to the main
park entrance, an excellent nature trail along Wolf Creek starts from the
Nature and Bridle Trail Staging area (parking lot) along Wolf Creek Pike just
west of Snyder Road.

Breeding birds commonly seen include Turkey Vulture, Red-tailed Hawk,
Yellow-billed Cuckoo, Great Horned Owl, Chimney Swift, Belted Kingfisher,
Willow Flycatcher, Eastern Phoebe, Great Crested Flycatcher, Eastern King-
bird, House Wren, Eastern Bluebird, Wood Thrush, Gray Catbird, Brown
Thrasher, Yellow Warbler, Common Yellowthroat, Yellow-breasted Chat,
Rufous-sided Towhee, Field, Chipping, and Song sparrows, Bobolink (casual),
Red-winged Blackbird, and Eastern Meadowlark.

Nearly all of Ohio's thrushes, vireos, and warblers are seen during migration. Large numbers of Sandhill Cranes have been observed flying over during
their fall migration. Long-eared Owls are frequently found in the pine groves
along either side of the creek along Nolan Road during winter. Winter may
produce an occasional Hermit Thrush.

Tawawa Forest   *Located just north of Wilberforce and*
Central State universities northeast of
Xenia on Ohio 42. (Map C–66)

Magnificent American beech trees, oaks, and maples still stand in this splendid
virgin woods which was damaged by the tornado of 1974. However, resultant
clearings have provided habitat for such edge-loving species as Yellow-billed
Cuckoo, Ruby-throated Hummingbird, Eastern Bluebird, Brown Thrasher,
Common Yellowthroat, Yellow-breasted Chat, Summer Tanager, Indigo Bunting, and Field and Song sparrows.

Taylorsville Reserve

In Montgomery County. Take I-75 north of Dayton; exit at Ohio 40 and proceed east to Brown School Road, or east and north along Ohio 40 to the several parts of the park. (Map C–67)

Noted for its spectacular ravines and geological formations, the reserve hosts segments of the Buckeye Trail. The area also includes remnants of the Miami-Erie Canal, sycamore- and cottonwood-lined trails along the Great Miami River bottomlands, an earthen flood-control dam, upland woods, several pine plantations, and extensive recreational parkland with plenty of picnic areas, hiking, and river fishing. Nearly six miles of trails, some rugged, cover this 865-acre Park District of Dayton-Montgomery County reserve. The grassy meadow south of the dam often attracts deer at sunset.

Great Blue and Green-backed herons, Wood Ducks, Mallards, and Belted Kingfishers occur along the river. A pair of Red-shouldered Hawks has nested nearby. Eastern Screech-Owls and Great Horned and Barred owls are resident breeders, along with Red-bellied, Downy, Hairy, and Pileated woodpeckers, Willow Flycatchers, Eastern Kingbirds, Carolina Chickadees, Tufted Titmice, White-breasted Nuthatches, House Wrens, Eastern Bluebirds, Northern Mockingbirds, Yellow-throated, Warbling, and Red-eyed vireos, Blue-winged, Yellow, Kentucky, and Hooded warblers, Common Yellowthroats, Yellow-breasted Chats, Summer and Scarlet tanagers, and Northern Orioles. A male Lawrence's Warbler paired with a female Blue-winged Warbler and nested for several years. The American Redstart is a rare nester. This is a good place to look for fall migrants, including hard-to-find species such as Olive-sided Flycatcher, Gray-cheeked Thrush, Philadelphia Vireo, and Golden-winged Warbler. Yellow-rumped Warblers are frequently seen during the early winter months. Long-eared and Northern Saw-whet owls occur during the cold months in the pine plantations.

Twin Lakes

Cross O'Shaughnessy Dam at the Columbus Zoo and go north on Ohio 745 for about 1.5 miles and turn left into the park just south of the inlet. (Map D–68)

There are trails running north and south along the stream at the west end of the park, which is reached by a cinder road paralleling the lagoon. When water levels are low in late summer and fall, shorebirds are sometimes found on the resulting mudflats. In winter and early spring, small flocks of ducks might be present, along with Ring-billed and Herring gulls.

Some of the nesting birds are Red-tailed Hawk, Yellow-billed Cuckoo,

Eastern Screech-Owl, Great Horned Owl, Red-headed Woodpecker, Northern Flicker, Eastern Wood-Pewee, Eastern Kingbird, House Wren, Eastern Bluebird, Gray Catbird, Yellow-throated and Red-eyed vireos, Yellow Warbler, Common Yellowthroat, Scarlet Tanager, Northern Cardinal, Indigo Bunting, Chipping, Field, and Song sparrows, and Northern Oriole.

Union Cemetery

Take Olentangy River Road in Columbus to just north of Dodridge Avenue. The cemetery is on the east side of the street. (Map D–69)

This is a good place to bird in both spring and fall. Large trees and undergrowth line the Olentangy River and a fine wooded trail extends south to Dodridge Avenue. During the warm months, look for Green-backed Herons, Wood Ducks, Mallards, Spotted Sandpipers, Chimney Swifts, Belted Kingfishers, and Northern Rough-winged and Barn swallows. During the spring and fall migrations, most of the arboreal species can be seen to good advantage. The wooded area above Dodridge Avenue is especially good in May for Ovenbirds and Kentucky, Connecticut, Mourning, Hooded, Wilson's, and Canada warblers.

Buckeye Swamp, OSU's wetland research park, is adjacent to the cemetery.

Walden Wildlife Refuge

See Blendon Woods Metropolitan Park.

Walter C. Tucker Nature Interpretive Center

See Blacklick Woods Metropolitan Park.

Whetstone Park

On North High Street in Columbus watch for the Park of Roses sign a few blocks south of Henderson Road and turn west on Hollenback Drive. (Map D–70)

This is an excellent place to observe migratory landbirds because of the park's proximity to the Olentangy River and the varied habitat of fields, woods, a creek, and a ravine. Occasional shorebirds such as Solitary and Spotted sandpipers can be seen along the river, in addition to Green-backed Herons, Wood Ducks, Mallards, and Belted Kingfishers. Among the rare birds that have been observed here are the Western Kingbird, Bell's Vireo, Golden-winged, Brewster's, Connecticut, and Mourning warblers.

Paths lead through a wooded corridor at the southwest corner of the park and continue south along the river to the smaller **Northmoor Park,** which can also be reached by car from North Broadway by turning north on Hennepin Road, then west on Kenworth Road, and north on Olentangy Boulevard. Another path meanders through the wooded ravine east of the small bridge.

Permanent residents include the American Kestrel, Eastern Screech-Owl, Downy Woodpecker, Blue Jay, American Crow, Carolina Chickadee, Tufted Titmouse, White-breasted Nuthatch, Northern Cardinal, and Song Sparrow.

Summer nesting birds commonly seen are Yellow-billed Cuckoos, Northern Flickers, Eastern Wood-Pewees, Great Crested Flycatchers, Northern Rough-winged Swallows, House Wrens, Wood Thrushes, Gray Catbirds, Cedar Waxwings, Red-eyed and Warbling vireos, Yellow Warblers, Common Yellowthroats, Indigo Buntings, Chipping Sparrows, Northern Orioles, and American Goldfinches.

Wright-Patterson Air Force Base   *Located northeast of Dayton in Greene County. Area C along Ohio 444 in Fairborn contains Huffman Prairie and Bass Lake. (Map C–71)*

Because this is an active air force base, this area is not open to the public. However, it is of great ecological significance since one of the last remnants of prairie occurs here alongside active runways. Huffman Prairie is 109 acres in size, and contains many rare and endangered prairie plants. The site is adjacent to Huffman Reserve and close to Eastwood Reserve and the Wright State University Woodlot. The prairie area has been proposed for inclusion in a National Historical Park, and in future years there may be access for the public.

The Dayton Audubon Society occasionally holds summer bird walks here and the area is included in the Christmas Bird Count by permission of military authorities. During the summer, grassland birds generally found include Upland Sandpiper, Sedge Wren (rare), Dickcissel, Vesper, Grasshopper and Henslow's sparrows, and Bobolinks. Migrant Sandhill Cranes and Short-eared Owls are sometimes seen. The winter season may produce a Snowy Owl, Lapland Longspurs, and Snow Buntings.

During the colder months, deep-water Bass Lake, normally a recreational lake, may host numerous waterfowl. Rare birds found here have included Red-necked Grebe, Oldsquaw, Black and Surf scoters.

The large open areas surrounding the runways provide excellent habitat for numerous thirteen-lined ground squirrels and meadow voles, which attract many raptors to the area. Hawks seen here include the Northern Harrier, Red-shouldered, Red-tailed, Rough-legged (winter), American Kestrel, and Merlin.

Henslow's Sparrow

Wright State University Woods

Located in northwest Greene County in Fairborn. Take the Wright State University exit off I-675 (North Fairfield Road); or follow U.S. 35 east to Woodman Drive, then go north to Colonel Glenn Highway, then east to the university. Park near the library. (Map C-72)

Located on the campus of Wright State University, this 200-acre woodlot is open to the public and includes a biology preserve containing mature trees in addition to second growth forest and fields which provide excellent habitat for resident birds as well as spring and fall migrants.

Commonly observed species include Turkey Vulture, Red-tailed Hawk, Eastern Screech-Owl, Great Horned Owl, Red-bellied, Downy, and Hairy woodpeckers, Northern Flicker, Pileated Woodpecker (particularly vocal), Carolina Chickadee, Tufted Titmouse, White-breasted Nuthatch, Brown Creeper, Carolina Wren, Eastern Bluebird, Gray Catbird, Brown Thrasher, Red-eyed Vireo, Northern Cardinal, Chipping, Field, Vesper, Grasshopper, Henslow's, and Song sparrows.

Birds seen during migration may include Yellow-bellied Sapsuckers, Acadian, Willow, Least, and Great Crested flycatchers, Eastern Kingbirds, Red-breasted Nuthatch, Winter Wren, thrushes and kinglets, Cedar Waxwings, a representative assortment of vireos and warblers, Scarlet Tanager, Rose-breasted Grosbeak, Indigo Bunting, Rufous-sided Towhee, Orchard and Northern orioles. Long-eared Owls occasionally winter. This area is close to Huffman Reserve, Eastwood Reserve, and Wright-Patterson Air Force Base.

PART III

The Southern and Eastern Unglaciated Counties

LAKE ERIE

STARK
COLUMBIANA
CARROLL
HOLMES
TUSCARAWAS
JEFFERSON
COSHOCTON
G
HARRISON
GUERNSEY
MUSKINGUM
BELMONT
FAIRFIELD
PERRY
NOBLE
MONROE
MORGAN
HOCKING
WASHINGTON
BUTLER
WARREN
CLINTON
ROSS
ATHENS
HAMILTON
HIGHLAND
VINTON
F
CLERMONT
PIKE
MEIGS
E
JACKSON
BROWN
ADAMS
GALLIA
SCIOTO
LAWRENCE

THERE ARE 35 counties in the unglaciated region, which extends from the rolling highlands of eastern Ohio and the hills and bluffs above the Ohio River to the urban sprawl of Cincinnati and beyond to Indiana. Northeastward the region juts almost to the center of the state. This vast area is the Allegheny Plateau, typified by river and mining towns, sleepy hamlets, industrial centers— and a reassuring number of city and state parks, nature preserves, wildlife areas, and some just plain wonderful spots that have escaped the onslaught of "civilization."

The southwestern counties, shown on Map E, are Adams, Brown, Butler, Clermont, Clinton, Hamilton, Highland, and Warren. Map F shows the south-central counties: Athens, Fairfield, Gallia, Hocking, Jackson, Lawrence, Meigs, Monroe, Morgan, Noble, Perry, Pike, Ross, Scioto, Vinton, and Washington. Map G covers the east-central section: Belmont, Carroll, Columbiana, Coshoc-ton, Guernsey, Harrison, Holmes, Jefferson, Muskingum, Stark, and Tus-carawas counties. Descriptions of, and directions to, the sites are presented in alphabetical order.

Adams Lake State Park *On Ohio 41 several miles north of West Union. (Map E-1)*

This 90-acre tract contains a 47-acre impounded lake, patches of woods, nature trails, and a picnic area. Established to protect a small relict prairie, the preserve is owned and operated by the Ohio Department of Natural Resources.

Among the nesting birds and summer visitors, look for the Green-backed Heron, Turkey Vulture, Red-shouldered and Red-tailed hawks, Ruffed Grouse, Northern Bobwhite, Killdeer, Yellow-billed and Black-billed cuckoos, Great Horned Owl, Whip-poor-will, Downy and Hairy woodpeckers, Eastern Phoebe, Eastern Kingbird, Purple Martin, Northern Rough-winged and Barn swallows, Carolina Chickadee, Carolina Wren, Eastern Bluebird, Gray Cat-bird, Northern Mockingbird, Brown Thrasher, White-eyed, Yellow-throated, Warbling, and Red-eyed vireos, Blue-winged, Yellow, Prairie, Cerulean, and Kentucky warblers, Louisiana Waterthrush, Common Yellowthroat, Yellow-breasted Chat, Orchard Oriole, Indigo Bunting, Rufous-sided Towhee, and Chipping, Field, and Song sparrows. Cruise nearby roads to find Grasshopper Sparrows and a few Henslow's Sparrows. In previous years, Lark Sparrows nested in the vicinity.

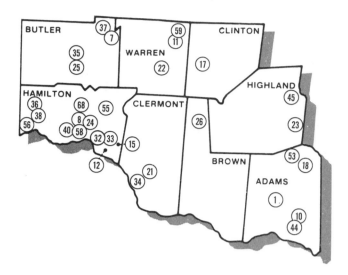

MAP E

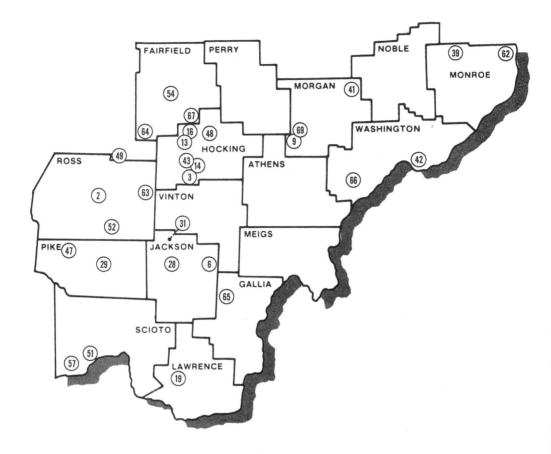

MAP F

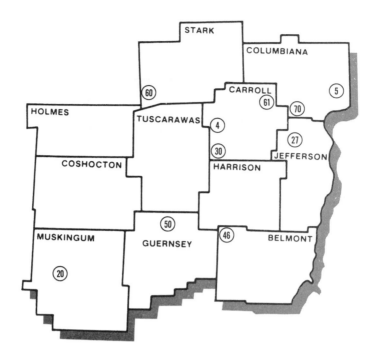

MAP G

Adena State Memorial   *On Ohio 104 to Allen Avenue, northwest*
                                        of Chillicothe. (Map F–2)

The early 19th-century home of Thomas Worthington, Ohio's founding father, this 300-acre estate is administered by the Ohio Historical Society. Open
daily except Mondays April through October, the mansion is situated on high
ground with a view of the surrounding hills. Besides the beautiful house with
its large barn, gardens, and orchard, there are acres of woodland and a ravine.

    Typical spring and summer birds include the Turkey Vulture, Red-tailed
Hawk, Northern Bobwhite, Yellow-billed Cuckoo, Chimney Swift, Ruby-
throated Hummingbird, Red-bellied Woodpecker, Eastern Phoebe, Eastern
Kingbird, Purple Martin, Barn Swallow, Carolina Chickadee, Tufted Titmouse,
House Wren, Blue-gray Gnatcatcher, Eastern Bluebird, Wood Thrush, Gray
Catbird, Brown Thrasher, Cedar Waxwing, White-eyed and Red-eyed vireos,
Blue-winged, Yellow, and Cerulean warblers, Ovenbird, Common Yellow-
throat, Summer Tanager, Northern Cardinal, Indigo Bunting, Rufous-sided
Towhee, Chipping, Field, and Song sparrows, Eastern Meadowlark, Northern
Oriole, and American Goldfinch. During the spring and fall, many warblers
and other migrant passerine birds can be found on the grounds and in the
surrounding countryside.

Ash Cave State Park   *Take U.S. 33 in Hocking County to Ohio*
                                       664, which is several miles northwest of
                                       Logan. Drive west about 10 miles to
                                       Route 374, turn left (south) and proceed
                                       about 4 miles to Route 56. Drive west
                                       less than a mile and follow signs to
                                       entrance. (Map F–3)

Part of the Hocking State Forest, the park's wooded hillsides of mixed hardwoods are accented by towering hemlocks. Centerpiece is a spectacular horseshoe-shaped sandstone overhang some 90 feet high and 700 feet wide with a
stream plunging from the top into a pool.

    This park can produce an impressive list of breeding warblers and other
specialties of the hills in May and June. Nesting birds include the Ruffed
Grouse, Yellow-billed and Black-billed cuckoos, Great Horned Owl, Ruby-
throated Hummingbird, Red-bellied Woodpecker, Acadian Flycatcher, Wood
Thrush, Yellow-throated Vireo, Northern Parula, Black-throated Green, Cerulean, and Black-and-white warblers, American Redstart, Ovenbird, Louisiana
Waterthrush, Kentucky and Hooded warblers, and Scarlet Tanager.

Ovenbird (front), Kentucky Warbler, and Hooded Warbler

Atwood Lake

In Carroll County southwest of Carrollton between Ohio 39 and Ohio 542. (Map G–4)

A part of the Muskingum Watershed Conservancy District, this impounded 1,540-acre lake is set amid dense woodlands, planted pine plantations, and rolling fields. Trails cross through the remote haunts of Ruffed Grouse. The males celebrate the spring with their weird drumming—an accelerating series of thumps produced with their wings—surely one of the great sounds of nature.

Green-backed Herons nest and small groups of waterfowl are seen in spring and fall; Great Horned and Barred owls are resident, and all six species of Ohio's commonly nesting woodpeckers are present. There are camping areas, cabins, and a beautiful state lodge.

Beaver Creek State Park

In southeastern Columbiana County on Ohio 7 about 8 miles north of East Liverpool. (Map G–5)

Natural scenery abounds in this 2,405-acre tract which contains a rushing creek, forested hills, and a deep gorge with hemlocks and Canadian yew. There are also extensive pine plantings, the remnants of an old canal, and a restored grist mill.

Warbling Vireos and Northern Orioles nest in sycamores and cottonwoods in open areas along the creek. The repetitious calling of Whip-poor-wills can be heard at night, along with the basso hooting of Great Horned Owls.

Sharp-shinned, Cooper's, and Red-tailed hawks nest, as do Belted King-fishers, Pileated Woodpeckers, Acadian Flycatchers, Yellow-throated Vireos, Cerulean Warblers, Ovenbirds, Louisiana Waterthrushes, Kentucky Warblers, and Scarlet Tanagers, especially in the area around the gorge.

Buckeye Furnace   *Take Ohio 35 to Ohio 124 in Jackson County; go east to County Road 58, then south to Township Road 167 and southwest to the furnace. (Map F–6)*

This 270-acre site features a restored charcoal furnace used to smelt iron ore in the late 19th century. One of the two nature trails winds around the abandoned ore pits and old roads once used in the operation of the furnace.

In the spring, migrant birds of many species may be seen along the nature trails and around the site itself. Among the nesting birds are Yellow-billed and Black-billed cuckoos, Red-bellied Woodpeckers, Eastern Wood-Pewees, Eastern Phoebes, Great Crested Flycatchers, Carolina Wrens, Blue-gray Gnatcatchers, Eastern Bluebirds, White-eyed, Yellow-throated, and Red-eyed vireos, Yellow, Cerulean, and Kentucky warblers, Ovenbirds, Louisiana Waterthrushes, Common Yellowthroats, Yellow-breasted Chats, Summer and Scarlet tanagers, Indigo Buntings, Chipping, Field, and Song sparrows, and Northern Orioles.

Bulls Run Arboretum   *In Middletown, Butler County. From the downtown area, take First and Central avenues east to Breiel Boulevard. Then north to Rosedale Road and left just under 0.5 mile to the parking lot and entrance (between Curryer and Red Bud). From I-75 take Ohio 122 (Roosevelt Boulevard) west, then north on Breiel Boulevard 1.2 miles to Rosedale Road. (Map E–7)*

About two miles from downtown Middletown in a pleasant suburban location, this excellent 11-acre area of trees, shrubs, and abundant undergrowth is great habitat for migrant passerines. Established in 1979 by the Middletown Historical Society, managed by the Friends of Bulls Run Arboretum, and owned by the City of Middletown, the arboretum is along historic Bulls Run Creek which was traveled by Miami Indians and pioneer hunters. A picnic shelter is available, and a feeding station is maintained. Nearby Miami University and Wildwood Golf Course offer additional habitat for migrants. Foxes call the park home, and deer sometimes pay a visit.

The woodland, containing more than 60 species of trees, attracts many migrants including thrushes, vireos, and warblers. Connecticut and Mourning warblers are sometimes seen in the dense undergrowth.

Burnet Woods

From I-75, take the Hopple Street exit and turn right (east) onto Hopple Street (which becomes Martin Luther King Drive). At the top of the long hill, turn left onto Clifton Avenue, then take the first right into the park. (Map E–8)

Weekday parking can be a problem because this 89-acre park is in the shadow of the University of Cincinnati. But perseverance might pay off, especially in late April and May, because the park attracts an excellent variety of passerine birds, including just about any warbler you would expect to see in Ohio. The small pond has even been a stopover for American Bitterns.

Burr Oak State Park

Off Ohio 78 north of Glouster and 15 miles north of Athens. (Map F–9)

Over 3,000 acres of wooded hills, fields, and hollows, a 664-acre lake, miles of hiking trails (including a portion of the Buckeye Trail), a luxurious lodge, 30 cabins, a full-service dining room, tennis courts, and lots of birds are some of the ingredients constituting this multipurpose park located in Wayne National Forest. Nearby attractions include the Borsari Stained Glass Studio, the Fenton Glass Outlet, the Button House, the Hocking Valley Scenic Railway, the Athens Dairy Barn Art Center, the Middletown Doll Company, and numerous antique and pottery shops.

In spring and fall, the lake attracts Pied-billed and Horned grebes, Common Loons, Double-crested Cormorants, Great Egrets, Bonaparte's, Ring-billed, and Herring gulls, Caspian and Common terns, and occasional Ospreys. Solitary and Spotted sandpipers along with a few "peeps" and Common Snipe are sometimes found in wet places and around the edges of the lake. Mute Swans, Canada Geese, Wood Ducks, and Mallards nest.

Nesting birds include Yellow-throated and Red-eyed vireos, Summer and Scarlet tanagers and the following warblers: Blue-winged, Northern Parula, Yellow, Prairie, Cerulean, Black-and-white, American Redstart, Ovenbird, Louisiana Waterthrush, Kentucky, Hooded, and Yellow-breasted Chat.

From the latter half of February through April, woodcocks perform their

courtship ritual where there are fields and wooded edges. Feeders are main-
tained around the lodge and at the old amphitheater, which also has a blind.
Birds commonly seen include Red-bellied and Downy woodpeckers, Carolina
Chickadees, Tufted Titmice, White-breasted Nuthatches, Carolina Wrens,
Northern Cardinals, Song Sparrows, American Goldfinches and, in winter, all
of the preceding plus American Tree and White-throated sparrows, Dark-eyed
Juncos, Pine Siskins and always possible Evening Grosbeaks.

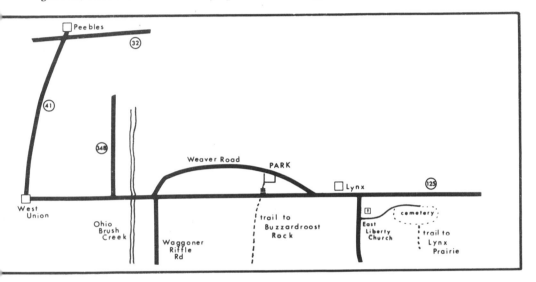

Buzzardroost Rock

*Drive east through West Union in Adams
County on Ohio Route 125 and cross the
bridge over Ohio Brush Creek. Take the
first road on the left, Weaver Road. Go
about 0.25 mile and park in the
designated area on the right. The trail
leaves the parking lot from the right-hand
corner, crosses the highway and proceeds up
to the ridge. (Map E–10)*

This is one of the 12 preserves constituting the Edge of Appalachia System,
owned and operated by the Cincinnati Museum of Natural History and the
Nature Conservancy. Rugged wooded hillsides, patches of prairie, streams, and
waterfalls are found on this 152-acre site.

Black and Turkey vultures soar overhead, while below the forest canopy
are Ruffed Grouse, Wild Turkeys, and Pileated Woodpeckers. From May
through the first half of July, look and listen for Pine, Cerulean, Worm-eating,

and Hooded warblers. In more open spaces there are Eastern Kingbirds, Eastern Bluebirds, Blue-winged and Prairie warblers, Common Yellowthroats, Yellow-breasted Chats, Orchard Orioles, and the possibility of Blue Grosbeaks.

Some of the birds found along the creek on the western side of the preserve on Waggoner Riffle Road include Wood Duck, an occasional Red-shouldered Hawk, Broad-winged Hawk, Eastern Screech-Owl, Barred Owl, Warbling Vireo, Northern Parula, and Prothonotary Warbler.

In spring and summer in open fields along nearby country roads, look for the following nesting sparrows: Chipping, Field, Vesper, Grasshopper, Henslow's, and Song. From late September to early May, brushy patches and hedgerows provide habitat for occasional Fox and Swamp sparrows and numerous White-throated and White-crowned sparrows.

For more details on the area see Ohio Brush Creek/Adams County account.

Caesar Creek State Park and Gorge Nature Preserve

In Warren County, east of Waynesville, take Ohio 73 toward Wilmington. Turn north to the park headquarters and beach just before the highway bisects the reservoir. Take Clarksville Road right from Ohio 73 to get to the Visitors Center. (Map E–11)

Caesar Creek Lake is a 2,830-acre reservoir situated in 10,186 acres licensed to the Ohio Department of Natural Resources. Much of the land has been incorporated into a state park. The lake was created by the U.S. Army Corps of Engineers between 1971 and 1978 as a flood control reservoir. Included in the area is a beach, picnicking facilities, campground, day lodge, pioneer village, and bridle trails.

The gently rolling terrain has acres of meadows and scattered woodlands in the south portion with heavily wooded, steep ravines in the north. Meadow and grain crops cover about half the area, and woodlands mixed with reverting fields make up the rest.

When the reservoir isn't frozen over, the lake can be good for overwintering ducks. During the early spring waterfowl migration, look for Common Loons (sometimes several dozen), Pied-billed and Horned grebes, Double-crested Cormorants, and a variety of ducks including Green-winged Teals, American Black Ducks, Mallards, Northern Pintails, Blue-winged Teals, Gadwalls, American Wigeon, Common Goldeneyes, Buffleheads, and Common Mergansers. Redheads, Lesser Scaup, and Red-breasted Mergansers sometimes occur in flocks of a hundred or more.

Ospreys and Bald Eagles are often seen soaring over the lake, and Ospreys have been known to summer. With the advent of warm weather, most of

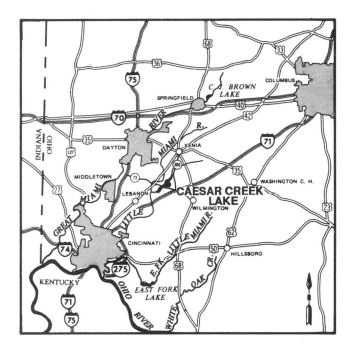

the waterbirds are usually seen in reverse ratio to the number of fishing and pleasure boats.

Other species observed here include Northern Harrier, Red-shouldered Hawk (rare), Red-tailed Hawk, Rough-legged Hawk (in winter), Northern Bobwhite, American Woodcock, Short-eared Owl, Red-headed Woodpecker, Yellow-bellied Sapsucker (October to May), Pileated Woodpecker, Yellow-billed Cuckoo, Tree Swallow, Eastern Bluebird (large numbers), Savannah Sparrow, and Eastern Meadowlark.

Rarities seen include Red-throated Loon, Red-necked Grebe, Eared Grebe, Brown Pelican, Little Blue Heron, Black Vulture, Northern Goshawk, Golden Eagle, Peregrine Falcon, Tundra Swan, Snow Goose, Oldsquaw, Surf Scoter, Ruddy Turnstone, Sanderling, Franklin's Gull, Black-legged Kittiwake, Sedge Wrens, and Henslow's Sparrow.

The State Park is relatively large, but many of the best birding spots are concentrated near where Ohio 73 crosses the lake. Be sure to check the boat ramp which is just opposite the road to the park headquarters. Gulls—Bonaparte's, Ring-billed, and Herring—frequently loaf on the beach beyond the headquarters building.

Luken's Cove Picnic Area (first road on the right after crossing the lake) provides access to scope much of the southern half of the lake, including a seasonal mudflat near the end of the road. A colony of Prairie Warblers nest in the cedars along this road. This area is good in winter for Eastern Bluebirds, kinglets, and Yellow-rumped Warblers. Consistently productive is **Merganser Bay,** as it is known to Dayton-area birders, an inlet at the end of Harveysburg Road just east of the town of Harveysburg. To get there, cross the lake from the park headquarters, and, after bypassing the town of Harveysburg on Ohio 73, turn left on Harveysburg Road and follow it to the lake. The large island visible from the end of the road sometimes harbors a large Turkey Vulture roost in summer. There are a number of other good access points around the lake, including **Pioneer Village** off Oregonia Road, **Mound Wildlife Area** (Ohio 380 north from Ohio 73; left on Center Road and then south on Mound Road), and **Saddle Dam** at the north end of the lake. This area is just two miles from Spring Valley State Wildlife Area. Both can be adequately birded in a single morning.

Just below the dam at the southern end of the lake is 482-acre **Caesar Creek Gorge Nature Preserve,** which is managed by the Ohio Department of Natural Resources. The gorge was created by tremendous glacial meltwaters; in some places the walls rise to 180 feet above the valley. Relatively untouched, the area is densely wooded with beech, maple, oak, and walnut trees. Prairie plants grow on the shallow soils of the cliffs. To get to the dam, Corps of Engineers Visitors Center, and gorge, take Ohio 73 east from Waynesville about one mile, then proceed right about two miles on Clarksville Road.

Cooper's and Red-tailed Hawks nest in the area, along with Eastern Screech-Owls, Great Horned Owls, Yellow-billed Cuckoo, Red-headed, Red-bellied, and Pileated woodpeckers, Acadian Flycatcher, Eastern Phoebe, Northern Parula, Prairie and Cerulean warblers, Ovenbird, Louisiana Waterthrush, Kentucky Warbler, Scarlet Tanager, and Rufous-sided Towhee. Wild Turkeys have been reintroduced and are successfully breeding. During April and October, the gorge is a good place to find Winter Wrens.

Stop by the Visitors Center to check the feeders during winter months. Purple Finches, Common Redpolls, and Pine Siskins sometimes occur.

California Woods   *Take U.S. 52 east from Cincinnati; the entrance is about a mile past the Little Miami River bridge at 5400 Kellog Avenue. (Map E–12)*

Situated at the confluence of the Little Miami and Ohio river valleys, this woodland features an interpretive nature center, trails, and seasonal nature programs. Habitat includes a remnant bottomland hardwood forest through which Lick Run flows. Over 50 species of trees have been identified on the tract; four of the trees are believed to be over 400 years old. Wildflowers abound in spring and summer and include ginseng, goldenseal, bent trillium, Canada lily, and lily-leaved twayblade. The creek is rich in fossils from the Ordovician period.

Nesting specialties include Great Horned Owls, Yellow-billed Cuckoos, Eastern Wood-Pewees, Acadian Flycatchers, Blue-gray Gnatcatchers, Red-eyed Vireos, Yellow-throated, Cerulean, Prothonotary, and Worm-eating warblers, Scarlet Tanagers, Indigo Buntings, and Rufous-sided Towhees.

Cantwell Cliffs State Park

Take U.S. 33 north of Logan in Hocking County to Ohio 374 and drive west about 6 miles. (Map F–13)

The northernmost component of the Hocking Hills State Park system, this site features a huge, horseshoe-shaped precipice 150 feet high. Trails go along the brink, descend into the valley, and thread the slopes. Plantations of red, white, and Scotch pines have been planted on the high ground, while mixed hardwoods and hemlocks grow in the valley and along the slopes.

A rich variety of breeding birds is found in the area during late May, June, and early July. Prominent among these are the Ruffed Grouse, Barred Owl, and Whip-poor-will.

Other specialties include Yellow-throated Vireo, Northern Parula, Black-throated Green, and Black-and-white warblers, American Redstart, Worm-eating, Kentucky, and Hooded warblers, Summer and Scarlet tanagers. During winter months, Pine Siskins, Red or White-winged Crossbills, and Evening Grosbeaks can occasionally be found. In late spring and summer, Grasshopper and Henslow's sparrows can often be found in hilltop fields along the unimproved road off Ohio 374 about 0.5 mile north of the park.

Cedar Falls State Park

Take U.S. 33 to the junction with Ohio 664 in Hocking County; go about 12 miles west to the park entrance. (Map F–14)

The wilderness atmosphere of this Hocking Hills State Park makes a visit here a memorable experience. Beneath the deeply grooved face of Cedar Falls is a wooded gorge of hemlocks, one of which, at 149 feet, is probably the tallest tree in the state. Early settlers mistook the towering trees for cedars—hence the name Cedar Falls. A three-mile section of the Buckeye Trail follows a succession of valleys rich in birdlife to Old Man's Cave State Park.

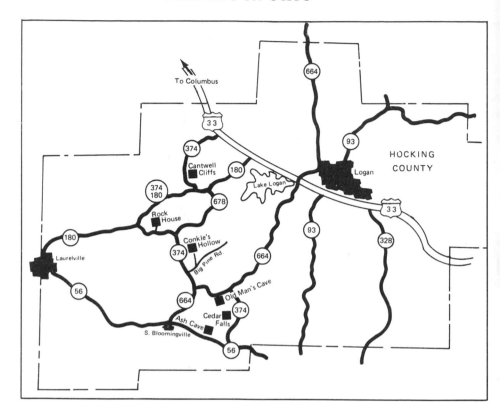

Hocking Hills State Park System

In recent years, breeding records have been established for five species—the Brown Creeper, Veery, Hermit Thrush, Solitary Vireo, and Blackburnian Warbler—which are beyond the normal limits of their ranges. Twelve other warbler species that nest are the Northern Parula, Black-throated Green, Cerulean, Black-and-white, American Redstart, Worm-eating, Ovenbird, Louisiana Waterthrush, Kentucky, Common Yellowthroat, Hooded, and Yellow-breasted Chat.

Mixed hardwoods are integrated with hemlocks on the slopes and cover the uplands. In these various habitats nesting species include the Ruffed Grouse, Wild Turkey, Yellow-billed and Black-billed cuckoos, Eastern Screech-Owl, Barred Owl, Whip-poor-will, Red-bellied and Pileated woodpeckers, Acadian Flycatcher, Eastern Phoebe, Carolina and House wrens, Gray Catbird, Brown Thrasher, Summer and Scarlet tanagers.

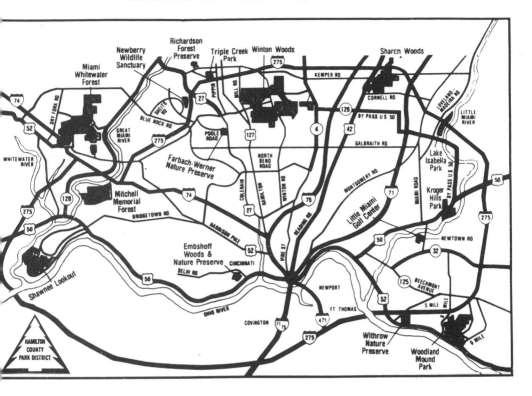

Cincinnati Area

Cincinnati Nature Center

Exit from I-275 onto Ohio 32, go east to Gleneste-Williamsville Road, then north to a three-way intersection. Turn east (right) and go about two blocks. (Map E–15)

This 680-acre center has a hardwood forest, ravines, brushy fields, and several ponds, making it a delightful place to hike and bird. The nature center has exhibits, a members' library, and up-to-date bird records. It is open to the public on weekdays all year round. Weekends are reserved for members and their guests, but permission for a weekend visit may be obtained by writing or phoning the Cincinnati Nature Center, 4949 Tealtown Road, Milford, Ohio 45150, phone (513) 831-1711.

During spring and fall, a few waterfowl visit the ponds; however, the big attraction is the large number of landbirds that can be seen any time of the year. Spring is most exciting with the mix of migrant warblers, tanagers, grosbeaks, and all their allies changing on a daily basis. Feeders bring many birds up close. In winter, woodpeckers, gleaners, sparrows, winter finches, and occasional Evening Grosbeaks can be viewed close-up. Northern Saw-whet Owls are frequently found.

Birds that nest or spend the summer in the area include the Green-backed Heron, Wood Duck, Turkey Vulture, Red-shouldered, Broad-winged, and Red-tailed hawks, American Kestrel, Northern Bobwhite, Yellow-billed Cuckoo, Eastern Screech-Owl, Great Horned and Barred owls, Red-bellied and Pileated woodpeckers, Acadian Flycatcher, Willow Flycatcher, Northern Rough-winged and Barn swallows, Carolina Wren, Eastern Bluebird, Northern Mockingbird, White-eyed, Yellow-throated, and Red-eyed vireos, Blue-winged, Yellow, Yellow-throated, Cerulean, and Kentucky warblers, Common Yellow-throat, Yellow-breasted Chat, Summer and Scarlet tanagers, Northern Cardinal, Rufous-sided Towhee, and Northern Oriole.

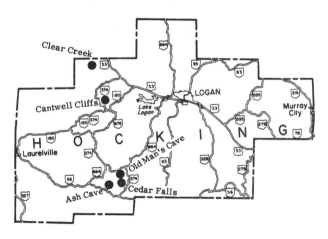

Clear Creek Valley

Take U.S. 33 south of Lancaster about 8.5 miles to the Clear Creek Road (Hocking County Road 116). (Map F–16)

The unglaciated portion of this lovely valley is about seven miles long and is bounded by outcroppings of rugged Black Hand conglomerate sandstone (see Black Hand Gorge account) for much of its length. Resting on glacial wash, the valley is a tapestry of tree-lined stream banks, swaths of scouring rushes, grasses, patches of brush, and strips of fallow fields. At its narrowest, the wooded slopes descend to the stream; in the wider parts of the valley, there are intervening meadows and a few cultivated fields. A profusion of native and introduced wildflowers flourish along the road and in the woods. Some trees typical of the valley are the dogwood, redbud, wild plum, sour gum, tulip, hemlock, sassafras, sourwood, pitch pine, Kentucky coffee, sweet birch, sycamore, willow; scarlet, black, and chestnut oaks; red maple, black walnut, and American beech. Vines and bushes common to the valley include the mountain laurel, wild grape, greenbrier, witch hazel, Virginia creeper, and bittersweet.

Over 3,000 acres of land in the Clear Creek Valley is owned by the Columbus and Franklin County Metropolitan Park District and has been dedicated as a state nature preserve. A gift of 1,159 acres in 1973 from the Allen F. Beck family provided the basis for the preserve that now bears his name. A recent gift of 661 acres from William E. and Emily P. Benua has also been dedicated as a state nature preserve and carries their name in recognition of the gift.

There is a gas station and convenience store at the intersection of Route 33 and the Clear Creek Road. It is all right to park at the west end of the parking lot. Killdeer nest in the adjacent field. Barn Swallows are sometimes joined by nesting Cliff Swallows in the barn across the road. Overhead, scrutinize the swirls of Turkey Vultures for individuals of the scarcer Black Vulture, a few of which nest in the vicinity, and occasional Red-shouldered or Red-tailed hawks.

Keep a sharp lookout to the sky for transiting Green-backed Herons, Pileated Woodpeckers, Eastern Bluebirds, Cedar Waxwings, Northern Rough-winged Swallows. Cedar Waxwings and Yellow Warblers nest in the trees behind the store. Listen for the rollicking yodel of the Carolina Wren, the repetitious *burry* notes of the Yellow-throated Vireo, the *churry churry* of the Scarlet Tanager, and the eggbeater-like song of the Cerulean Warbler.

About 0.4 mile from Route 33, a driveway leads up a hill to Neotoma, a long wooded hollow that once was owned and extensively studied for many years by Edward S. Thomas, Curator of Natural History at the old Ohio State Museum, and his colleagues. It is now administered by the Metro Parks, which must be contacted for permission to enter the tract. The birdlife at Neotoma during the nesting season is always of interest. Around the old cabin, look and listen for Yellow-billed and Black-billed cuckoos, Acadian Flycatchers, Carolina Chickadees, Blue-gray Gnatcatchers, Wood Thrushes, Northern Parula, Cerulean, Black-and-white, and, rarely, Pine warblers. Ovenbirds, American Redstarts, and Scarlet Tanagers visit the clearing around the cabin; a pair of Summer Tanagers frequently nest nearby.

Several trails lead down the wooded hollow, which follows a small stream. Here there are Red-bellied and Pileated woodpeckers, Yellow-throated Vireos, Worm-eating and Kentucky warblers, several pairs of Louisiana Waterthrushes, and Rufous-sided Towhees. At the head of the valley and below the cabin, listen for Willow Flycatchers, Blue-winged Warblers, Common Yellowthroats, and Yellow-breasted Chats. At dusk, listen for Whip-poor-wills.

The area around Leaning Lena (a great chunk of sandstone that towers over the road) is good for Black-billed Cuckoos, Yellow-breasted Chats, and Summer Tanagers.

About 1.8 miles from Route 33, Starner Road leads to the south; an old iron bridge crosses Clear Creek and the road meanders along for a while between the creek and a slope of magnificent hemlocks. There are plenty of places to park off the side of the road. A small nesting colony of Great Blue Herons can be seen atop one of the hills south of the creek from the Clear Creek Road. Phoebes, Blue-gray Gnatcatchers, Yellow-throated Warblers, and Louisiana Waterthrushes nest near the bridge. Some years, a pair of Magnolia Warblers nests in the hemlocks.

Down the Clear Creek Road 2.5 miles from U.S. 33, pull off the road and park near the wooded hollow on the right. A pair of Canada Warblers frequently nests back along the hemlock-covered slope. Veeries nest in the vicinity, in addition to a fine assortment of warblers. Among the latter are Blue-winged, Northern Parula, Yellow, Magnolia (rare), Black-throated Green, Yellow-throated, Cerulean, Black-and-white, American Redstart, Worm-eating, Ovenbird, Louisiana Waterthrush, and Common Yellowthroat. Pileated Woodpeckers and a pair of Broad-winged Hawks nest nearby, and a short walk down the road in either direction will reveal Kentucky and Hooded warblers.

Continuing along the road, at 4.8 miles from U.S. 33 is Written Rock, a graffiti-covered sandstone cliff at the edge of the road. Hundreds of initials are inscribed here, most of the recent ones with spray paint that unfortunately obscures some of the chiseled inscriptions, some of which are well over 150 years old. A pair of Eastern Phoebes and several pairs of Northern Rough-winged Swallows sometimes nest in crannies on the face of the cliff. Sycamores along the creek attract nesting Eastern Kingbirds, Warbling Vireos, Northern Orioles and an occasional pair of Orchard Orioles. Other birds to look for in the vicinity, including the field across the creek, are Red-tailed Hawk, Ruby-throated Hummingbird, Belted Kingfisher, Red-bellied Woodpecker, Willow Flycatcher, Barn Swallow, Eastern Bluebird, White-eyed, Yellow-throated, and Red-eyed vireos, Northern Parula (in the evergreens high atop Written Rock), Yellow and Yellow-throated warblers, Common Yellowthroat, Yellow-breasted Chat, and Summer Tanager.

From Written Rock, continue westward to the entrance leading to Barneby Center, once an environmental training station operated by The Ohio State University. The Solitary Vireo has been found nesting here, along with such specialties as Broad-winged Hawk, Black-billed Cuckoo, Rose-breasted Grosbeak, Prairie Warbler, and at least 15 other members of its clan.

About a mile farther down the Clear Creek Road a new concrete bridge has replaced an old iron one that once crossed the creek. Near the new bridge, look for Blue-gray Gnatcatchers, Cedar Waxwings, Blue-winged, Yellow-throated, and Cerulean warblers, Ovenbirds, Common Yellowthroats, Yellow-breasted Chats, Summer and Scarlet tanagers, Indigo Buntings, Rufous-sided Towhees, and Song Sparrows. Green-backed Herons, Belted Kingfishers, and Northern Rough-winged Swallows can frequently be seen flying along the creek. Listen for Wild Turkeys along the edges of nearby fields. The part of the valley between Rich Hollow Road and an old covered bridge farther on provides a final encore to the wonderful birdlife of the region.

A few Eastern Screech Owls and one or two pairs of Great Horned and Barred owls inhabit the valley but are difficult to find except at night with the help of a tape recorder. Eight to ten pairs of Whip-poor-wills can be heard calling on territory each year. In a population study of the valley, the author has recorded 114 species of nesting birds. A pair of Common Ravens was present from 1987 through 1989. One of the adults was seen feeding a fledgling in 1987. Other unusual birds seen in the valley include Common Loon, Osprey, Peregrine Falcon, Golden Eagle, Say's Phoebe, Bewick's Wren (nested), Lawrence's Warbler (hybrid), Great-tailed Grackle, and Evening Grosbeak.

If you are headed back toward Columbus on U.S. 33 and have never been to **Chestnut Ridge Metropolitan Park**, maybe this is the day for a new adventure. This magnificent 486-acre tract on Winchester Road west of Carroll features a forested ridge that rises up out of the surrounding fields like a mountainous island, two miles of trails including a high-altitude boardwalk, a trailside stream, rolling meadows, and a man-made lake. Nesting birds include American Woodcock, Red-headed and Pileated woodpeckers, Tree Swallows, Wood Thrushes, White-eyed, Yellow-throated, and Red-eyed vireos, Scarlet Tanagers, the following warblers—Blue-winged, Yellow, Prairie, Cerulean, Black-and-white, Ovenbird, Kentucky, Common Yellowthroat, Hooded, and Yellow-breasted Chat—and Orchard and Northern orioles.

Cowan Lake State Park	*Southwest of Wilmington in Clinton*
Sugar Grove Cemetery	*County. From Wilmington, follow Ohio*
	730 southwest to the spillway; or take
	U.S. 68 south, then west on Ohio 350 to
	the several park entrances. (Map E–17)

This 700-acre lake, centered in an attractive state park of 1,076 acres, offers boating, fishing, camping, cabins, a beach, picnicking, and a marina, in addition to hiking and birding. The lake usually attracts flocks of migrant waterfowl from February through April, and again in October and November; however, hunting is permitted during the fall. Mallards, American Wigeons, Redheads, Ring-necked Ducks, and all three mergansers are usually most numerous. Common Loons and a few Pied-billed and Horned grebes are also likely to be seen at such times. The beach, picnic, and camping areas are good for spotting waterfowl and the occasional Osprey.

Summering birds include Great Blue and Green-backed herons, Turkey Vulture, Red-shouldered and Red-tailed hawk, American Kestrel, Northern Bobwhite, Killdeer, Spotted Sandpiper, Yellow-billed Cuckoo, Barred Owl, Red-headed and Pileated woodpeckers, Acadian and Willow (rare) flycatchers, Eastern Kingbird, Tree, Northern Rough-winged and Barn swallows, Eastern Bluebird, Wood Thrush, Yellow-throated, Warbling, and Red-eyed vireos, Yellow Warbler, Yellow-breasted Chat (rare), Common Yellowthroat, and Northern Oriole.

When conditions are right, the spillway area, below the dam at the west end of the lake along Ohio 730, attracts shorebirds such as Semipalmated Plover, Killdeer, Greater and Lesser yellowlegs, Solitary, Spotted, Semipalmated, Least, and Pectoral sandpipers. More unusual species seen there include Yellow-crowned Night-Heron, Ruddy Turnstone, Sanderling, White-rumped and Baird's sandpipers, Short-billed Dowitcher, and Wilson's Phalarope. During migration, especially when the weather is inclement or cool, large flocks of swallow species sometimes congregate. There is a parking lot just south of the spillway which gives excellent access to the area.

When the water level is down, mudflats at the east end of the lake are good for shorebirds and on one occasion attracted a flock of nearly 100 Sandhill Cranes. Rarities seen out in the lake from this location have included Red-necked Grebe, White-winged Scoter, and Oldsquaw.

Lotus Cove Nature Trail, off Dalton Road at the northeast end of the lake, provides access to mixed woods, brush, and marsh habitat favorable to Great Blue and Green-backed herons, Ospreys, Tree Swallows, Blue-gray Gnatcatchers, and White-eyed Vireos.

Another nearby birding spot is Cowan Creek Road. Summer nesters found along the creek include Eastern Screech-Owl, Acadian Flycatcher, Eastern Phoebe, Yellow-throated and Red-eyed vireos, Northern Parula, Yellow-throated, Cerulean, Black-and-white, Kentucky, and Hooded warblers, Louisiana Waterthrush, Yellow-breasted Chat, and Summer and Scarlet tanagers. Cowan Creek Road is accessible from Old State Road which runs from Ohio 730 north of the spillway south to the intersection of Ohio 730 and 350 (follow signs to Spillway Lodge). Cowan Creek Road runs northwest about two miles to Clarksville Road.

About seven miles northeast of the lake in nearby Wilmington is **Sugar Grove Cemetery**, which can be very good during migration and in the winter. Yellow-bellied Sapsuckers, Pine Siskins, and Red Crossbills have all been observed during winter in the older conifers. To reach the cemetery from downtown Wilmington, follow South Street (U.S. 68) south two blocks, then right on Ohio 730 (Truesdell Street) to the cemetery on the right.

Cumberland Mine Area   *See Ohio Power Recreation Area.*

Davis (Edwin H.) State Memorial   *Take Ohio 41 to the south edge of Peebles,*
go east on Steam Furnace Road, then
southeast about 2.3 miles to Township
Road 129. Go east on this road for about
2.5 miles. (Map E–18)

This 88-acre tract, administered by the Ohio Historical Society, affords birders
the opportunity to observe a good cross-section of southwestern Ohio birds in
a setting of rugged dolomite cliffs, a cave, a canebrake, prairie openings, a
stream, and a woodland composed of arborvitae, Virginia pine, red cedar, red
and chestnut oaks, tulip, and sugar maple trees. Some of the birds found in
these varied habitats include Red-shouldered Hawk, Ruffed Grouse, Barred
Owl, Whip-poor-will, Eastern Wood-Pewee, Wood Thrush, Red-eyed Vireo,
Cerulean and Kentucky warblers, Ovenbird, Louisiana Waterthrush, Scarlet
Tanager, Rufous-sided Towhee, and Chipping Sparrow. Along the South Trail–
one of two nature trails–typical breeding birds are the Carolina Wren, Gray
Catbird, Brown Thrasher, Yellow-throated Vireo, Summer Tanager, Indigo
Bunting, and Field Sparrow.

Dean State Forest and Lake   *Take Ohio 93 in Lawrence County north*
Vesuvius Recreation Area   *from Ironton: 7 miles to Lake Vesuvius,*
15 miles to Dean State Forest.
(Map F–19)

Both areas combine rugged wooded hills, streams, fallow fields, and hiking
trails. Cooper's, Broad-winged, and Red-tailed hawks nest at both sites, as do
Ruffed Grouse, Whip-poor-wills, and Pileated Woodpeckers. Breeding warblers include the Yellow, Prairie, Cerulean, Black-and-white, American Redstart, Worm-eating, Ovenbird, Louisiana Waterthrush, Kentucky, Common
Yellowthroat, Hooded, and Yellow-breasted Chat.

Dillon State Park and Reservoir   *Take Ohio 146 north of Zanesville about*
8 miles to the park entrance.
(Map G–20)

There is a diversity of habitat at this site including substantial areas of marshy
shoreline, a large impounded lake, wooded hillsides, ravines, and brushy fields.

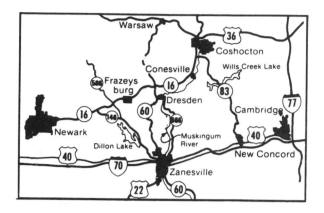

Ohio 146 parallels the lake most of its length with a number of access roads leading to the shore. Common Loons, Pied-billed and Horned grebes, occasional Double-crested Cormorants and Tundra Swans, and sizeable assemblages of ducks and geese rest and feed here during their seasonal migrations. Great Blue Herons are present in all but the coldest months; Green-backed Herons can be found from late April to mid-September, and rarer wading birds such as the Great Egret, Little Blue Heron, and Cattle Egret, and small flocks of Black-crowned Night-Herons, are sometimes found in spring and late summer.

A few of the breeding bird specialties include the Wood Duck, Red-shouldered and Red-tailed hawks, Ruffed Grouse, Black-billed Cuckoo, Eastern Screech-Owl, Great Horned and Barred owls, Whip-poor-will, Pileated Woodpecker, Marsh Wren, Yellow-throated Vireo, Yellow Warbler, Cerulean Warbler, Ovenbird, Summer and Scarlet tanagers, and Rufous-sided Towhee.

East Fork State Park and Reservoir

Located in Clermont County southeast of Cincinnati. From I-275 east of Cincinnati, take Ohio 125 east about 9 miles to Bantam, turn left (north) and follow park signs. (Map E–21)

Situated in the Little Miami River Basin amid wooded hills, open meadows, and remnant prairies, this 10,580-acre site combines 2,166-acre Harsha Lake, campgrounds with 416 sites including electric hookups, drinking water, and showers, an equestrian camp, 30 miles of bridle trails, a swimming beach, boat ramps, Rent-A-Camp facilities (by reservation only), and miles of hiking trails, including an eight-mile section of the Buckeye Trail.

Adena and Hopewell Indians and early mound builders once inhabited the area. A mound near Elklick Road on the northwestern edge of the park

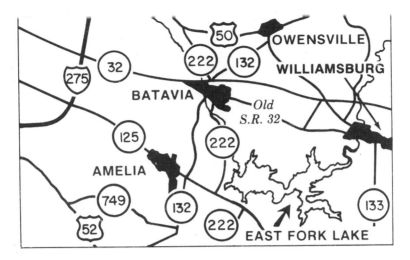

was probably built by the Adenas. Two gold mines operated in the vicinity shortly after the Civil War; one at Elklick consisted of a flume for separating flakes of gold from gravel, another near Twin Bridges was a tunnel to reach deposits encased in bedrock.

The lake often attracts good numbers of waterfowl in the spring and fall. Common Loons, Pied-billed and Horned grebes, Double-crested Cormorants, most of Ohio's dabbling and diving ducks, gulls, and terns are seen with regularity. Herons, egrets, and shorebirds occur in modest numbers. Ospreys and Bald Eagles are frequently seen.

Representative breeding birds are Green-backed Heron, Wood Duck, Cooper's, Red-shouldered, Broad-winged (uncommon), and Red-tailed hawks, American Kestrel, Ruffed Grouse (rare), Wild Turkey, Bobwhite, Killdeer, Spotted Sandpiper, American Woodcock, Yellow-billed Cuckoo, Eastern Screech-Owl, Great Horned and Barred owls, Whip-poor-will, Ruby-throated Hummingbird, Belted Kingfisher, Red-headed, Hairy, and Pileated woodpeckers, Eastern Wood-Pewee, Acadian Flycatcher, Eastern Phoebe, Great Crested Flycatcher, Eastern Kingbird, all the swallows except Cliff, Wood Thrush, Cedar Waxwing, White-eyed, Yellow-throated, and Red-eyed vireos, Summer and Scarlet tanagers, Indigo Bunting, Rufous-sided Towhee, Chipping, Field, Grasshopper, Henslow's (fairly common), and Song sparrows, Orchard and Northern orioles, and American Goldfinch.

Breeding warblers are Blue-winged, Northern Parula, Yellow, Yellow-throated, Prairie, Cerulean, Prothonotary, Louisiana Waterthrush, Kentucky, Common Yellowthroat, and Yellow-breasted Chat.

Winter visitors include Northern Harriers, Sharp-shinned Hawks, Rough-legged Hawks (scarce), increased numbers of Horned Larks, Brown Creepers,

Golden-crowned Kinglets, Yellow-rumped Warblers, American Tree, Field, Fox (occasional), Song, Swamp, White-throated, and White-crowned sparrows, Dark-eyed Juncos, Purple Finches, and Pine Siskins (erratic).

Rarities have included Red-throated Loon, Red-necked Grebe, American White Pelican, Tricolored Heron, Tundra Swan, Northern Goshawk, American Avocet, Ruddy Turnstone, Sanderling, White-rumped Sandpiper, Lapland Longspur, Laughing Gull, Franklin's Gull, Snow Bunting, and Common Redpoll.

Fort Ancient State Memorial

In Warren County, take I-71 to the Lebanon exit, proceed southeast a short distance on Ohio 123, then turn left onto Ohio 350 and drive about 5 miles to the entrance (entrance fee required; limited hours). There is also unlimited access along the Little Miami River to the Scenic River Forest Preserve, an excellent birding area. Park in the lot just west of the bridge along Ohio 350, and walk south along the river. (Map E–22)

Approximately 1,500 years ago the Hopewell Indians built these important prehistoric earthworks, which circle the crest of a 270-foot-high bluff over the Little Miami River, Ohio's first national and state-designated Scenic River. Centuries later, the Fort Ancient Indians occupied the same site. The area is maintained by the Ohio Historical Society and a museum displays many of the artifacts of both cultures.

Deeply forested ravines and streams extend from the earthworks to the river valley below. Dominant trees include the American beech, sugar maple, white, scarlet, red, and chestnut oaks, hickory and, in the river bottom, sycamore and cottonwood. There are trails that lead to scenic overlooks, past brushy fields, and extensive parklands.

Summer birds include the Black and Turkey vultures, Cooper's, Red-shouldered, and Red-tailed hawks, American Kestrel, Wild Turkey, Northern Bobwhite, Black-billed Cuckoo, Pileated Woodpecker, Eastern Phoebe, Eastern Bluebird, Wood Thrush, Northern Mockingbird, White-eyed, Yellow-throated, Warbling, and Red-eyed vireos, Summer and Scarlet tanagers, Rose-breasted Grosbeak, Rufous-sided Towhee, Chipping, Field, and Song sparrows, Orchard and Northern orioles, and the following warblers: Blue-winged, Northern Parula, Yellow-throated, Cerulean, Black-and-white, American Redstart (nests near the canoe livery), Prothonotary (along the river), Worm-eating, Louisiana Waterthrush, Kentucky, Common Yellowthroat, and Hooded.

Fort Hill State Memorial   *In eastern Highland County on County*
Road 256, which can be reached from
Ohio 41. (Map E–23)

This 1,197-acre tract, a property of the Ohio Historical Society, includes remnants of prehistoric Indian earthworks in rugged terrain that ranges from dense forest and cool wooded slopes to hot arid hillsides and brushy bottomlands. Wild cherry and white and red oaks are abundant, and there are some sugar maples and tulip trees over 100 feet tall. A moist limestone gorge harbors such uncommon plants as the Canadian yew, *Sullivantia,* walking fern, and Canby's mountain lover. On the slopes are moss phlox, dwarf larkspur, wood-sorrel, and a splendid mosaic of other wildflowers and ferns.

Breeding and summer birds include Wood Duck, Turkey Vulture, Sharp-shinned, Cooper's, Broad-winged, and Red-tailed hawks, American Kestrel, Northern Bobwhite, Yellow-billed and Black-billed cuckoos, Eastern Screech-Owl, Barred Owl, Whip-poor-will, Ruby-throated Hummingbird, Belted Kingfisher, Red-headed, Red-bellied, Downy, and Hairy woodpeckers, Northern Flicker, Pileated Woodpecker, Eastern Wood-Pewee, Acadian Flycatcher, Eastern Phoebe, Great Crested Flycatcher, Eastern Kingbird, Purple Martin, Northern Rough-winged and Barn swallows, Blue Jay, and American Crow.

Other typical breeding species are the Carolina Chickadee, Tufted Titmouse, White-breasted Nuthatch, Carolina and House wrens, Blue-gray Gnatcatcher, Eastern Bluebird, Wood Thrush, Gray Catbird, Northern Mockingbird, Brown Thrasher, Cedar Waxwing, White-eyed, Yellow-throated, and Red-eyed vireos, Blue-winged Warbler, Northern Parula, Yellow, Yellow-throated, Prairie, Cerulean, and Black-and-white warblers, American Redstart, Worm-eating warblers, Ovenbird, Louisiana Waterthrush, Kentucky Warbler, Common Yellowthroat, Yellow-breasted Chat, Summer and Scarlet tanagers, Northern Cardinal, Indigo Bunting, Rufous-sided Towhee, and Chipping, Field, and Song sparrows. The Bewick's Wren and Bachman's Sparrow once nested here.

French Park   *On the east side of Cincinnati, exit I-71 at*
Ridge Road (exit 8) and proceed north to
Section Road, thence to the entrance. From
I-75 South, exit at Galbraith Road
(10B), turn left and go east on Galbraith
Road to Ridge Road. Turn right and
proceed to Section Road. (Map E–24)

A 270-acre park of varied habitats that attracts a nice variety of spring and fall passerine migrants. Still remembered for a one-time occurrence of a Black-throated Gray Warbler.

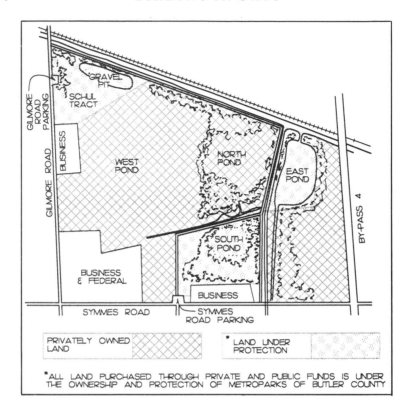

Gilmore Ponds Preserve

In southeast Butler County, just east of Fairfield and Hamilton. From I-75 take the Tylersville Road (Exit 22) and go west about 6 miles to bypass 4. Turn left (south), and proceed about 0.25 mile, then turn right (west) onto Symmes Road. Or from downtown Hamilton, take Ohio 4 south about 2 miles to Symmes Road. Follow Symmes Road about 1.5 miles to Berk Boulevard. Park opposite Berk Boulevard in front of the guard rail. Follow the dike north to the ponds. From I-275 take Ohio 4 north, then right on Ohio Bypass 4 to Symmes Road, then left to parking area. (Map E–25)

Located in a bustling industrial area within the city limits of Hamilton and adjacent to a remnant section of the Miami-Erie Canal, this area of about 250 acres is nearly hidden by an industrial park and an airport. It contains a vestige of interesting wetland habitat, a small portion of which is currently protected (about one-fourth) and managed by the Metro Parks of Butler County. Current efforts to expand and save this important site are being undertaken by the Gilmore Ponds Conservancy.

Several drainage ditches empty here and are flanked by a series of dikes that divide the water into three separate impoundments—a transient lake, a shallow pond to the south, and a deeper, triangular pond to the east. Remnants of the historic Miami-Erie Canal still flow through the area. White-tailed deer, rabbits, groundhogs, red fox, muskrats, raccoons, mink, and weasels can all be found.

The transient lake reaches its fullest stage only after periods of heavy rainfall. During the spring migration, hundreds of diving and dabbling ducks feed in the flooded vegetation. Soras and Common Snipe can be found along the edges. In the wooded area at the center of the lake, large concentrations of Rusty Blackbirds congregate from late February through April. As the lake begins to dry up, large areas of mudflat are exposed, attracting a variety of shorebirds. When the lake is full, shorebirds can be found in nearby flooded farmland, especially across the railroad tracks to the north. All of the common shorebirds have been recorded, plus such uncommon species as Piping Plover, Upland Sandpiper, Sanderling, Stilt, White-rumped, Baird's, and Buff-breasted sandpipers, Long-billed Dowitcher, and Wilson's and Red-necked phalaropes.

The shallow cattail pond to the south is bordered by a willow swamp. Pied-billed Grebes, Least Bitterns, Blue-winged Teals, Hooded Mergansers, Soras, and American Coots have nested here. American Bitterns and Marsh Wrens are sometimes seen during migration. American Woodcock are common and can be observed displaying at dawn and dusk from March through early May, especially in the field to the west.

It is difficult to traverse the ditch necessary to reach the east pond, but it can sometimes be well worth the effort. The pond is choked with dead and dying willows which provide excellent cover for nesting Black-crowned Night-Herons and Wood Ducks.

Additional nesting waterbirds include Green-backed Heron, Canada Goose, Mallard, Virginia Rail, Sora, Killdeer, Spotted Sandpiper, and Belted Kingfisher.

The area also has an interesting variety of landbirds. The brushy thickets along the dikes are good places to look for Willow Flycatchers, Eastern Kingbirds, Warbling Vireos, Yellow Warblers, Prothonotary Warblers, Common Yellowthroats, Yellow-breasted Chats, Orchard and Northern orioles. Red-tailed Hawks, American Kestrels, and Northern Bobwhites inhabit the area.

Many other unusual species have been sighted over the years including Snowy and Cattle egrets, Tundra Swan, Oldsquaw, Black Vulture, Peregrine Falcon, King Rail, Piping Plover, Wilson's Phalarope, Least Tern, Barn and

Northern Saw-whet owls, Sedge Wren, Worm-eating, Mourning, and Kirtland's warblers, Dickcissel, Bobolink, and Brewer's Blackbird.

Winter species include some ducks, occasional Northern Harriers and accipiters, Horned Larks, and numerous sparrows. Minimum amounts of water collect in the area during drought years. Check with local birders as to conditions.

The ponds are not far from the Miami and Erie Canal Park.

Goetz (Christian and Emma)   *See Buzzardroost Rock.*
Nature Preserve

Greenbelt Nature Preserve   *See Winton Woods.*

Hocking Hills State Park   *See Cantwell Cliffs, Cedar Falls, etc.*

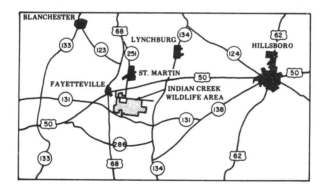

Indian Creek State Wildlife Area   *In Brown County on Ohio 50 1 mile east*
                                                      of Fayetteville. (Map E–26)

Birdlife and small mammals abound in this 1,540-acre tract of rolling hills, ponds, streams, bits of marsh, and oak-hickory woods.

Wood Ducks and Mallards nest in wet areas and a few migratory species such as Blue-winged Teals and American Wigeons are present during the spring months. Greater and Lesser yellowlegs and Solitary and Spotted sandpipers can be found in the spring, late summer, and fall. During the spring months, wooded and brushy areas sometimes teem with transient flycatchers, vireos, warblers, sparrows, and finches.

Just a few of the nesting birds are the Green-backed Heron, Red-tailed Hawk, Ring-necked Pheasant, American Woodcock, Belted Kingfisher, Red-headed Woodpecker, Willow Flycatcher, Eastern Kingbird, Eastern Bluebird, Cedar Waxwing, Warbling Vireo, Yellow Warbler, and Northern Oriole.

Jefferson Lake State Park   *In Jefferson County on Ohio 43 about 4 miles west of Richmond. (Map G–27)*

A fine oak-hickory forest graces this 933-acre site which features rolling hills and ravines around a lovely lake, and adjacent marsh. Wood Ducks nest in boxes set out for them. Ruffed Grouse occur sparingly, and Spotted Sandpipers sometimes nest. Other nesting birds include Eastern Screech-Owl, Great Horned Owl, Whip-poor-will, Ruby-throated Hummingbird, Belted Kingfisher, five species of woodpeckers, Eastern Wood-Pewee, Acadian Flycatcher, Eastern Phoebe, Great Crested Flycatcher, Eastern Kingbird, Purple Martin, Northern Rough-winged and Barn swallows, Carolina Chickadee, Tufted Titmouse, and White-breasted Nuthatch. House Wrens are common in brushy places and around human habitations. Blue-gray Gnatcatchers and Cedar Waxwings are widespread and fairly common. Also look and listen for Yellow-throated and Red-eyed vireos, Blue-winged, Yellow, Cerulean, and Black-and-white warblers, Louisiana Waterthrushes, Kentucky Warblers, Common Yellowthroats, Yellow-breasted Chats, Scarlet Tanagers, Vesper and Grasshopper sparrows in surrounding fields, and Northern Orioles.

Lake Katherine (Edwin A. Jones and James J. McKitterick Memorial Wildlife Sanctuary)   *In Jackson County, take U.S. 35 about 3.3 miles north of Jackson; turn west on County Road 59, cross Little Salt Creek, go 1 mile to County Road 59A and turn south. (Map F–28)*

A splendid array of habitats are preserved in this 1,467-acre preserve through the foresight of two longtime business partners, Edwin A. Jones and the late James J. McKitterick, who donated the land to the Ohio Department of Natural Resources.

High sandstone bluffs festooned with gnarled Virginia pines overlook the lake. Ferns, mosses, a myriad of wildflowers and rare plants, including several endangered species of Ohio orchids, make this a botanist's paradise. Hemlocks, mountain laurel, and sweet birch in the bottoms vie for attention with several hundred bigleaf magnolias and an undisturbed forest of oaks, maples, and beech trees.

Sharp-shinned, Cooper's, Broad-winged, and Red-tailed hawks, Eastern Screech-Owls, Great Horned and Barred owls nest in the area regularly. Other breeding species are Turkey Vulture, American Kestrel, Ruffed Grouse, Black-billed Cuckoo, Whip-poor-will, Pileated Woodpecker, and the following warblers: Yellow, Cerulean, Black-and-white, Ovenbird, Louisiana Waterthrush, Kentucky, Common Yellowthroat, Hooded, and Yellow-breasted Chat.

Lake White   *In Pike County, a few miles south of*
                                           Waverly, Ohio. Routes 104, 220, 551,
                                           and 552 circle the lake. (Map F–29)

Thousands of Canada Geese gather here in the winter, usually along the north shore, occasionally accompanied by a small Richardson's Goose or a few Snow Goose stragglers. Tundra Swans and sometimes a Mute Swan or two stop over, usually in late fall and again in March. Common Loons, when they do appear, seldom remain longer than a day or two, but mixed flocks of ducks, along with Pied-billed and Horned grebes, sometimes build up to respectable numbers.

Nesting passerines around the lake include Eastern Wood-Pewee, Eastern Phoebe, Carolina and House wrens, Wood Thrush, Gray Catbird, Cedar Waxwing, White-eyed, Yellow-throated, Warbling, and Red-eyed vireos, Blue-winged, Yellow, and Prairie warblers, Ovenbird, Kentucky Warbler, Common Yellowthroat, Yellow-breasted Chat, Scarlet Tanager, Indigo Bunting, Rufous-sided Towhee, Field and Chipping sparrows, Orchard and Northern orioles.

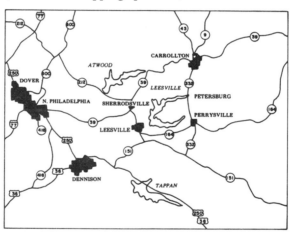

Leesville Lake and Vicinity

Leesville Lake   *In southern Carroll County north of the village*
                                           of Leesville. Roads lead to the lake from Ohio
                                           212 and Ohio 164. (Map G–30)

This 1,000-acre lake and its wooded shoreline is part of the Muskingum Watershed Conservancy District. Modest numbers of waterfowl stop here during migration, along with flocks of Ring-billed Gulls, small numbers of terns, and occasional Ospreys. There are pleasant forest trails which provide an opportunity to flush Ruffed Grouse, catch a glimpse of a Pileated Woodpecker and, if you are fortunate, hear the melancholy notes of the Black-billed Cuckoo. Belted Kingfishers nest, and a colony of Great Blue Herons is located on a wooded ridge bordering the lake.

Leo Petroglyph State Memorial

From U.S. 35 about 5 miles north of Jackson, take County Road 28 east about 2 miles. (Map F–31)

Prehistoric Indians carved images of birds, fish, a bear, footprints, and animal tracks on a large stone outcropping at this twelve-acre site owned by the Ohio Historical Society. Trails meander beneath tall oaks and through cool moist spots carpeted with a fine variety of wildflowers, ferns, and mosses.

Turkey Vultures and a pair of Red-tailed Hawks are frequently seen soaring overhead. In the wooded areas in spring and summer, there are Yellow-billed Cuckoos, Whip-poor-wills, Red-bellied Woodpeckers, Eastern Wood-Pewees, Acadian and Great Crested flycatchers, Carolina Chickadees, Wood Thrushes, Red-eyed Vireos, Cerulean Warblers, Ovenbirds, Louisiana Water-thrushes, Scarlet Tanagers, and Rufous-sided Towhees.

In more open spaces, look and listen for Eastern Phoebes, Carolina and House wrens, Eastern Bluebirds, Blue-winged and Yellow warblers, Common Yellowthroats, Yellow-breasted Chats, Indigo Buntings, Chipping and Song sparrows, and Northern Orioles.

Little Miami River Overlook

Drive east in Cincinnati on U.S. 52 to Reservoir Road and turn right toward the Ohio River to a parking lot and marina. (Map E–32)

A variety of ducks can be seen here from late October to April. Look for American Black Ducks, Mallards, Northern Pintails, American Wigeons, Canvasbacks, Redheads, Common Goldeneyes, and Hooded, Common, and Red-breasted mergansers. At such times, Bonaparte's, Ring-billed, and Herring gulls are sometimes present. A few Caspian Terns are sometimes encountered in April and May and in late summer along with small flocks of Common and Black terns. Ospreys, Broad-winged Hawks, and other raptors have a tendency to follow the Little Miami River north during spring migration. In early May, the willows and shrubs in the area yield good numbers of warblers and other transients.

Lunken Airport

Southeast of downtown Cincinnati in the floodplain of the Little Miami and Ohio rivers. From I-75 take Red Bank Road (exit 9) south to U.S. 50. Proceed SW on 50 to Ohio 125. Turn left (east) and almost immediately exit onto Wilmer Avenue. (Map E-33)

From its northern access at the playground parking lot to its southern access at Airport Road, a three-mile bike-hike trail atop a flood control levee offers broad views of the airport and a variety of habitat. Good birding is provided as the trail parallels the Little Miami River, bottomland forests, stretches of thickets, second-growth trees, and seasonally flooded swales and wet spots in grasslands adjacent to the airport.

The airport is noted for up to a dozen Short-eared Owls that arrive in November and remain through the first part of April. Some of the best views can be obtained from the rear of the Wilmer Avenue firehouse. Sometimes the friendly firefighters allow observations from their second story enclosed airport observation deck.

At dawn and dusk in early spring, American Woodcocks can be seen and heard displaying, and modest numbers of shorebirds and waterfowl can be seen in the wet areas. Spring and fall songbird migration can be good to excellent along the levee. Grassy areas attract Northern Harriers, Horned Larks, Water Pipits, and Savannah Sparrows.

Meldahl (Anthony) Dam

Take U.S. 52 southeast of Cincinnati to Moscow (about 30 miles). Just beyond town turn right toward the Ohio River. (Map E-34)

An excellent variety of waterbirds can be seen from the dam or the parking lot from October through April. Look for the Common Loon, Pied-billed and Horned grebes, Canada Goose, Green-winged Teal, American Black Duck, Mallard, Northern Pintail, Gadwall, American Wigeon, Canvasback, Redhead, Lesser Scaup, Common Goldeneye, and all three mergansers. Gulls of several species are frequently present and, in spring, small companies of terns can be seen flying over the water. A few Ospreys are recorded each spring and fall and Bald Eagles are regular visitors. There is a colony of Cliff Swallows. To compensate for the distance to the river, a spotting scope is a necessity for birding at this site. Rarities have included American White Pelican and Eurasian Wigeon. Congregations of shorebirds on a large gravel bar below the dam can best be seen from the Kentucky shore. To get there, take I-75 across the river at Cincinnati, exit onto Kentucky 8 and drive east about 30 miles.

Miami and Erie Canal Park   *Northeast of Hamilton, in Butler County.*
From Hamilton take Ohio 4 northeast,
then take Reigart Road north less than 1
mile to the park. There is also access to
the Miami-Erie Canal along Headgates
and Canal roads. (Map E–35)

This 226-acre park with 0.5 mile frontage along the Great Miami River is managed by the Metro Parks of Butler County. Features include several recreation areas with picnic facilities and shelters, playgrounds, amphitheater, fitness court, nature and hiking trails, woodland (Rentschler Forest Preserve), and restored portions of the old canal. Activities include canoeing along the river, hiking, fishing, and birding. Plans are currently being made to expand the park with construction of a Visitors Center and canal museum. Several scenic vistas overlooking the Great Miami River are excellent places to look for migrating warblers and other arboreal species during the spring migration.

Birds commonly seen in early summer include the Green-backed Heron, Spotted Sandpiper, Belted Kingfisher, Yellow-billed Cuckoo, Red-bellied Woodpecker, Northern Flicker, Eastern Kingbird, Northern Rough-winged Swallow, Carolina Chickadee, Carolina and House wrens, Gray Catbird, Cedar Waxwing, Yellow-throated, Warbling, and Red-eyed vireos, Yellow and Cerulean warblers, Common Yellowthroat, and Northern Oriole. White-winged Crossbill sometimes occur in winter.

Nearby are the **Miller Brewery fields,** an area that often attracts open country birds. Surrounding the brewery, a large expanse of cultivated fields has been allowed to go fallow. The area is annually mowed to arrest normal succession, and thus attracts grassland and open country species that are otherwise rare or absent in this region. During winter months, large flocks of Horned Larks and lesser numbers of Snow Buntings and Lapland Longspurs sometimes occur after heavy snowfalls. An abundance of meadow voles attract Northern Harriers, Rough-legged Hawks, and American Kestrels.

Dickcissels, Horned Larks, Grasshopper, Savannah, and Vesper sparrows, and occasional Bobolinks nest here. Winter records include Short-eared Owls and, rarely, Grasshopper and Savannah sparrows. To reach the area, return to Ohio 4 and go northeast to Liberty-Fairfield Road, then turn left and proceed 2.2 miles across the Great Miami River to the brewery fields. Ask permission to park at the first farm south of the brewery or, if the ground is dry, park along the road across from the farm.

Miami Whitewater Forest   *Take I-74 west of Cincinnati; at the Dry*
                                              Fork exit go north about 2 miles.
                                              (Map E-36)

One of the older preserved forest areas in the state, this 2,000-acre tract once knew the tread of Indian feet and, during the Civil War, sheltered Morgan's Raiders. White-tailed deer roam the woods and fields. There is a braille trail, as well as a trail to Reservoir Overlook with views of Ohio, Indiana, and Kentucky. Among the breeding birds are the Wood Duck, Cooper's, Red-shouldered, Broad-winged, and Red-tailed hawks, Northern Bobwhite, American Woodcock, Yellow-billed Cuckoo, Eastern Screech-Owl, Great Horned and Barred owls, Red-headed, Red-bellied, Hairy, and Pileated woodpeckers, Eastern Wood-Pewee, Acadian and Willow flycatchers, Eastern Phoebe, Great Crested Flycatcher, Carolina Chickadee, Tufted Titmouse, White-breasted Nuthatch, Carolina, House, and Sedge wrens, Eastern Bluebird, Wood Thrush, Gray Catbird, Northern Mockingbird, Brown Thrasher, Cedar Waxwing, and White-eyed, Yellow-throated, Warbling, and Red-eyed vireos.

Warblers that nest are the Blue-winged, Yellow, Cerulean, Black-and-white, Worm-eating, Ovenbird, Louisiana Waterthrush, Kentucky, Common Yellowthroat, Hooded, and Yellow-breasted Chat. Other typical breeding birds include Summer and Scarlet tanagers, an abundance of Northern Cardinals and Indigo Buntings, Rufous-sided Towhees, Chipping, Field, Savannah, Grasshopper, and Song sparrows, and Northern Orioles.

Middletown Airport   *Located in northeast Butler County. From*
and Smith Park   *the center of downtown Middletown, take*
                                              Verity Parkway north (Ohio 4), then go
                                              left on Tytus Avenue to the park entrance.
                                              To view both the airfield and river,
                                              continue west on Tytus to Reinartz
                                              Boulevard, then to Carmody Boulevard
                                              and proceed north. (Map E-37)

Hook Field, the municipal airport, lies beside the Great Miami River, on the west, and Smith Park on the south. Open grassy areas provide habitat for thirteen-lined ground squirrels, occasional Upland Sandpipers in spring, and Rough-legged Hawks in winter. The best viewing is in Smith Park (see below).

The Great Miami River along Carmody Blvd. (which runs along the flood-wall levee for some distance), contains a number of gravel bars which attract migrating shorebirds and their kin. Commonly seen are Killdeer, Black-bellied and Semipalmated plover, Greater and Lesser yellowlegs, Solitary, Spotted, Semipalmated, Least, and Pectoral sandpipers. Unusual birds have included Double-crested Cormorant, Black-crowned Night-Heron, Oldsquaw, White-winged Scoter, Osprey, Bald Eagle, Sandhill Crane, Lesser Golden-Plover, American Avocet, Ruddy Turnstone, Short-billed Dowitcher, and Snow Bunting. The City of Middletown has begun a project to straighten and chan-nel the river in this area, which will likely have a negative impact on this productive area.

Smith Park contains a pond, a small lake, and a flock of domestic geese and ducks which attract a few wild waterfowl, particularly when the river is rough. Snow Buntings have been found around the lake when it is frozen. There is a picnic area, athletic fields, restored remnants of the old Miami and Erie Canal, and a Canal Museum maintained by the Middletown Historical Society. Paved jogging and hiking trails line the perimeter of the park and afford excellent views of the airfield.

Mitchell Memorial Forest   *West of Cincinnati, exit I-74 at Rybolt Road (exit 11) eastbound, drive a short distance on Harrison Avenue, then turn immediately onto Rybolt Road southbound. At Wesselman or Taylor Road turn right (west) and proceed to Zion Hill and finally onto Zion Road which leads to the forest. (Map E-38)*

"A beautiful forest with magnificent views," this 1,318-acre tract encompasses several large pine plantations, abandoned fields, and hardwood forests, some of the areas undeveloped and difficult to access.

Resident birds include Cooper's and Red-shouldered hawks, Northern Bobwhite, Barred Owl, Hairy and Pileated woodpeckers, Eastern Bluebird, and Cedar Waxwings.

At least 11 warbler species nest: Blue-winged, Yellow, Yellow-throated, Pine (rare), Cerulean, Ovenbird, Louisiana Waterthrush, Kentucky, Common Yellowthroat, Hooded, and Yellow-breasted Chat. During the winter, look for Yellow-bellied Sapsucker, Red-breasted Nuthatch, Winter Wren, Fox Sparrows, White-crowned Sparrows, and Pine Siskins. Northern Saw-whet Owls some-times occur in evergreens and grapevine thickets.

Monroe Lake State Wildlife Area   *In Monroe County on Ohio 800 5 miles north of Woodsfield. (Map F-39)*

Densely wooded slopes descend to 39-acre Monroe Lake on this 1,332-acre tract of forest, pine plantings, streams, cultivated fields, and roadside thickets. A nature trail that circles the lake provides vantage points for observing small

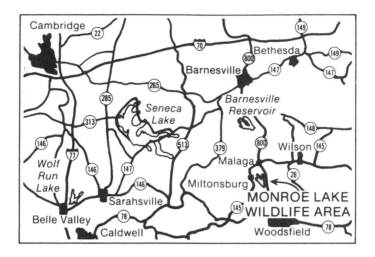

groups of transient waterfowl. About 70 species of birds nest in the area, including Ruffed Grouse and Pileated Woodpeckers. Many other species—including Ospreys—are seen in migration.

Mt. Airy Forest

In Cincinnati, take I-74 to the northbound exit for U.S. 27 (Colerain Avenue), proceed up a long hill and look for the park entrance on the left. After entering, bear right and turn right again after about 100 yards and enter the arboretum. (Map E-40)

The 120-acre arboretum is probably the best place to start your explorations in this wonderful 1,460-acre park. The mixture of mature trees, shrubs, and open lawns makes bird finding easy. Plantings of evergreens native to more northern climes attract boreal species such as Yellow-bellied Sapsuckers, Red-breasted Nuthatches, Golden-crowned Kinglets, Tennessee, Magnolia, Cape May, and Canada warblers, and Pine Siskins, among many others. Pine Warblers may be present during the summer.

Areas of mature hardwood forest are home to Eastern Screech-Owl, Great Horned and Barred owls, Red-bellied, Hairy, and Pileated woodpeckers, Carolina Chickadees, and Rufous-sided Towhees. In the summer, they are joined by Yellow-billed Cuckoos, Great Crested Flycatchers, Red-eyed and Yellow-throated vireos, Cerulean, Kentucky, and Hooded Warblers, Summer and Scarlet tanagers, and Orchard and Northern orioles.

Neotoma   *See Clear Creek Valley.*

Newberry Wildlife Sanctuary   *See Winton Woods.*

Newell's Run and Leith Run   *In Washington County, on State Route 7*
Embayments   *about 11 miles and 20 miles east*
                                        of I-77. (Map F–41)

Snuggled alongside the Ohio River, these two backwaters were formed when
the Willow Island Dam was built. You can drive around Newell's Run (Newport Twp. Road 443) and come back onto Ohio 7. Waterbirds present in early
spring, late fall and winter include Pied-billed and Horned grebes, Double-
crested Cormorants, a variety of dabbling ducks, Canvasbacks, Redheads,
Lesser Scaup, Hooded, Common, and Red-breasted mergansers, and American Coots. Canada Geese nest and, in the summer, there are Great Blue and
Green-backed herons, Wood Ducks, and Mallards. On the backside of Newell's Run, Newport Twp. Road 19 doglegs up a wooded valley. In early May, it
is resplendent with wildflowers and, throughout the month, is a good place to
look for migrant cuckoos, thrushes, vireos, and most of Ohio's warblers.

From Newell's Run, continue north on Ohio 7 another 8.5 miles, through
the village of Newport, thence to Leith Run. There are several trails back to the
embayment and along the river. Improvements underway include overnight
camping facilities and the planned addition of an observation platform which
will overlook the shallow water area. When mudflats are present during migration they attract Semipalmated Plovers, both yellowlegs, Solitary, Spotted, and
Pectoral sandpipers, and Common Snipe. A Whimbrel and Black-bellied Plover have been seen here.

Some of the nesting species are Willow Flycatchers, Blue-winged, Golden-
winged, Yellow, and Prothonotary warblers, Common Yellowthroats, Summer
and Scarlet tanagers, Orchard and Northern orioles.

Ospreys and Bald Eagles are seen along the river with increasing frequency. Look for them in flight, sitting in trees along the river's edge, or out on
islands. Both of these species are seen mostly in the spring and fall but in recent
years have been spotted almost every month of the year. On Middle Island,
above Newport, there is a Great Blue Heron colony of 30 or more nests.

From the Willow Island Dam observation tower river boats and barges
can be seen navigating their way through the locks. While there, scan the river
for waterfowl, Ospreys, and Bald Eagles. On the highway between the dam
and Newell's Run, during the winter months, watch the telephone poles and
fence posts for Northern Harriers and Rough-legged Hawks. One year a
Snowy Owl spent several weeks in this area.

Ohio Power Recreation Area
(Cumberland Mine Area)

Located largely in Morgan County, sections
spill over into Guernsey, Noble, and
Muskingum counties. Best reached by
taking Ohio 83 south from New Concord
or Ohio 146 and Ohio 284 southeast
from Zanesville. (Map F–42)

Once stripped for coal, this vast area embracing 100,000 acres is largely re-claimed land and boasts 320 stocked lakes and ponds, 34 million planted tree seedlings, campsites, shelters, and picnic areas. Literature, maps, and camping permits may be obtained by stopping at any Ohio Power Company office, or writing to Ohio Power Company, P.O. Box 328, McConnelsville, Ohio 43756, or the Publication Center, Ohio Department of Natural Resources, Fountain Square, Building C, Columbus, Ohio 43224.

Bird species that have returned or adapted to the area are as numerous as the varied habitats, which include ravines, marshes, streams, extensive fields, and farmland. The most successful are birds of the open countryside.

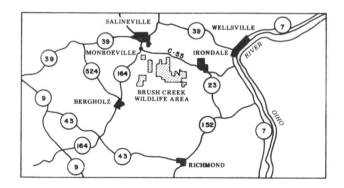

Ohio Brush Creek
Adams County

Take Ohio 125 in Adams County about 8
miles east of West Union just after crossing
Ohio Brush Creek; go south on Waggoner
Riffle Road 5 miles, look for a bridge
crossing the creek, and park at the side of
the road. (Map E–43)

This region, famed for its botanical treasures, is also home to a wide variety of interesting bird species. Most notable is the Chuck-will's-widow, a bird of the deep south, which regularly occurs here in one of its northernmost breeding outposts. They can be heard in the valley after dark along with Whip-poor-wills from May through July.

Chuck-will's-widow

All of Adams County is of ornithological interest because of its proximity to the Ohio River and the fact that it comprises two distinct topographies: the glaciated northwest corner and the unglaciated remainder. The glaciated section with low rolling hills and agricultural fields is a good place to look for grassland species such as Vesper, Savannah, Grasshopper, and Henslow's sparrows, and the possibility of a pair of Loggerhead Shrikes or Blue Grosbeaks. Prior to the late 1970s, a few pairs of Lark Sparrows nested on rocky, eroded slopes interspersed with scraggy vegetation and small trees.

An eye to the sky will net Black Vultures most any season. In the rugged hills of the unglaciated part of the county, up the hollows and along the creek beds, look for Ruffed Grouse, Wild Turkey, Warbling Vireo, Blue-winged Warbler, Northern Parula, Yellow and Yellow-throated warblers, Louisiana Waterthrushes, Worm-eating warblers, Ovenbirds, Kentucky and Hooded warblers, and Scarlet Tanagers.

Where there are stands of pine trees, listen for the chipping trill of Pine Warblers. Hillside pockets of blackberry and scrub often produce Prairie Warblers—listen for their thin, high-pitched song which Roger Tory Peterson likens to "a mouse with a toothache"—and in mixed habitats of fallow fields, small trees and shrubs, listen for the lazy *bee-buzz* of Blue-winged Warblers. Bewick's Wrens formerly nested in the area.

Some of the best birding in Adams County is in and around the Edge of Appalachia Preserve System, owned and operated jointly by the Cincinnati Museum of Natural History and the Nature Conservancy. Much of this preserve is not open to the public. For further information, contact the Cincinnati Museum of Natural History at 1/513/287-7020, or the Nature Conservancy at

1/614/486-4194. Also see the Buzzardroost Rock account. A checklist of the birds of Adams County can be obtained from the Soil and Conservation Office in West Union (1/513/544-2651).

Old Man's Cave State Park

Take U.S. 33 to Ohio 374 or Ohio 664 and proceed southwest about 15 miles to the park entrance. (Map F-44)

This dramatic park combines awesome overhangs of Black Hand sandstone (see Black Hand Gorge State Nature Preserve), a gorge with tunnels, rock stairways, waterfalls, precipitous ledges and cliffs, and trails that ultimately lead to the Devil's Bathtub and Old Man's Cave. A canopy of mixed hardwoods and conifers cloak the hills and gorges creating a cool, damp environment for wildflowers, ferns, and mosses.

With the exception of Yellow-throated Warblers, which nest in sycamores near the parking lot, resident and breeding birds are essentially the same as those listed for Ash Cave and Cantwell Cliffs State Parks,

In April, early May, and again in late September and early October, this is a fine place to find such transients as the Broad-winged Hawk; Yellow-bellied Sapsucker; Red-breasted Nuthatch; Winter Wren; Veery; Gray-cheeked, Swainson's, and Hermit thrushes; Solitary Vireo; Nashville, Magnolia, Cape May, Yellow-rumped, Blackburnian, and Bay-breasted warblers; Northern Waterthrush; Wilson's and Canada warblers; and Rose-breasted Grosbeak.

Paint Creek Reservoir and State Park

Take U.S. 50 about 5 miles west of Bainbridge and turn north following the signs to the park. (Map E-45)

In 1973 Paint Creek was impounded about five miles below the confluence of Paint and Rattlesnake creeks. The habitat at the lake is diverse, including the 1,200-acre lake, streams, floodplain, heavily wooded hillsides, agricultural land, and extensive nearby grasslands.

The chances for encountering waterfowl are good between late February and the first of May and from October through December. A few Common Loons and Pied-billed Grebes are usually seen each season; small numbers of ducks make brief stops, and up to a hundred or more American Coots are often present. The majority of shorebirds are usually seen in late summer and fall when there are mudflats. American Avocets have been recorded, and a few Ospreys put in an appearance each spring and fall.

Nesting species include the Green-backed Heron, Wood Duck, Turkey Vulture, Red-tailed Hawk, American Kestrel, Northern Bobwhite, Spotted

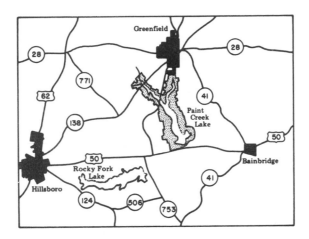

Sandpiper, American Woodcock, Yellow-billed Cuckoo, Eastern Screech-Owl, Great Horned and Barred owls, Ruby-throated Hummingbird, Belted Kingfisher, Red-headed and Red-bellied woodpeckers, Acadian Flycatcher, Eastern Phoebe, Eastern Kingbird, Northern Rough-winged and Barn swallows, Eastern Bluebird, Wood Thrush, Northern Mockingbird, Cedar Waxwing, White-eyed, Yellow-throated, Warbling, and Red-eyed vireos, Blue-winged, Yellow, and Cerulean warblers, Ovenbird, Kentucky Warbler, Common Yellowthroat, Yellow-breasted Chat, Orchard and Northern orioles, Summer and Scarlet tanagers, Rufous-sided Towhee, and Chipping, Field, and Song sparrows. There is some evidence that Tree Swallows and Prothonotary Warblers nest in small numbers.

Piedmont Lake   *Take U.S. 22 to Smyrna or Piedmont and take any one of several county roads south to the lake, which is in northwestern Belmont County. (Map G–46)*

This Muskingum Conservancy District lake comprises 2,270 acres with an additional 4,330 acres of wooded parkland. Beech-maple and oak-hickory woods border the lake and cover the surrounding hills. Additional acres have been planted in pines. The dam across Stillwater Creek is near the village of Piedmont.

Rafts of diving ducks composed of Canvasbacks, Redheads, Ring-necked Ducks, and Lesser Scaups congregate on the lake in March, early April, and again in late October and November. Modest numbers of surface-feeding ducks—American Black Ducks, Mallards, Northern Pintails, Northern Shovel-

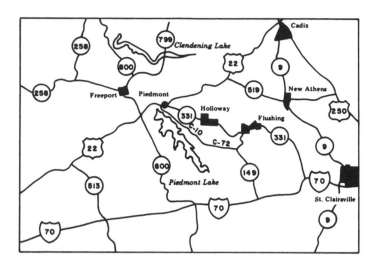

ers, Gadwalls, and American Wigeons—occur along with the divers. Flocks of Canada Geese are common and a few Tundra Swans sometimes appear, usually in mid-March.

Some of the breeding birds include Cooper's and Red-tailed hawks, Ruffed Grouse, Black-billed Cuckoo, Eastern Screech-Owl, Great Horned and Barred owls, Whip-poor-will, Ruby-throated Hummingbird, Belted Kingfisher, Red-bellied and Hairy woodpeckers, Acadian and Great Crested flycatchers, Yellow, Cerulean, and Worm-eating warblers (rare), Ovenbird, Kentucky Warbler, Summer and Scarlet tanagers, Rufous-sided Towhees, Orchard and Northern orioles.

Pike State Forest and Pike Lake　　*In Pike County south of U.S. 50 on Ohio*
State Park　　　　　　　　　　　　*41. (Map F-47)*

The 13-acre lake is in the northeast section of the forest and attracts small numbers of migrant waterfowl and occasional wading birds in all but the winter months. Roads and trails give access to the 10,586-acre forest, and another trail circles the lake.

Breeding bird specialties are the Broad-winged Hawk, Ruffed Grouse, Whip-poor-will, Pileated Woodpecker, White-eyed Vireo, and the following warblers: Blue-winged, Yellow, Pine, Prairie, Black-and-white, American Redstart, Worm-eating, Ovenbird, Louisiana Waterthrush, Kentucky, Common Yellowthroat, and Hooded. Summer Tanagers and Orchard Orioles can be found in clearings and around houses.

Rockbridge State Nature Preserve   *In Hocking County about 1.5 miles south of the village of Rockbridge. Turn east off U.S. 33 at Crawford-Stamer Road and proceed to the parking area. (Map F–48)*

The largest natural rock bridge in the state arcs over a feeder stream of the Hocking River in this secluded nature preserve. From the parking area, follow the trail through the narrow fenced-in corridor, past elderberry groves and pawpaw trees until it reaches a scenic open field hilltop. From this high point, the trail descends into a climax forest and follows a winding stream that eventually plunges 50 feet to the ravine floor below the bridge. The trail continues through an area rich in wildflowers to a wooded hilltop.

Breeding bird specialties include Green-backed Heron, Wood Ducks, Great Crested Flycatchers, Rough-winged Swallows, Carolina Wrens, Blue-gray Gnatcatchers, Wood Thrushes, Cedar Waxwings, White-eyed, Yellow-throated, Warbling, and Red-eyed vireos, Summer and Scarlet tanagers, the following warblers—Blue-winged, Northern Parula, Yellow, Yellow-throated, Cerulean, Ovenbird, Louisiana Waterthrush, Kentucky, Common Yellowthroat, Hooded, and Yellow-breasted Chat—and Orchard and Northern orioles.

Ross-Pickaway County Line Road   *Follow U.S. 23 south through Circleville and about 6 miles beyond. Turn right onto the road just north of a highway overpass. Follow this road south to the intersection with County Line Road, which passes over Route 23 and continues east to Kingston and Adelphi-Laurelville. (Map F–49)*

One of the best places in Ohio to see raptors during the winter season is along this road in south-central Ohio. Most of the action starts in November and continues through March. On a Christmas Bird Count on December 19, 1976, participants recorded 20 Black Vultures; 25 Turkey Vultures; 68 Northern Harriers; 2 Sharp-shinned Hawks; 5 Cooper's Hawks; 1 Northern Goshawk; 65 Red-tailed Hawks; 49 Rough-legged Hawks; 132 American Kestrels; 1 Merlin; 2 Common Barn-Owls; 1 Eastern Screech-Owl; 4 Great Horned Owls, and 4 Short-eared Owls. Look for hawks perched in trees, on utility wires and fences, and in the air, both high and low.

The section of the road east of Kingston is especially productive for birds of prey. In late afternoon, Northern Harriers are sometimes found in fields east of Whistler Road where they roost during the night in the clumps of tall grasses.

Conclaves of Short-eared Owls are also known to frequent the Whistler

Road area and are best seen around sundown. Sometimes as many as two dozen gather together during the cold months.

In winter, it is not uncommon to find large numbers of Horned Larks, flocks of Eastern Bluebirds, a few Water Pipits, an occasional Loggerhead Shrike, a few Savannah Sparrows, large assemblages of American Tree Sparrows, rarely, a few Lapland Longspurs and Snow Buntings, and groups of Eastern Meadowlarks.

County Line Road can be interesting at other times of the year because of its wide fertile fields and its proximity to the hills of Ross, Hocking, and Vinton counties. Abundant rainfall in the spring creates sky ponds that sometimes attract flocks of Lesser Golden-Plover, Greater and Lesser yellowlegs, Upland and Pectoral sandpipers, and Common Snipes. A few pairs of Upland Sandpipers nest in the vicinity.

Other breeding birds include Northern Harrier, Red-tailed Hawk, American Kestrel, Ring-necked Pheasant, Northern Bobwhite, Killdeer, Mourning Dove, Common Barn-Owls and Short-eared Owls (both rare), Red-headed Woodpecker, Northern Flicker, Eastern Kingbird, Horned Lark, American Crow, Eastern Bluebird, Northern Mockingbird, Yellow Warbler, Common Yellowthroat, Northern Cardinal, Indigo Bunting, Chipping, Field, Vesper, Grasshopper, Henslow's (erratic), and Song sparrows, Bobolink, Eastern Meadowlark, and American Goldfinch.

Salt Fork State Park

On Ohio 22 about 8 miles northeast of Cambridge in Guernsey County. (Map G–50)

This 20,000-acre state park contains a 2,052-acre lake with bits of marsh in the upper ends, and integrated woodlots, fallow fields, and farms. A large state lodge, cabins, and recreational facilities are available.

In spring and fall, most of the common species of Ohio waterfowl are found on the lake. Wading birds, a few rails, and bitterns are in marsh habitat, and small gatherings of shorebirds occur in season. Peregrine Falcons and Bald Eagles have been reported. Breeding birds include such diverse species as the Green-backed Heron, Wood Duck, Red-shouldered Hawk, Ruffed Grouse, American Woodcock, Black-billed Cuckoo, Pileated Woodpecker, American Redstart, and Summer Tanager.

Scioto Bottoms

In Scioto County, just west of Portsmouth on U.S. 52 turn right and proceed north on Ohio 73 and 104 to the junction with Ohio 239. Turn left onto 239 and drive south on 239 back to 52. (Map F–51)

Just west of Portsmouth on U.S. 52, the Scioto River empties into the Ohio River. An extensive floodplain reaches from the city flood defenses to the hills on the west side of the valley. During wet springs these bottomlands retain huge "lakes" of water that are attractive to grebes, cormorants, herons, egrets, geese, swans, ducks, gulls, and terns. Ospreys often perch in bordering trees. The directions above form a triangle of excellent roads with many pulloffs. On Ohio 239, a small church with a parking lot in the rear is a good place to observe migrant waterfowl and shorebirds.

Return to U.S. 52 and drive west about four miles from the city to a country road named Moores Lane. Turn south and, in the spring, watch the hedgerows for White-throated and White-crowned sparrows and Brown Thrashers as kestrels lead the way down the power lines. In the fields, look for Northern Harriers, Rough-legged Hawks (in the colder months), and Horned Larks.

From March through May, wet spots are frequented by yellowlegs and peeps. Near the Ohio River, the road turns west. The Jack Blake farm on the right breeds some exotic birds. Stop nearby and look and listen for Bobolinks. Keep an eye out for Ospreys, Bald Eagles, and hawks in the large sycamores along the river. Turkey Creek flows into the Ohio River at the end of the road. A slough often has a complement of ducks and geese. Watch the river for gulls and terns.

Another birding route from U.S. 52 is to follow the Scioto River north on Ohio 104. In the spring, Great Blue Herons and Great Egrets can be seen along the riverbanks. Flocks of Bonaparte's and Ring-billed gulls flutter over newly plowed fields or congregate around sky ponds.

In Portsmouth, Greenlawn Cemetery is good for spring warblers, Monk Parakeets roost along some streets, and high water can be viewed from several side streets south and west of Scioto Trail along the flood defense system. There's even a beer garden where one can sit on the verandah and watch herons and egrets in the bottoms.

Scioto Trail State Park and Forest   *In Ross County, located east of U.S. 23 about 7 miles south of Chillicothe. From U.S. 23, take Ohio 372 to the park entrance. (Map F–52)*

The 9,400-acre park consists of rugged hills, hiking trails, and two lakes: Caldwell Lake and Stewart Lake. Camping with electricity is available at Caldwell Lake, while primitive camp sites are situated near Stewart Lake. Picnic areas are located at both lakes. Boating, fishing, and horseback riding are other recreational options that are available. Maps and other information can be obtained at the park office.

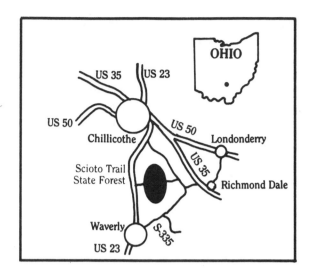

Although Pine Warblers can be found in stands of pine trees throughout the park, in early spring you can get a sneak preview approximately 0.5 mile from U.S. 23 where a fire tower is set in a grove of pines. Listen for their song, a trill which Roger Tory Peterson describes as looser and more musical than the song of the Chipping Sparrow.

From the fire tower, if you proceed on Road #3 (Lake Road), you will traverse a ridge where numerous migrants and nesting species can be found. After 1.3 miles, the road forks. The road to the right descends into the camping area at Caldwell Lake. The left fork follows the ridge another 3.5 miles and finally deadends at Stoney Creek Road. Turn right to return to park headquarters.

Yellow-throated Warblers and Louisiana Waterthrushes nest along many of the streams within the park. As a rule, look for the tail-wagging water-thrushes down low, the warblers up high in sycamore trees. The song of the waterthrush consists of slurry notes, loud and ringing. The Yellow-throated Warbler sounds a bit like an Indigo Bunting but with the last note rising.

Breeding birds include Ruffed Grouse, Wild Turkey, Red-bellied and Pile-ated woodpeckers, Eastern Wood-Pewee, Acadian and Willow flycatchers, Eastern Phoebe, Great Crested Flycatcher, Blue-gray Gnatcatcher, White-eyed, Yellow-throated, Warbling, and Red-eyed vireos, Summer and Scarlet tanagers, and Rufous-sided Towhee.

Additional nesting warblers include Blue-winged, Golden-winged, North-ern Parula, Yellow, Prairie, Cerulean, Black-and-white, American Redstart, Worm-eating, Ovenbird, Kentucky, Common Yellowthroat, Hooded, and Yel-low-breasted Chat.

Serpent Mound State Memorial   *In northern Adams County on Ohio 73 4 miles northwest of Locust Grove.*
(Map E–53)

This attractive park on the east bluff of Ohio Brush Creek contains the largest known effigy mound in the United States. One-quarter mile long with seven deep curves, the serpent is in the act of uncoiling; in its open jaws lies a small mound—possibly representing an egg. The Adena Indians built this ceremonial earthworks sometime between 1000 B.C. and A.D. 400. Both the mound and a five-mile-wide crater may be seen from the observation tower.

A few of the nesting birds of the area include Whip-poor-will, Ruby-throated Hummingbird, Eastern Phoebe, Carolina Wren, Blue-gray Gnat-catcher, Wood Thrush, Yellow-throated Vireo, Blue-winged and Yellow warblers, Common Yellowthroat, Yellow-breasted Chat, Summer and Scarlet tanagers, Indigo Bunting, Chipping and Song sparrows, and Northern Oriole.

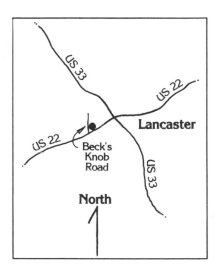

Shallenberger Nature Preserve   *In Fairfield County, take U.S. 22 3 miles southwest of Lancaster and turn onto Beck's Knob Road for 0.2 mile.*
(Map F–54)

This 87-acre site is dominated by Allen Knob, a promontory of Black Hand sandstone (see Black Hand Gorge State Nature Preserve) rising 270 feet above a creek on its north side. Chestnut oaks, mountain laurel, and remnants of American chestnuts clothe the knob, and mixed deciduous trees cover the lower slopes.

Breeding birds include American Kestrels, Black-billed Cuckoos, Eastern Wood-Pewees, Acadian Flycatchers, Great Crested Flycatchers, Wood Thrushes, Yellow-throated Vireos, Cerulean and Black-and-white warblers, Ovenbirds, Louisiana Waterthrushes, Common Yellowthroats, Yellow-breasted Chats, and both tanagers.

Sharon Woods County Park

Take I-275 north of Cincinnati to U.S. 42 and drive south to the park entrance. (Map E-55)

This 740-acre Hamilton County Park District tract includes a creek and waterfalls; a lake; a climax forest of oak, beech, and maple; a gorge famed for rare fossils; an Indian mound; and many hiking trails.

During late April and May, large numbers of transient landbirds swarm through the area and listing 50 or 60 species in a single morning isn't unusual. Over 50 species have nested within the park, including Acadian Flycatchers and Yellow-throated and Kentucky warblers.

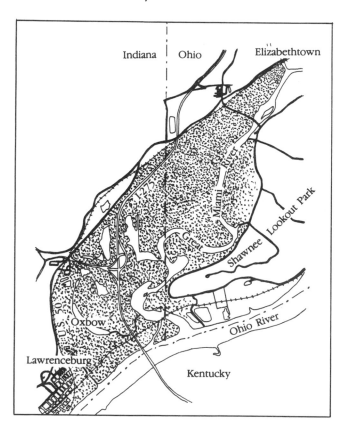

Shawnee Lookout County Park   *Exit U.S. 50 and head west on Mt. Nebo Road. Turn right on River Road which becomes Lawrenceburg Road. The park entrance is on the left. (Map E–56)*

This 1,010-acre Hamilton County Park District site at the mouth of the Great Miami River features a fort built by Indians about 2,000 years ago and later used as a lookout by the Shawnees.

One of the best all-round places to go birding in southwestern Ohio, the park attracts shorebirds, waterfowl, birds of prey, and large numbers of landbirds. It is one of the few places in Ohio where the Black Vulture nests.

Black Vulture

Along the river, in early spring look for Canada Geese, Green-winged Teal, American Black Ducks, Mallards, Northern Pintails, Blue-winged Teal, Northern Shovelers, Gadwalls, American Wigeons, Canvasbacks, Redheads, Ring-necked Ducks, Lesser Scaups, Common Goldeneyes, Buffleheads, all three merganser species, and Ruddy Ducks.

Breeding bird species include Wild Turkey, Black and Turkey vultures, Cooper's and Red-tailed hawks, Northern Bobwhite, Yellow-billed Cuckoo, Great Horned Owl, Ruby-throated Hummingbird, Belted Kingfisher, Red-headed and Red-bellied woodpeckers, Eastern Phoebe, Great Crested Fly-catcher, Carolina Chickadee, Tufted Titmouse, White-breasted Nuthatch, Carolina and House wrens, Eastern Bluebird, Gray Catbird, Northern Mock-ingbird, Brown Thrasher, White-eyed, Yellow-throated, Warbling, and Red-eyed vireos, Blue-winged, Yellow, and Cerulean warblers, American Redstart, Prothonotary Warbler, Ovenbird, Kentucky Warbler, Common Yellowthroat, Yellow-breasted Chat, Summer and Scarlet tanagers, Northern Cardinal, Indigo Bunting, Rufous-sided Towhee, and Northern Oriole.

Across the Great Miami River from Shawnee Lookout Park is **The Oxbow,** a fine place to find shorebirds and a variety of waterbirds. Spring visitors include Pied-billed and Horned grebes, occasional Double-crested Cormorants, Great Blue and Green-backed herons and Black-crowned Night-Herons, Bonaparte's and Ring-billed gulls, and Caspian, Common, and Black terns. Shorebirds to look for are Black-bellied Plover, Lesser Golden-Plover, Semipalmated Plover, Killdeer, Greater and Lesser yellowlegs, Spotted, Semipalmated, Least, White-rumped, Baird's, and Pectoral sandpipers, Dunlin, Stilt and Buff-breasted Sandpipers (rare), and Common Snipe. Many of the shorebirds are seen only in late summer and fall.

Additional rarities have included Tundra Swan, Eurasian Wigeon, Black Scoter, Sandhill Crane, American Avocet, and Willet.

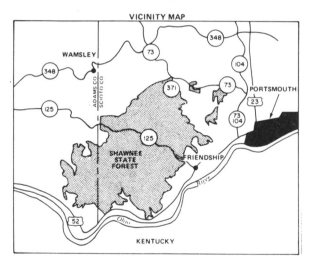

Shawnee State Forest and State Park

Take U.S. 52 west from Portsmouth about 7 miles and turn onto Route 125; continue northwest about 4 miles. (Map F–57)

With 58,165 acres of rugged woodland, this sprawling tract north of the Ohio River is the largest forest in the state. Three lakes—Bear, Turkey Creek, and Roosevelt—attract occasional Common Loons, Pied-billed Grebes, small rafts of ducks, and American Coots. There is also a small pond that is sometimes good for waterbirds on U.S. 52 a short distance west of Ohio 125 just past the Friendship School.

Wild Turkeys can be seen in the vicinity of Bear Creek Reservoir; Broad-winged Hawks soar over the wooded hills, and Yellow-throated Warblers frequent the sycamores along many of the creeks. Pine Warblers are common in the stands of red and white pines, especially along Forest Road 1 off Route 125. Make a circuit of the Panorama-McBride-Shawnee roads for some good birding. Ruffed Grouse can be found in any of the wooded areas.

Bird specialties to look for in spring and summer include both cuckoos, Whip-poor-wills, Ruby-throated Hummingbirds, Eastern Wood-Pewees, Acadian Flycatchers, Eastern Phoebes, Great Crested Flycatchers, Eastern Kingbirds, Purple Martins, Northern Rough-winged and Barn swallows, House Wrens, Blue-gray Gnatcatchers, Wood Thrushes, Cedar Waxwings, and White-eyed, Yellow-throated, Warbling (in cottonwoods along the streams), and Red-eyed vireos.

Additional nesting warblers include Blue-winged, Golden-winged (rare), Northern Parula (in hemlocks), Yellow, Black-throated Green, Prairie, Cerulean, Black-and-white, American Redstart, Worm-eating, Ovenbird, Louisiana Waterthrush (in ravines and along creeks), Kentucky, Common Yellowthroat, Hooded, and Yellow-breasted Chat. Eastern Meadowlarks are common in the fields, and Orchard and Northern orioles are fond of clearings, groves of trees, and roadside streams. Northern Cardinals, Indigo Buntings, and American Goldfinches are abundant everywhere but in the deepest woods.

Birds found in winter may include the Turkey Vulture, Cooper's, Red-shouldered, and Red-tailed hawks, Eastern Screech-Owl, Great Horned, Barred, and Long-eared (rare) owls, all of the woodpeckers regular in Ohio, Eastern Phoebe, Blue Jay, American Crow, Carolina Chickadee, Tufted Titmouse, Red-breasted and White-breasted nuthatches, Brown Creeper, Eastern Bluebird, Hermit Thrush, Cedar Waxwing, Yellow-rumped Warbler, Rufous-sided Towhee, American Tree, Field, Fox (scarce), Song, White-throated, and White-crowned sparrows, Dark-eyed Junco, Pine Siskin, American Goldfinch, and Evening Grosbeak (erratic).

Spring Beauty Dell   *See Winton Woods.*

Spring Grove Cemetery   *Take the Mitchell Avenue exit from I-75*
                                       in Cincinnati; drive north to Spring Grove
                                       Avenue, turn left and proceed about 0.5
                                       mile. (Map E–58)

An excellent place to go birding for spring migrants, this site combines large parklike areas with smaller niches of natural habitat including wooded ravines and native stands of beech, oak, and maple.

In late April and May, large numbers of birds stop over, rest and feed a day or two, and then are on their way again. On a red-letter day, the trees are alive with Least Flycatchers and other *Empidonax,* a variety of vireos, and all of the common migrant warblers. Heavily wooded and brushy areas yield such species as the Veery, Gray-cheeked and Swainson's thrushes, Worm-eating Warbler, Northern Waterthrush, Kentucky, Connecticut (rare), Mourning (rare), Hooded, Wilson's, and Canada warblers. Sometimes one tree will be full of warblers plus Scarlet Tanagers, Northern Orioles, and Rose-breasted Grosbeaks.

A surprising number of these new arrivals remain to nest along with the resident birds. A partial list of breeding birds would include the Wood Duck, American Kestrel, Yellow-billed Cuckoo, Eastern Screech-Owl, Barred Owl, Ruby-throated Hummingbird, Downy and Hairy woodpeckers, Northern Flicker, Eastern Wood-Pewee, Great Crested Flycatcher, Blue Jay, Carolina Chickadee, Tufted Titmouse, White-breasted Nuthatch, Carolina and House wrens, Wood Thrush, American Robin, Gray Catbird, Northern Mockingbird, Brown Thrasher, Cedar Waxwing, Red-eyed Vireo, Yellow, Cerulean, Black-and-white, and Kentucky warblers, Common Yellowthroat, Scarlet Tanager, Indigo Bunting, and Chipping and Field sparrows.

Because of the numerous hemlock, spruce, pine, sweet gum and alder trees, Spring Grove is an excellent place in winter to find such visitors as the Red-breasted Nuthatch, Purple Finch, both crossbills, Pine Siskin, American Goldfinch, and Evening Grosbeak.

Spring Valley State Wildlife Area
In Warren County, take U.S. 42 2.5 miles south of the village of Spring Valley, turn east on Roxanna-New Burlington Road, go 1.4 miles to Pence Jones Road; follow the signs to the north and south parking lots. (Map E–59)

Consistently one of southwest Ohio's best birding spots, this superb area managed by the Ohio Department of Natural Resources is located on the county line between Greene and Warren counties. It includes a 150-acre lake and marsh with overgrown channels, underbrush, fields and an upland woods. A boardwalk, which is entered from the north parking lot, crosses the north end of the marsh and is accessible during the spring and summer. Wide trails circle the lake passing through a variety of habitats. The marshy and wet areas provide a haven for the rare Massasauga Rattlesnake.

Grebes, geese, and all the common ducks can be seen here in good numbers during migrations. Rarely, loons and swans may be spotted as well. When water levels are low, the area can be excellent for shorebirds.

Nesting species include the Pied-billed Grebe, Least Bittern, Green-backed

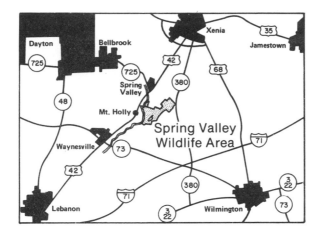

Heron, Canada Goose, Wood Duck, Mallard, Blue-winged Teal (rare), Hooded Merganser (rare), Virginia Rail, Sora, Common Moorhen, American Coot, American Woodcock, Eastern Screech-Owl, Great Horned and Barred owls, Belted Kingfisher, Red-headed, Red-bellied, and Pileated woodpeckers, Willow Flycatcher, Eastern Kingbird, Tree Swallow, Marsh Wren, Brown Thrasher, White-eyed, Yellow-throated, and Warbling vireos (the latter along the old railroad right-of-way), Yellow Warbler, Prothonotary Warbler (rare), Common Yellowthroat, Rose-breasted Grosbeak (rare), Orchard (uncommon) and Northern orioles. Ospreys are sometimes seen in the summer.

American Bitterns are sometimes found along the boardwalk during the spring. Swamp Sparrows and Rusty Blackbirds occur during spring and fall migrations. Winter brings Purple Finches and Pine Siskins, in addition to White-throated and White-crowned sparrows. Common Snipe are also found during some winters.

In March and early April, migrant Fox Sparrows like the hedgerows near the upper parking lot. Chimney Swifts and all of the swallows that occur in Ohio may be found in good numbers skimming the lake. Kinglets and Yellow-rumped and Palm warblers are followed by wave after wave of other warblers and passerines through late April and May. Northern Waterthrushes and Lincoln's Sparrows find lots of suitable habitat.

More than 230 species have been seen at Spring Valley Wildlife Area. Species that can sometimes be found include Double-crested Cormorant, Great Egret, Bald Eagle, Northern Harrier, Sharp-shinned, Cooper's, and Red-shoul-dered hawks, Black Tern, Short-eared Owl, Olive-sided and Alder flycatchers, American Pipit, Worm-eating, Connecticut, and Mourning warblers, and Savannah Sparrow.

Rarities have included Red-necked Grebe, Little Blue Heron, Cattle Egret,

Yellow-crowned Night-Heron, White Ibis, Mute Swan, Greater White-fronted
Goose, Snow Goose, Oldsquaw, Black Vulture, Golden Eagle, Merlin, Yellow,
Black and King rails, Purple Gallinule, Sandhill Crane, Willet, Baird's Sand-
piper, Wilson's Phalarope, Sedge Wren, Clay-colored Sparrow, and Brewer's
Blackbird.

Stark Wilderness Center

*On U.S. 250 in Stark County, 1 mile
northwest of Wilmot. (Map G–60)*

Trails radiate out from a nature interpretive center to lead the birder through
three woods, across fields, along creeks, and past a marsh and two ponds.
Sigrist Woods boasts oaks 400 years old, in addition to mature beech and
maple trees.

The center was founded in 1964 by the Canton Audubon Society in
cooperation with the National Audubon Society and with grants from large
corporations, foundations, and other interested organizations. Hunting, fishing,
trapping, and camping are prohibited. Waterfowl have responded to the protection they receive here and increasing numbers of geese and ducks feed and rest
on the largest pond, especially in the spring. Pied-billed Grebes, Green-backed
Herons, occasional American Bitterns and Soras, and groups of American
Coots are found at the lake or in the marsh.

Typical breeding birds are the Red-headed Woodpecker, Eastern Phoebe,
Great Crested Flycatcher, Eastern Kingbird, Barn Swallow, Black-capped
Chickadee, Wood Thrush, Red-eyed Vireo, Yellow and Cerulean warblers,
Ovenbird, Scarlet Tanager, Rufous-sided Towhee, and Northern Oriole.

Still Fork Swamp (Specht Marsh)

*In Carroll County, follow an improved
county road north 1.5 miles from
Mechanicstown, then turn west about 3
miles to just beyond Watheys.
(Map G–61)*

This 125-acre marsh was obtained by the Nature Conservancy and is administered by Kent State University. Forest W. Buchanan has done extensive field-
work in the area from which most of the data presented here are derived.

Plant species include swamp rose, wool-grass, marsh fern, cattail, giant
bur-reed, arrowhead, duckweed, pondweed, spatterdock, and pickerelweed. Alders and several species of ash grow in and around the marsh.

Buchanan has established or verified the following breeding records for the
marsh: American Bittern, Least Bittern, Wood Duck, American Black Duck,
Blue-winged Teal, Northern Harrier, Virginia Rail, Sora, American Woodcock,
Willow Flycatcher, Marsh Wren, Yellow Warbler, and Swamp Sparrow.

Sunfish Creek State Forest   *On Ohio 7 in Monroe County 4 miles*
                                                  north of Clarington. (Map F–62)

Forested hills and wooded overlooks along the Ohio River descend to the meandering configurations of Sunfish Creek. Turkey Vultures and Cooper's and Red-tailed hawks nest in forest areas, along with Eastern Screech-Owls, Great Horned and Barred owls. Other woodland breeders are the Ruffed Grouse, Yellow-billed and Black-billed cuckoos, Whip-poor-wills, Red-bellied and Pileated woodpeckers, Acadian Flycatchers, Wood Thrushes, and Scarlet Tanagers.

Eastern Phoebes, Carolina and House wrens, Blue-gray Gnatcatchers, Eastern Bluebirds, Gray Catbirds, Warbling Vireos, and Northern Orioles nest along the creek and in clearings.

Tar Hollow State Forest   *Take Ohio 56 southeast to Adelphi in*
and State Park   *southeastern Pickaway County; pick up*
                                                  Ohio 327 and go south about 10 miles to
                                                  the access road. (Map F–63)

This beautiful 16,126-acre tract is an enjoyable place to go birding any time of the year. A dammed stream has created a lake, and there are extensive wooded hills—most of them oak-hickory and beech maple—with sizeable plantings of pine. Deer are abundant, along with many smaller mammals.

During the spring, birds are conspicuous along Route 327 all the way to the park, especially during the early morning hours when newly arrived swifts twitter across the sky, Barn Swallows dip and dart over the road, and every patch of woods and brush seems to harbor a host of singing birds. Listen for the *turtle-turtle-turtle* song of the Kentucky Warbler, and the more emphatic *teacher-teacher-teacher* song of the Ovenbird. On a favorable May morning, warblers of many species and the entire entourage of birds that move north with them can be seen and heard along the park roads, around the lake and its attendant stream, and on the hillsides.

Typical breeding birds are Turkey Vulture, Cooper's, Broad-winged, and Red-tailed hawks, American Kestrel, Ruffed Grouse, Northern Bobwhite, Black-billed and Yellow-billed cuckoos, Eastern Screech-Owl, Great Horned and Barred owls, Whip-poor-will, Ruby-throated Hummingbird, Belted Kingfisher, Red-headed, Red-bellied, and Pileated woodpeckers, Eastern Wood-Pewee, Acadian Flycatcher, Eastern Phoebe, Great Crested Flycatcher, Eastern Kingbird, Carolina Chickadee, Tufted Titmouse, White-breasted Nuthatch, Carolina and House wrens, Blue-gray Gnatcatcher, Eastern Bluebird, Wood Thrush, Gray Catbird, Northern Mockingbird, Brown Thrasher, White-eyed, Yellow-throated, Warbling, and Red-eyed vireos.

Warblers that nest are the Blue-winged, Northern Parula, Yellow, Yellow-throated, Pine, Prairie, Cerulean, Black-and-white, American Redstart, Worm-eating, Ovenbird, Louisiana Waterthrush, Kentucky, Common Yellowthroat, Hooded, and Yellow-breasted Chat.

Other breeders include Summer and Scarlet tanagers, Indigo Bunting, Rufous-sided Towhee, Field and Song sparrows, and American Goldfinch. In nearby farm fields look for Grasshopper and Henslow's sparrows, Bobolink, and Eastern Meadowlark.

Wintering birds, in addition to resident species, frequently include the Yellow-bellied Sapsucker, Red-breasted Nuthatch, Black-capped Chickadee, Brown Creeper, Golden- and Ruby-crowned (rare) kinglets, Yellow-rumped Warbler, American Tree, Field, Song, White-throated, and White-crowned sparrows, Dark-eyed Junco, Red and White-winged crossbills (rare and erratic), and Pine Siskin (erratic).

Tarlton Cross Mound

Southeast of Circleville, take Ohio 159 to the village of Tarlton; turn west and go several blocks to Redding Street (County Road 12); turn north and go .5 mile to the entrance on the left side of the road. (Map F-64)

This pleasant 16-acre tract is the site of an unusual cross-shaped Hopewell Indian ceremonial earthwork. A footbridge crosses a small stream and one trail leads to the mound; others meander through the oak-maple woods. Birds present in the spring and summer are the Yellow-billed Cuckoo, Northern Flicker, Eastern Wood-Pewee, Acadian and Great Crested flycatchers, Blue Jay, Tufted Titmouse, White-breasted Nuthatch, Blue-gray Gnatcatcher, Wood Thrush, Yellow-throated and Red-eyed vireos, Yellow Warbler, American Redstart, Ovenbird, Louisiana Waterthrush, Kentucky Warbler, Scarlet Tanager, Northern Cardinal, and Rufous-sided Towhee.

In the sycamores along the creek, look for a pair or two of Yellow-throated Warblers. In the brushy areas along the creek and around the perimeter of the small park, there are House Wrens, Gray Catbirds, Yellow-breasted Chats, Indigo Buntings, Chipping Sparrows, and American Goldfinches. On the far western side of the woods is a shallow gully with a few sycamores, willows, cottonwoods, and shrub-dotted upland fields. Among the nesting birds are Brown Thrashers, White-eyed Vireos, Blue-winged and Prairie warblers, and Field Sparrows.

Trillium Trails   *See Winton Woods.*

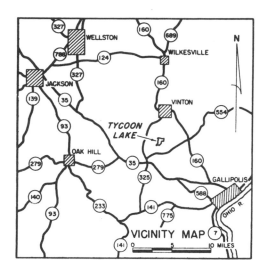

Tycoon Lake State Wildlife Area   *Take Ohio 554 in Gallia County several miles northeast of Rio Grande to the access road on the left. (Map F–65)*

The lake and attendant marsh, woodland, brushy areas, fields, and surrounding farmland provide mixed habitats for an abundance of diversified bird species.

Green-backed Herons, Wood Ducks, migrant Soras, Solitary and Spotted sandpipers, and Common Snipe inhabit the marsh. Red-tailed Hawks nest nearby. Ruffed Grouse are sometimes encountered; the Northern Bobwhite was plentiful before 1976 and is making a comeback.

Some of the frequently found breeding birds are the Yellow-billed Cuckoo, Barred Owl, Whip-poor-will, Ruby-throated Hummingbird, Pileated Woodpecker, Willow Flycatcher, Eastern Bluebird, Wood Thrush, Northern Mockingbird, Cedar Waxwing, Kentucky and Hooded warblers, Summer and Scarlet tanagers, and Rufous-sided Towhee.

Vesuvius, Lake   *See Dean State Forest.*

Veto Lake State Wildlife Area   *On Ohio 339 about 8 miles northwest of Belpre in Washington County. (Map F–66)*

Mallards, Blue-winged Teals, Northern Shovelers, American Wigeons, Redheads, Ring-necked Ducks, and Lesser Scaup are typical of the waterfowl attracted in spring to this 160-acre lake set in a tract of mixed hardwoods. In April, all of the swallows seen in Ohio can be found skimming over the water and, by the end of the month, the surrounding woods and countryside resound with the songs of a multitude of newly arrived birds. Lincoln's Sparrows lurk in brushy areas, and an occasional Swamp Sparrow can be flushed from wet tangles.

Marshy spots along the lakeshore attract Great Blue and Green-backed herons and occasional shorebirds such as Greater and Lesser yellowlegs. On big migration days in May, look for Summer Tanagers and Orchard Orioles.

Breeding birds commonly present are Red-tailed Hawk, Northern Bobwhite, Black-billed Cuckoo, Red-bellied Woodpecker, Willow Flycatcher, Eastern Phoebe, Barn Swallow, House Wren, Eastern Bluebird, Yellow-throated Vireo, Yellow Warbler, Common Yellowthroat, Yellow-breasted Chat, Summer Tanager, Indigo Bunting, Field and Song sparrows.

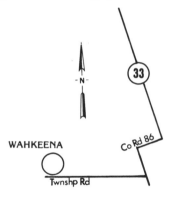

Wahkeena State Memorial

Take U.S. 33 6 miles south from Lancaster and turn right onto County Road 86, then left onto Pumping Station Road about 2 miles to the entrance. (Map F-67)

Mr. and Mrs. Frank Warner bequeathed this 150 acres of wooded hills, a small lake, and lodge to the Ohio Historical Society to be used as an outdoor nature laboratory. Black Hand sandstone (see Black Hand Gorge State Nature Preserve) outcroppings provide a scenic backdrop to many of the trails. Native trees include hemlock, pitch, scrub, and white pines, flowering dogwood, redbud, common alder, chestnut, black walnut, tulip, black cherry, mocker nut hickory, shingle, pin, rock chestnut, and white oaks, sassafras, red maple, sourwood, red elm, sweet birch, bigtooth aspen, white ash, black locust, American beech, and ironwood.

Wahkeena is a delightful place to study spring wildflowers. A few of the many to be found are creeping phlox, fire-pink, wild columbine, bluebells, bluets, Jacob's ladder, long-spurred violet, common periwinkle, wild cranesbill, speedwell, swamp buttercup, hairy Solomon's seal, kidney-leaf crowfoot, marsh marigold, spring avens, bloodroot, bulbous bitter cress, false Solomon's seal, large-flowered trillium, May-apple, rue anemone, spring beauty, striped white violet, wild strawberry, showy orchis, and pink lady's slipper.

Rhododendron and mountain laurel are plentiful, and the cool, wooded hillsides and rocky damp spots provide fine habitat for many species of ferns, among them the ostrich, Christmas, wood, marginal shield, fragile, common polypody, ebony spleenwort, interrupted, sensitive, cinnamon, upland lady, rattlesnake, marsh, broad beech, maidenhair, silvery spleenwort, New York, evergreen wood, bulblet, blunt-lobed woodsia, and water clover, or pepperwort.

There are birds aplenty, too. A pair of Wood Ducks nest every year in a box at the northeastern end of the lake. Pied-billed Grebes, Mallards, Blue-winged Teals, and Northern Shovelers sometimes show up; a pair of Spotted Sandpipers sometimes nest nearby, and Belted Kingfishers are resident as long as the water is open. Most years, a pair of Green-backed Herons nest in the trees near the lake. The lake is also a favorite feeding spot for Northern Rough-winged and Barn Swallows.

Red-tailed Hawks are seen year-round and, in summer, a pair of Broad-winged Hawks are frequently noted soaring overhead. During spring and fall migrations, a full spectrum of flycatchers, thrushes, vireos, warblers, orioles, tanagers, and finches are often present after a big migration wave.

Nesting species readily seen and heard around the lodge and lake include Ruby-throated Hummingbird, Downy Woodpecker, Northern Flicker, Eastern Phoebe, Blue Jay, Carolina Chickadee, Tufted Titmouse, White-breasted Nuthatch, Carolina Wren, Blue-gray Gnatcatcher, American Robin, Gray Catbird, Brown Thrasher, Cedar Waxwing, White-eyed and Warbling vireos, Blue-winged and Yellow-throated warblers, Common Yellowthroat, Yellow-breasted Chat, Summer Tanager, Northern Cardinal, Indigo Bunting, Song Sparrow, American Goldfinch, and Northern Oriole.

Birds that usually nest in the deeper woods are the Ruffed Grouse, Eastern Screech-Owl, Barred Owl, Red-bellied and Hairy woodpeckers, Eastern Wood-Pewee, Acadian and Great Crested flycatchers, Wood Thrush, Yellow-throated and Red-eyed vireos, and the following warblers: Cerulean, Black-and-white, American Redstart, Worm-eating, Ovenbird, Louisiana Waterthrush, Kentucky, and Hooded. Also Scarlet Tanager and Rufous-sided Towhee.

Hiking along the trails at Wahkeena is invigorating any time of the year, and winter is no exception. An occasional Pileated Woodpecker is sometimes heard or seen flying across a clearing; Yellow-bellied Sapsuckers and Hairy

Woodpeckers are frequently present, and a nice variety of birds can be seen at the feeders around the lodge.

Winton Woods   *Located in north central Hamilton County*
                                    north of Cincinnati. From I-75 take
                                    I-275 west to Winton Road (Exit 39),
                                    then south on Winton Road about 3 miles
                                    to the park entrance. (Map E–68)

A multi-recreational 2,233-acre park has handicapped access to a paved bike-hike trail, many paved sidewalks, picnic areas, and a Visitors Center. Other attractions are camping, boating, fishing, horseback riding, Frisbee golf, an 18-hole golf course, and miles of hiking trails. Birding habitats include a 188-acre lake with 22 miles of winding shoreline, a shallow swampy strip, a small cattail marsh, a wooded stream, and heavily forested areas in all stages of succession, including mature stands of oak, maple, beech, pine plantings, brushy thickets, and extensive overgrown fields.

As many as 20 warbler species are possible on a good May morning with the added expectations of small numbers of herons and egrets, waterfowl, shorebirds, and an occasional Osprey.

Northern Saw-whet Owl

Representative nesting birds include Green-backed Heron, Canada Goose, Wood Ducks, Mallards, Cooper's, Red-shouldered, Broad-winged (rare), and Red-tailed hawks, American Kestrel, Northern Bobwhite, Killdeer, Spotted Sandpiper, American Woodcock, Yellow-billed Cuckoo, Eastern Screech-Owl,

LONG-EARED OWL

Long-eared Owl

Great Horned and Barred owls, Ruby-throated Hummingbird, Belted King-fisher, Hairy and Pileated woodpeckers, Eastern Wood-Pewee, Acadian Fly-catcher, Eastern Phoebe, Great Crested Flycatcher, Eastern Kingbird, Purple Martin, Tree, Northern Rough-winged, and Barn swallows, White-breasted Nuthatch, Carolina and House wrens, Blue-gray Gnatcatcher, Eastern Blue-bird, Wood Thrush, Gray Catbird, Northern Mockingbird, Brown Thrasher, Cedar Waxwing, White-eyed, Yellow-throated, Warbling, and Red-eyed vireos.

Breeding warblers are: Blue-winged, Northern Parula, Yellow, Yellow-throated, Pine, Cerulean, Prothonotary, Louisiana Waterthrush, Kentucky, Common Yellowthroat, and Yellow-breasted Chat. Also Summer and Scarlet tanagers, Northern Cardinal, Indigo Bunting, Rufous-sided Towhee, Chipping, Field, and Song sparrows, Red-winged Blackbird, Eastern Meadowlark, Or-chard and Northern orioles, and American Goldfinch.

Black-crowned Night-Herons and other waders are best observed at dusk in the shallows west of the Visitors Center. American Woodcocks can be seen displaying in early spring at dawn and dusk in the fields near the dam. Pine Warblers can be seen and heard from late March through the nesting season in the pine plantings at East Woods.

In winter, Canada Geese, American Black Ducks, and large numbers of Mallards keep a hole in the ice open and are joined by occasional other water-fowl. Typical wintering birds include Sharp-shinned Hawk, Red-breasted Nut-hatch (especially in the pines), Brown Creeper, Winter Wren (uncommon), Golden-crowned Kinglet, Hermit Thrush, Yellow-rumped Warbler, American Tree, Field, Fox (uncommon), Song, Swamp, White-throated, and White-crowned sparrows, Dark-eyed Junco, Pine Siskin (erratic), and a few Purple Finches.

Rare and unusual species that have been recorded include Yellow-crowned Night-Heron, Snowy Egret, Little Blue Heron, Merlin, Sandhill Crane, Long-eared and Northern Saw-whet owls, Golden-winged Warbler, Blue Grosbeak, Bachman's Sparrow, Snow Bunting, and Brewer's Blackbird.

Wolf Creek Wildlife Area   *Both Ohio 78 and Ohio 555 in Morgan*
                                          County lead to the area, which is just
                                          south and east of Ringgold. (Map F–69)

The rolling terrain of this 3,500-acre scenic area combines forests, pastures, cropland, fallow fields, and brushy stream edges, providing a rich ecological mix for a diversity of birdlife. A three-tier nine-acre lake just off Ohio 78 near County Road 13 attracts small numbers of waterbirds.

In areas of scrubby growth, forest and stream edges, from late April through most of the summer, look for these nesting birds: Northern Bobwhite, Eastern Phoebe, Eastern Kingbird, Northern Rough-winged, Cliff, and Barn

Yellow-throated (front) and Cerulean Warblers

swallows, Northern Mockingbird, White-eyed and Warbling vireos, Blue-winged, Yellow, and Prairie warblers, Common Yellowthroat, Yellow-breasted Chat, Summer Tanager, Indigo Bunting, and Orchard and Northern orioles.

Species nesting in wooded situations include the Cooper's and Red-tailed hawks, Ruffed Grouse, American Woodcock, Yellow-billed Cuckoo, Eastern Screech-Owl, Great Horned Owl, Whip-poor-will, Pileated Woodpecker, Great Crested Flycatcher, Wood Thrush, Yellow-throated Vireo, Cerulean Warbler, American Redstart, Louisiana Waterthrush, Kentucky Warbler, and Scarlet Tanager.

In winter, a number of half-hardy species—Eastern Bluebird, American Robin, Yellow-rumped Warbler, Rufous-sided Towhee, Field, Song, Swamp, White-throated, and White-crowned sparrows, Purple Finch, and American Goldfinch—are frequently encountered.

Yellow Creek State Forest   *On Ohio 39 in southern Columbiana County about 10 miles east of Salineville. (Map G–70)*

Hemlocks, pitch pines, and red cedars shade the deep ravines of this 756-acre retreat, while oaks, tulip trees, and maples clothe the upland hills. Ruffed Grouse and Whip-poor-wills are found in the woods; Great Horned Owls occur, and the Long-eared Owl has been known to nest nearby. The Sharp-shinned Hawk is a rare breeding bird, and there is a record of the Brown Creeper nesting in the vicinity. Warblers that nest are the Yellow, Cerulean, Black-and-white, Worm-eating, Ovenbird, Louisiana Waterthrush, Kentucky, Common Yellowthroat, Hooded, and Yellow-breasted Chat.

PART IV

The Birds of Ohio

Checklist of Ohio Birds

The purpose of this expanded checklist is to provide an up-to-date list of the bird species recorded in Ohio from historic time to the present day. The list includes all species that have been authenticated as occurring in the state, with common and scientific names, status, and check-off boxes for maintaining a personal list.

Guidelines for species inclusion are based in part on American Birding Association criteria:

(a) An extant specimen identified by a recognized authority together with convincing evidence that the specimen was obtained within our defined (geographical) limits; or
(b) one or more photographs or tape-recordings that clearly demonstrate definitive characteristics; or
(c) a sight record backed by detailed documentation which includes the date, time, and location of the observation, names of other observers, distance from the subject, optics used, and a detailed description of the bird.

An asterisk (*) denotes that the species has been documented as nesting in Ohio either at the present time or at some time in the past. The nomenclature and taxonomic sequence follow that of the American Ornithologists' Union (1983; 1985), and the American Birding Association *Checklist: Birds of the Continental United States and Canada*, fourth edition (1990). Common names of species are followed by the scientific names.

Following the scientific names are brief résumés of the numerical status, times of year most often observed, and geographical distribution of each species. Although great care was taken to make these indicators as accurate as possible, there are bound to be many exceptions to the rule. The late Edward S. Thomas, when he was curator of the Ohio State Museum, once explained it to me very succinctly: "Birds have wings," he said with a smile.

Designations of Abundance

Common: A species that occurs routinely or is conspicuously present in season
in its habitat and easily found. Depending on the species, numbers seen in
one locality, or in one day, might run from 10 to 50 or more.
Fairly common: Fewer numbers than the *Common* category, a bit harder to find,
more localized, with numbers that might run from 5 to 9.
Infrequent: Not always found in any given season or year. Often more localized, sometimes with more restrictive habitat requirements. When found,
numbers in a given location or on one day are apt to be fewer than 5.
Rare: Can refer to seasonal numbers or the aggregate status of a species. Includes situations when just a few individuals are seen in a season or in an
entire region. Sometimes records of occurrence are separated by a number
of years.
Accidental: Extremely rare or casual. Includes birds that have wandered beyond their normal range, storm-driven individuals, disoriented migrants,
or species that are in the process of being extirpated.
Extirpated: A species that may occur elsewhere, but is no longer found in Ohio.
Extinct: A species that does not survive anywhere.

Loons and Grebes

☐ **Red-throated Loon,** *Gavia stellata.* Rare migrant; accidental in winter
☐ **Pacific Loon,** *Gavia pacifica.* Accidental
☐ **Common Loon,** *Gavia immer.* Fairly common-common migrant; rare sum-
mer visitor; rare in winter
☐ ***Pied-billed Grebe,** *Podilymbus podiceps.* Fairly common-common migrant; infre-
quent and local in summer; fairly common Lake Erie breeder. Rare in winter
☐ **Horned Grebe,** *Podiceps auritus.* Fairly common migrant, infrequent in winter
☐ **Red-necked Grebe,** *Podiceps grisegena.* Rare migrant, accidental in winter
☐ **Eared Grebe,** *Podiceps nigricollis.* Rare migrant
☐ **Western Grebe,** *Aechmophorus occidentalis.* Accidental-rare migrant

Petrels, Gannets, and Pelicans

☐ **Wilson's Storm-Petrel,** *Oceanites oceanicus.* Accidental
☐ **Black-capped Petrel,** *Pterodroma hasitata.* Accidental

☐ **Leach's Storm-Petrel,** *Oceanodroma leucorhoa.* Accidental

☐ **Northern Gannet,** *Sula bassanus.* Accidental

☐ **American White Pelican,** *Pelecanus erythrorhynchos.* Accidental-rare migrant, summer visitor

CORMORANTS

☐ ***Double-crested Cormorant,** *Phalacrocorax auritus.* Irregular-fairly common migrant, infrequent summer and winter visitor. Common Lake Erie migrant, fairly common in summer, infrequent in winter

HERONS, BITTERNS, AND IBISES

☐ **Anhinga,** *Anhinga anhinga.* Accidental

☐ **Magnificent Frigatebird,** *Fregata magnificens.* Accidental

☐ ***American Bittern,** *Botaurus lentiginosus.* Rare-infrequent migrant, local summer resident; accidental in winter

☐ ***Least Bittern,** *Ixobrychus exilis.* Rare migrant, summer resident, most frequent in Lake Erie marshes

☐ ***Great Blue Heron,** *Ardea herodias.* Fairly common-locally common migrant, summer resident. Infrequent in winter.

☐ ***Great Egret,** *Casmerodius albus.* Rare-infrequent migrant, summer visitor; common in Lake Erie marshes. Rare in winter

☐ ***Snowy Egret,** *Egretta thula.* Rare migrant, local summer visitor

☐ ***Little Blue Heron,** *Egretta caerulea.* Rare migrant, local summer visitor

☐ **Tricolored Heron,** *Egretta tricolor.* Accidental. Rare migrant, local summer resident in Lake Erie marshes

☐ ***Cattle Egret,** *Bubulcus ibis.* Rare migrant, local summer visitor

☐ ***Green-backed Heron,** *Butorides striatus.* Fairly common migrant; infrequent in summer except near Lake Erie; accidental in winter

☐ ***Black-crowned Night-Heron,** *Nycticorax nycticorax.* Infrequent migrant, summer visitor. Fairly common summer resident Lake Erie. Rare in winter

☐ ***Yellow-crowned Night-Heron,** *Nycticorax violaceus.* Rare migrant, infrequent and local in summer

☐ **White Ibis,** *Eudocimus albus.* Accidental

□ **Glossy Ibis,** *Plegadis falcinellus.* Accidental migrant; rare summer visitor on Lake Erie

□ **White-faced Ibis,** *Plegadis chihi.* Accidental

□ **Roseate Spoonbill,** *Ajaia ajaja.* Accidental

□ **Wood Stork,** *Mycteria americana.* Accidental

SWANS, GEESE, AND DUCKS

□ **Fulvous Whistling-Duck,** *Dendrocygna bicolor.* Accidental migrant, summer visitor

□ **Tundra Swan,** *Cygnus columbianus.* Infrequent migrant, rare in winter. Fairly common-common Lake Erie migrant

□ **Trumpeter Swan,** *Cygnus buccinator.* Accidental/extirpated

□ ***Mute Swan,** *Cygnus olor.* Rare-infrequent migrant, visitor

□ **Greater White-fronted Goose,** *Anser albifrons.* Rare migrant; accidental in winter

□ **Snow Goose,** *Chen caerulescens.* Infrequent migrant but fairly common on Lake Erie. Accidental in summer; rare in winter

□ **Ross' Goose,** *Chen rossii.* Accidental

□ **Brant,** *Branta bernicla.* Accidental migrant, more frequent on Lake Erie

□ ***Canada Goose,** *Branta canadensis.* Common migrant, permanent resident.

□ ***Wood Duck,** *Aix sponsa.* Fairly common migrant, summer resident. Rare in winter

□ ***Green-winged Teal,** *Anas crecca.* Fairly common migrant. Rare summer visitor in Lake Erie marshes; rare in winter

□ ***American Black Duck,** *Anas rubripes.* Fairly common-common migrant, winter visitor; infrequent in summer in Lake Erie marshes

□ ***Mallard,** *Anas platyrhynchos.* Common migrant, permanent resident

□ ***Northern Pintail,** *Anas acuta.* Infrequent-fairly common migrant. Infrequent summer visitor in Lake Erie marshes; rare in winter

□ ***Blue-winged Teal,** *Anas discors.* Fairly common-common migrant. Rare-infrequent in summer except in Lake Erie marshes. Rare in winter

□ **Cinnamon Teal,** *Anas cyanoptera.* Accidental

□ ***Northern Shoveler,** *Anas clypeata.* Infrequent-fairly common migrant; rare summer visitor in Lake Erie marshes. Rare in winter

☐ ***Gadwall,** *Anas strepera.* Fairly common migrant; infrequent in winter and as a summer visitor in Lake Erie marshes

☐ **Eurasian Wigeon,** *Anas penelope.* Rare migrant

☐ ***American Wigeon,** *Anas americana.* Fairly common-common migrant. Rare summer visitor in Lake Erie marshes. Infrequent in winter

☐ **Canvasback,** *Aythya valisineria.* Fairly common migrant; common winter visitor Lake Erie; rare summer visitor in Lake Erie marshes

☐ ***Redhead,** *Aythya americana.* Fairly common-common migrant; rare summer visitor in Lake Erie marshes; fairly common winter visitor on Lake Erie

☐ **Ring-necked Duck,** *Aythya collaris.* Common migrant; rare summer resident and winter visitor

☐ **Greater Scaup,** *Aythya marila.* Rare migrant, winter visitor. Common on Lake Erie in winter

☐ ***Lesser Scaup,** *Aythya affinis.* Common migrant; common on Lake Erie in winter. Rare summer visitor in Lake Erie marshes

☐ **Common Eider,** *Somateria mollissima.* Accidental

☐ **King Eider,** *Somateria spectabilis.* Accidental; rare winter visitor on Lake Erie

☐ **Harlequin Duck,** *Histrionicus histrionicus.* Accidental; rare Lake Erie migrant, winter visitor

☐ **Oldsquaw,** *Clangula hyemalis.* Rare migrant, winter visitor

☐ **Black Scoter,** *Melanitta nigra.* Rare migrant, winter visitor, more frequent on Lake Erie

☐ **Surf Scoter,** *Melanitta perspicillata.* Rare migrant, winter visitor, more frequent on Lake Erie

☐ **White-winged Scoter,** *Melanitta fusca.* Rare migrant, winter visitor, more frequent on Lake Erie

☐ **Common Goldeneye,** *Bucephala clangula.* Fairly common-common migrant, winter visitor; accidental in summer

☐ **Barrow's Goldeneye,** *Bucephala islandica.* Accidental

☐ **Bufflehead,** *Bucephala albeola.* Fairly common migrant, winter visitor; accidental in summer

☐ ***Hooded Merganser,** *Lophodytes cucullatus.* Fairly common-common migrant; rare in winter. In summer, infrequent in Lake Erie marshes; rare elsewhere

☐ **Common Merganser,** *Mergus merganser.* Fairly common migrant, winter visitor, more common on Lake Erie. Accidental in summer

☐ **Red-breasted Merganser,** *Mergus serrator.* Fairly common migrant, winter visitor, more common on Lake Erie. Accidental in summer

☐ ***Ruddy Duck,** *Oxyura jamaicensis.* Fairly common migrant, winter visitor, more common on Lake Erie. Accidental in summer

VULTURES

☐ ***Black Vulture,** *Coragyps atratus.* Accidental-rare; locally in unglaciated counties, an infrequent-fairly common resident

☐ ***Turkey Vulture,** *Cathartes aura.* Fairly common-common migrant, summer resident. Accidental in winter except locally in unglaciated counties

OSPREYS, KITES, EAGLES, AND HAWKS

☐ ***Osprey,** *Pandion haliaetus.* Infrequent migrant; rare summer visitor

☐ **American Swallow-tailed Kite,** *Elanoides forficatus.* Accidental

☐ **Mississippi Kite,** *Ictinia mississippiensis.* Accidental

☐ ***Bald Eagle,** *Haliaeetus leucocephalus.* Rare migrant, permanent resident; along W. Lake Erie, infrequent permanent resident

☐ ***Northern Harrier,** *Circus cyaneus.* Infrequent migrant, winter visitor. Rare in summer

☐ ***Sharp-shinned Hawk,** *Accipiter striatus.* Infrequent migrant; fairly common along W. Lake Erie. Rare-infrequent in summer. Infrequent in winter

☐ ***Cooper's Hawk,** *Accipiter cooperii.* Fairly common migrant, permanent resident; common migrant Lake Erie

☐ **Northern Goshawk,** *Accipiter gentilis.* Rare migrant, winter visitor

☐ **Harris' Hawk,** *Parabuteo unicinctus.* Accidental

☐ ***Red-shouldered Hawk,** *Buteo lineatus.* Infrequent migrant, permanent resident; fairly common migrant Lake Erie

☐ ***Broad-winged Hawk,** *Buteo platypterus.* Infrequent migrant, more numerous along Lake Erie. Infrequent summer resident, mostly in northeastern and southern Ohio

☐ **Swainson's Hawk,** *Buteo swainsoni.* Accidental

☐ ***Red-tailed Hawk,** *Buteo jamaicensis.* Fairly common-common permanent resident; common Lake Erie migrant

☐ **Rough-legged Hawk,** *Buteo lagopus.* Infrequent winter visitor and migrant; more numerous along Lake Erie

☐ **Golden Eagle,** *Aquila chrysaetos*. Rare migrant, winter visitor, most often seen along Lake Erie

Falcons

☐ *****American Kestrel,** *Falco sparverius*. Fairly common migrant, permanent resident
☐ *****Merlin,** *Falco columbarius*. Rare migrant, winter visitor
☐ *****Peregrine Falcon,** *Falco peregrinus*. Rare migrant, summer resident. Rare in winter.
☐ **Gyrfalcon,** *Falco rusticolus*. Accidental winter visitor
☐ **Prairie Falcon,** *Falco mexicanus*. Accidental

Game Birds

☐ *****Gray Partridge,** *Perdix perdix*. Introduced, now extirpated
☐ *****Ring-necked Pheasant,** *Phasianus colchicus*. Introduced. Infrequent-fairly common permanent resident
☐ *****Ruffed Grouse,** *Bonasa umbellus*. Infrequent permanent resident in southern and eastern Ohio
☐ *****Greater Prairie-Chicken,** *Tympanuchus cupido*. Extirpated
☐ *****Wild Turkey,** *Meleagris gallopavo*. Infrequent-fairly common permanent resident, mostly in southern and eastern counties
☐ *****Northern Bobwhite,** *Colinus virginianus*. Rare-infrequent permanent resident, mostly in southern and eastern counties

Rails, Gallinules, and Coots

☐ *****Yellow Rail,** *Coturnicops noveboracensis*. Rare migrant; accidental summer visitor
☐ **Black Rail,** *Laterallus jamaicensis*. Rare migrant; accidental summer visitor
☐ *****King Rail,** *Rallus elegans*. Accidental; in Lake Erie marshes a rare migrant, summer visitor. Accidental in winter

□ ***Virginia Rail,** *Rallus limicola.* Infrequent migrant, summer visitor, more frequent in Lake Erie marshes. Accidental in winter

□ ***Sora,** *Porzana carolina.* Infrequent-fairly common migrant, summer resident, especially in Lake Erie marshes; accidental in winter

□ ***Purple Gallinule,** *Porphyrula martinica.* Accidental

□ ***Common Moorhen,** *Gallinula chloropus.* Rare migrant, summer resident, more frequent in Lake Erie marshes

□ ***American Coot,** *Fulica americana.* Common migrant; infrequent summer resident. Common summer resident in Lake Erie marshes. Infrequent in winter

CRANES

□ ***Sandhill Crane,** *Grus canadensis.* Rare migrant, summer resident; accidental in winter

PLOVERS

□ **Black-bellied Plover,** *Pluvialis squatarola.* Infrequent-fairly common migrant, most numerous along Lake Erie

□ **Lesser Golden-Plover,** *Pluvialis dominica.* Infrequent-fairly common migrant, most numerous along Lake Erie

□ **Snowy Plover,** *Charadrius alexandrinus.* Accidental

□ **Wilson's Plover,** *Charadrius wilsonia.* Accidental

□ **Semipalmated Plover,** *Charadrius semipalmatus.* Infrequent migrant; fairly common-common along Lake Erie

□ ***Piping Plover,** *Charadrius melodus.* Rare migrant

□ ***Killdeer,** *Charadrius vociferus.* Common migrant, summer resident; infrequent winter resident

STILTS AND AVOCETS

□ **Black-necked Stilt,** *Himantopus mexicanus.* Accidental

□ **American Avocet,** *Recurvirostra americana.* Rare migrant

SANDPIPERS AND ALLIES

□ **Greater Yellowlegs,** *Tringa melanoleuca*. Fairly common migrant, most numerous along Lake Erie

□ **Lesser Yellowlegs,** *Tringa flavipes*. Common migrant, most numerous along Lake Erie

□ **Spotted Redshank,** *Tringa erythropus*. Accidental

□ **Solitary Sandpiper,** *Tringa solitaria*. Infrequent-fairly common migrant; accidental in winter

□ **Willet,** *Catoptrophorus semipalmatus*. Rare migrant

□ ***Spotted Sandpiper,** *Actitis macularia*. Fairly common migrant; infrequent in summer; accidental in winter

□ ***Upland Sandpiper,** *Bartramia longicauda*. Rare-infrequent migrant; rare in summer

□ **Eskimo Curlew,** *Numenius borealis*. Extirpated

□ **Whimbrel,** *Numenius phaeopus*. Rare migrant

□ **Long-billed Curlew,** *Numenius americanus*. Accidental

□ **Hudsonian Godwit,** *Limosa haemastica*. Accidental migrant; rare along Lake Erie

□ **Marbled Godwit,** *Limosa fedoa*. Accidental migrant, rare-infrequent along Lake Erie

□ **Ruddy Turnstone,** *Arenaria interpres*. Rare migrant; fairly common along Lake Erie. Accidental in winter

□ **Red Knot,** *Calidris canutus*. Rare-infrequent Lake Erie migrant. Accidental inland

□ **Sanderling,** *Calidris alba*. Rare-infrequent migrant; fairly common migrant along Lake Erie

□ **Semipalmated Sandpiper,** *Calidris pusilla*. Fairly common migrant; common along Lake Erie

□ **Western Sandpiper,** *Calidris mauri*. Rare migrant

□ **Rufous-necked Stint,** *Calidris ruficollis*. Accidental

□ **Least Sandpiper,** *Calidris minutilla*. Fairly common migrant; common along Lake Erie

□ **White-rumped Sandpiper,** *Calidris fuscicollis*. Rare migrant; infrequent-fairly common along Lake Erie

□ **Baird's Sandpiper,** *Calidris bairdii*. Rare migrant; accidental in winter

□ **Pectoral Sandpiper,** *Calidris melanotos*. Fairly common-common migrant, more numerous along Lake Erie

☐ **Sharp-tailed Sandpiper,** *Calidris acuminata.* Accidental

☐ **Purple Sandpiper,** *Calidris maritima.* Rare Lake Erie fall and winter visitor

☐ **Dunlin,** *Calidris alpina.* Fairly common-common migrant, more numerous along Lake Erie; rare in winter

☐ **Curlew Sandpiper,** *Calidris ferruginea.* Accidental; rare migrant along Lake Erie

☐ **Stilt Sandpiper,** *Calidris himantopus.* Rare-fairly common migrant; fairly common-common along Lake Erie

☐ **Buff-breasted Sandpiper,** *Tryngites subruficollis.* Rare migrant

☐ **Ruff,** *Philomachus pugnax.* Rare migrant

☐ **Short-billed Dowitcher,** *Limnodromus griseus.* Fairly common migrant; fairly common-common along Lake Erie

☐ **Long-billed Dowitcher,** *Limnodromus scolopaceus.* Rare migrant; infrequent-fairly common along Lake Erie; accidental in winter

SNIPES AND WOODCOCKS

☐ ***Common Snipe,** *Gallinago gallinago.* Fairly common-locally common migrant; rare summer resident northern Ohio, accidental elsewhere. Infrequent in winter

☐ **Eurasian Woodcock,** *Scolopax rusticola.* Accidental

☐ ***American Woodcock,** *Scolopax minor.* Fairly common migrant, summer resident; accidental in winter

PHALAROPES

☐ ***Wilson's Phalarope,** *Phalaropus tricolor.* Rare; infrequent migrant along Lake Erie; accidental-rare summer resident

☐ **Red-necked Phalarope,** *Phalaropus lobatus.* Rare migrant

☐ **Red Phalarope,** *Phalaropus fulicaria.* Rare migrant, accidental in winter

JAEGERS, GULLS, AND KITTIWAKES

☐ **Pomarine Jaeger,** *Stercorarius pomarinus.* rare migrant along Lake Erie, Accidental inland

☐ **Parasitic Jaeger,** *Stercorarius parasitidus.* Rare-infrequent migrant along Lake Erie. Accidental inland

☐ **Long-tailed Jaeger,** *Stercorarius longicaudus.* Accidental migrant

☐ **Laughing Gull,** *Larus atricilla.* Rare migrant, summer visitor

☐ **Franklin's Gull,** *Larus pipixcan.* Infrequent migrant, summer visitor

☐ **Little Gull,** *Larus minutus.* Rare-infrequent Lake Erie visitor, most often seen in winter. Accidental inland

☐ **Common Black-headed Gull,** *Larus ridibundus.* Rare Lake Erie migrant; rare winter and summer visitor

☐ **Bonaparte's Gull,** *Larus philadelphia.* Infrequent-fairly common migrant inland; common Lake Erie migrant; rare-infrequent at other times

☐ **Heerman's Gull,** *Larus heermanni.* Accidental on Lake Erie

☐ **Mew Gull,** *Larus canus.* Accidental on Lake Erie

☐ ***Ring-billed Gull,** *Larus delawarensis.* Common migrant, infrequent-fairly common resident. Most common on Lake Erie

☐ **California Gull,** *Larus californicus.* Accidental on Lake Erie

☐ ***Herring Gull,** *Larus argentatus.* Fairly common-common migrant, irregular and local other times. Most numerous at all seasons on Lake Erie

☐ **Thayer's Gull,** *Larus thayeri.* Rare Lake Erie migrant, winter visitor

☐ **Iceland Gull,** *Larus glaucoides.* Rare Lake Erie migrant, winter visitor. Accidental inland

☐ **Lesser Black-backed Gull,** *Larus fuscus.* Rare Lake Erie migrant, winter visitor

☐ **Glaucous Gull,** *Larus hyperboreus.* Infrequent Lake Erie migrant, winter visitor. Accidental at other times. Accidental inland

☐ **Great Black-backed Gull,** *Larus marinus.* Fairly common-common Lake Erie visitor. Rare inland

☐ **Black-legged Kittiwake,** *Rissa tridactyla.* Rare Lake Erie migrant, winter visitor. Accidental inland

☐ **Sabine's Gull,** *Xema sabini.* Rare migrant along Lake Erie. Accidental inland

☐ **Ivory Gull,** *Pagophila eburnea.* Accidental

TERNS

☐ **Caspian Tern,** *Sterna caspia.* Fairly common Lake Erie migrant, rare summer visitor. Infrequent migrant elsewhere

☐ *Common Tern, *Sterna hirundo.* Infrequent migrant, summer visitor, more numerous along Lake Erie

☐ Arctic Tern, *Sterna paradisaea.* Accidental

☐ Forster's Tern, *Sterna forsteri.* Infrequent-fairly common Lake Erie migrant, non-breeding summer visitor. Less numerous inland

☐ Least Tern, *Sterna antillarum.* Accidental

☐ Large-billed Tern, *Phaetusa simplex.* Accidental

☐ *Black Tern, *Chlidonias niger.* Infrequent Lake Erie migrant, rare summer resident. Rare-infrequent inland

Murres, Murrelets, and Puffins

☐ Thick-billed Murre, *Uria Lomvia.* Accidental

☐ Ancient Murrelet, *Synthliboramphus antiquus.* Accidental

☐ Atlantic Puffin, *Fratercula arctica.* Accidental

Doves and Pigeons

☐ *Rock Dove, *Columba livia.* Common permanent resident

☐ *Mourning Dove, *Zenaida macroura.* Common permanent resident

☐ *Passenger Pigeon, *Ectopistes migratorius.* Extinct

Parakeets

☐ *Carolina Parakeet, *Conuropsis carolinensis.* Extinct

Cuckoos and Anis

☐ *Black-billed Cuckoo, *Coccyzus erythropthalmus.* Infrequent migrant, summer resident

☐ ***Yellow-billed Cuckoo,** *Coccyzus americanus*. Infrequent-fairly common migrant, summer resident

☐ **Groove-billed Ani,** *Crotophaga sulcirostris*. Accidental

OWLS

☐ ***Common Barn-Owl,** *Tyto alba*. Rare permanent resident

☐ ***Eastern Screech-Owl,** *Otus asio*. Fairly common permanent resident

☐ ***Great Horned Owl,** *Bubo virginianus*. Fairly common-common permanent resident

☐ **Snowy Owl,** *Nyctea scandiaca*. Rare winter visitor, more numerous along Lake Erie

☐ **Northern Hawk-Owl,** *Surnia ulula*. Accidental winter visitor northern Ohio

☐ **Burrowing Owl,** *Athene cunicularia*. Accidental

☐ ***Barred Owl,** *Strix varia*. Fairly common permanent resident

☐ **Great Gray Owl,** *Strix nebulosa*. Accidental

☐ ***Long-eared Owl,** *Asio otus*. Rare-infrequent migrant, winter visitor; rare summer resident northern Ohio

☐ ***Short-eared Owl,** *Asio flammeus*. Infrequent migrant, winter visitor; rare summer resident

☐ ***Northern Saw-whet Owl,** *Aegolius acadicus*. Infrequent migrant, winter visitor. Rare summer resident

GOATSUCKERS

☐ ***Common Nighthawk,** *Chordeiles minor*. Fairly common migrant, summer resident

☐ ***Chuck-will's-widow,** *Caprimulgus carolinensis*. Rare-infrequent summer resident locally in southern Ohio. Accidental-rare migrant elsewhere

☐ ***Whip-poor-will,** *Caprimulgus vociferus*. Infrequent-fairly common migrant, summer resident, most numerous in southern Ohio

SWIFTS

☐ ***Chimney Swift,** *Chaetura pelagica*. Common migrant, summer resident

HUMMINGBIRDS

☐ *Ruby-throated Hummingbird, *Archilochus colubris*. Infrequent migrant, summer resident; fairly common-common in southern Ohio

☐ Rufous Hummingbird, *Selasphorus rufus*. Accidental

KINGFISHERS

☐ *Belted Kingfisher, *Ceryle alcyon*. Fairly common migrant, summer resident; rare-infrequent in winter

WOODPECKERS

☐ *Red-headed Woodpecker, *Melanerpes erythrocephalus*. Infrequent migrant, permanent resident

☐ *Red-bellied Woodpecker, *Melanerpes carolinus*. Infrequent migrant, permanent resident; fairly common-common in southern Ohio

☐ *Yellow-bellied Sapsucker, *Sphyrapicus varius*. Fairly common migrant; infrequent in winter; rare summer resident locally in northern Ohio

☐ *Downy Woodpecker, *Picoides pubescens*. Common permanent resident

☐ *Hairy Woodpecker, *Picoides villosus*. Infrequent permanent resident

☐ Red-cockaded Woodpecker, *Picoides borealis*. Accidental

☐ Black-backed Woodpecker, *Picoides arcticus*. Accidental

☐ *Northern Flicker, *Colaptes auratus*. Common migrant, summer resident; infrequent in winter

☐ *Pileated Woodpecker, *Dryocopus pileatus*. Infrequent permanent resident; fairly common in southern and eastern counties

☐ Ivory-billed Woodpecker, *Campephilus principalis*. Extinct

FLYCATCHERS

☐ *Olive-sided Flycatcher, *Contopus borealis*. Rare-infrequent migrant; accidental in summer

□ *Eastern Wood-Pewee, *Contopus virens*. Fairly common summer resident

□ Yellow-bellied Flycatcher, *Empidonax flaviventris*. Rare-infrequent migrant

□ *Acadian Flycatcher, *Empidonax virescens*. Fairly common migrant, summer resident; common summer resident in unglaciated counties

□ *Alder Flycatcher, *Empidonax alnorum*. Rare migrant, infrequent summer resident northern Ohio

□ *Willow Flycatcher, *Empidonax traillii*. Infrequent migrant, summer resident

□ *Least Flycatcher, *Empidonax minimus*. Fairly common-common migrant; fairly common summer resident in northern counties

□ *Eastern Phoebe, *Sayornis phoebe*. Infrequent-fairly common migrant, summer resident, most numerous in unglaciated counties. Rare in winter

□ Say's Phoebe, *Sayornis saya*. Accidental

□ Vermilion Flycatcher, *Pyrocephalus rubinus*. Accidental

□ *Great Crested Flycatcher, *Myiarchus crinitus*. Fairly common migrant, summer resident

□ Western Kingbird, *Tyrannus verticalis*. Accidental

□ *Eastern Kingbird, *Tyrannus tyrannus*. Infrequent-fairly common migrant, summer resident

□ Scissor-tailed Flycatcher, *Tyrannus forficatus*. Accidental

LARKS

□ *Horned Lark, *Eremophila alpestris*. Fairly common permanent resident, more numerous in winter

SWALLOWS

□ *Purple Martin, *Progne subis*. Infrequent-locally common migrant, summer resident

□ *Tree Swallow, *Tachycineta bicolor*. Fairly common migrant, summer resident; common summer resident along Lake Erie; accidental in winter

□ *Northern Rough-winged Swallow, *Stelgidopteryx serripennis*. Fairly common migrant, summer resident

□ *Bank Swallow, *Riparia riparia*. Fairly common migrant; infrequent summer resident, but common along Lake Erie

□ *Cliff Swallow, *Hirundo pyrrhonota*. Rare-infrequent migrant, summer resident, locally fairly common

□ *Barn Swallow, *Hirundo rustica*. Common migrant, summer resident

Jays, Crows, and Ravens

□ *Blue Jay, *Cyanocitta cristata*. Fairly common permanent resident and migrant; common Lake Erie migrant

□ Black-billed Magpie, *Pica pica*. Accidental

□ *American Crow, *Corvus brachyrhynchos*. Common permanent resident

□ *Common Raven, *Corvus corax*. Accidental; rare in southern Ohio

Chickadees and Titmice

□ *Black-capped Chickadee, *Parus atricapillus*. Fairly common permanent resident northern Ohio. Infrequent-fairly common sporadic migrant

□ *Carolina Chickadee, *Parus carolinensis*. Fairly common-common permanent resident

□ Boreal Chickadee, *Parus hudsonicus*. Accidental

□ *Tufted Titmouse, *Parus bicolor*. Fairly common-common permanent resident

Nuthatches

□ *Red-breasted Nuthatch, *Sitta canadensis*. Infrequent-fairly common sporadic migrant, winter resident; accidental in summer

□ *White-breasted Nuthatch, *Sitta carolinensis*. Fairly common-common permanent resident

Creepers

□ *Brown Creeper, *Certhia americana*. Fairly common migrant, winter resident; rare summer resident northern Ohio

WRENS

☐ **Rock Wren,** *Salpinctes obsoletus.* Accidental

☐ ***Carolina Wren,** *Thryothorus ludovicianus.* Infrequent-fairly common permanent resident, more numerous in southern Ohio

☐ ***Bewick's Wren,** *Thryomanes bewickii.* Accidental

☐ ***House Wren,** *Troglodytes aedon.* Fairly common-common migrant, summer resident; accidental in winter

☐ ***Winter Wren,** *Troglodytes troglodytes.* Infrequent-fairly common migrant; rare summer resident locally in northeastern and southeastern counties; infrequent winter resident

☐ ***Sedge Wren,** *Cistothorus platensis.* Rare migrant, locally distributed summer resident; accidental in winter

☐ ***Marsh Wren,** *Cistothorus palustris.* Infrequent migrant, summer resident, most numerous in Lake Erie marhes

KINGLETS AND GNATCATCHERS

☐ ***Golden-crowned Kinglet,** *Regulus satrapa.* Common migrant; rare summer resident in northeastern Ohio; infrequent-fairly common winter resident

☐ **Ruby-crowned Kinglet,** *Regulus calendula.* Common migrant; rare winter visitor

☐ ***Blue-gray Gnatcatcher,** *Polioptila caerulea.* Infrequent-fairly common migrant, summer resident, most numerous in southern and eastern Ohio

THRUSHES

☐ **Northern Wheatear,** *Oenanthe oenanthe.* Accidental

☐ ***Eastern Bluebird,** *Sialia sialis.* Fairly common migrant, summer resident, most numerous in southern Ohio. Infrequent in winter

☐ **Townsend's Solitaire,** *Myadestes townsendi.* Accidental

☐ ***Veery,** *Catharus fuscescens.* Fairly common migrant, summer resident in northeastern Ohio. Rare summer resident in southeastern Ohio

☐ **Gray-cheeked Thrush,** *Catharus minimus.* Infrequent migrant, most numerous along Lake Erie

□ **Swainson's Thrush,** *Catharus ustulatus.* Fairly common-common migrant, accidental in winter

□ ***Hermit Thrush,** *Catharus guttatus.* Fairly common-common migrant, rare winter resident; accidental-rare summer resident in southeastern and northeastern Ohio

□ ***Wood Thrush,** *Hylocichla mustelina.* Fairly common-common migrant, summer resident, most numerous in eastern and southern Ohio. Accidental in winter

□ ***American Robin,** *Turdus migratorius.* Common migrant, summer resident; infrequent-fairly common in winter

□ **Varied Thrush,** *Ixoreus naevius.* Accidental winter visitor

MIMICS

□ ***Gray Catbird,** *Dumetella carolinensis.* Fairly common-common migrant, summer resident; rare in winter

□ ***Northern Mockingbird,** *Mimus polyglottos.* Infrequent-fairly common permanent resident

□ ***Brown Thrasher,** *Toxostoma rufum.* Fairly common migrant, summer resident; rare in winter

PIPITS

□ **Water Pipit,** *Anthus spinoletta.* Infrequent-fairly common migrant, rare in winter

□ **Sprague's Pipit,** *Anthus spragueii.* Accidental

WAXWINGS

□ **Bohemian Waxwing,** *Bombycilla garrulus.* Accidental winter visitor northern Ohio

□ ***Cedar Waxwing,** *Bombycilla cedrorum.* Fairly common-common migrant, summer resident; infrequent in winter

SHRIKES

☐ **Northern Shrike,** *Lanius excubitor.* Accidental; rare winter visitor in northern Ohio

☐ ***Loggerhead Shrike,** *Lanius ludovicianus.* Rare migrant, permanent resident

STARLINGS

☐ ***European Starling,** *Sturnus vulgaris.* Introduced. Common permanent resident

VIREOS

☐ ***White-eyed Vireo,** *Vireo griseus.* Fairly common migrant, summer resident, common in southern Ohio

☐ ***Bell's Vireo,** *Vireo bellii.* Rare migrant, accidental summer resident

☐ ***Solitary Vireo,** *Vireo solitarius.* Fairly common migrant, rare summer resident in northeastern and southeastern Ohio

☐ ***Yellow-throated Vireo,** *Vireo flavifrons.* Infrequent-fairly common migrant, summer resident

☐ ***Warbling Vireo,** *Vireo gilvus.* Fairly common migrant, summer resident

☐ **Philadelphia Vireo,** *Vireo philadelphicus,* Rare-infrequent migrant

☐ ***Red-eyed Vireo,** *Vireo olivaceus.* Common migrant, summer resident

WOOD WARBLERS

☐ ***Blue-winged Warbler,** *Vermivora pinus.* Infrequent migrant, summer resident; more numerous in eastern and southern counties

☐ ***Golden-winged Warbler,** *Vermivora chrysoptera.* Rare migrant, summer resident

☐ **Tennessee Warbler,** *Vermivora peregrina.* Common migrant

☐ **Orange-crowned Warbler,** *Vermivora celata.* Rare-infrequent migrant, accidental in winter

☐ *Nashville Warbler, *Vermivora ruficapilla*. Common migrant, accidental summer resident northern Ohio; accidental in winter

☐ *Northern Parula, *Parula americana*. Infrequent migrant, infrequent-fairly common summer resident in unglaciated counties

☐ *Yellow Warbler, *Dendroica petechia*. Infrequent-fairly common migrant, summer resident, most numerous along Lake Erie

☐ *Chestnut-sided Warbler, *Dendroica pensylvanica*. Fairly common-common migrant, rare summer resident in northwest and southeast counties

☐ *Magnolia Warbler, *Dendroica magnolia*. Fairly common-common migrant, rare summer resident in northeastern and southeastern counties

☐ Cape May Warbler, *Dendroica tigrina*. Fairly common-common migrant

☐ *Black-throated Blue Warbler, *Dendroica caerulescens*. Infrequent-fairly common migrant, rare summer resident northeastern Ohio

☐ Yellow-rumped Warbler, *Dendroica coronata*. Common migrant, infrequent in winter

☐ Black-throated Gray Warbler, *Dendroica nigrescens*. Accidental

☐ Townsend's Warbler, *Dendroica townsendi*. Accidental

☐ *Black-throated Green Warbler, *Dendroica virens*. Fairly common-common migrant, infrequent summer resident in northeastern and southeastern Ohio

☐ *Blackburnian Warbler, *Dendroica fusca*. Fairly common-common migrant, rare summer resident in northeastern and southeastern Ohio

☐ *Yellow-throated Warbler, *Dendroica dominica*. Rare-infrequent migrant, summer resident. Fairly common in southern Ohio. Accidental in winter

☐ *Pine Warbler, *Dendroica pinus*. Rare-infrequent migrant, summer resident, most numerous in southeastern Ohio

☐ Kirtland's Warbler, *Dendroica kirtlandii*. Accidental-rare migrant

☐ *Prairie Warbler, *Dendroica discolor*. Infrequent migrant, summer resident, most numerous in southeastern Ohio

☐ Palm Warbler, *Dendroica palmarum*. Fairly common-common migrant, rare in winter

☐ Bay-breasted Warbler, *Dendroica castanea*. Fairly common-common migrant

☐ Blackpoll Warbler, *Dendroica striata*. Fairly common-common migrant

☐ *Cerulean Warbler, *Dendroica cerulea*. Infrequent migrant, summer resident; fairly common in southeastern Ohio

☐ *Black-and-white Warbler, *Mniotilta varia*. Fairly common migrant, rare in summer; fairly common in southeastern Ohio

☐ ***American Redstart,** *Setophaga ruticilla*. Fairly common-common migrant, infrequent summer resident, most numerous in unglaciated counties

☐ ***Prothonotary Warbler,** *Protonotaria citrea*. Rare migrant, infrequent and local summer resident

☐ ***Worm-eating Warbler,** *Helmitheros vermivorus*. Rare migrant, infrequent-fairly common summer resident in southern and eastern Ohio

☐ **Swainson's Warbler,** *Limnothlypis swainsonii*. Accidental

☐ ***Ovenbird,** *Seiurus aurocapillus*. Fairly common-common migrant, infrequent summer resident; common in unglaciated counties

☐ ***Northern Waterthrush,** *Seiurus noveboracensis*. Infrequent-fairly common migrant, rare summer resident northeastern Ohio; accidental in winter

☐ ***Louisiana Waterthrush,** *Seiurus motacilla*. Infrequent migrant, summer resident except in unglaciated counties where it is fairly common

☐ ***Kentucky Warbler,** *Oporornis formosus*. Rare-infrequent migrant, fairly common-common summer resident in unglaciated counties

☐ **Connecticut Warbler,** *Oporornis agilis*. Rare migrant

☐ ***Mourning Warbler,** *Oporornis philadelphia*. Rare migrant, accidental-rare summer resident in northern and southeastern Ohio

☐ ***Common Yellowthroat,** *Geothlypis trichas*. Fairly common-common migrant, summer resident; accidental in winter

☐ ***Hooded Warbler,** *Wilsonia citrina*. Rare-uncommon migrant, summer resident; fairly common in eastern and southern counties

☐ **Wilson's Warbler,** *Wilsonia pusilla*. Infrequent-fairly common migrant

☐ ***Canada Warbler,** *Wilsonia canadensis*. Infrequent-fairly common migrant, rare summer resident northeastern and southeastern Ohio

☐ **Painted Redstart,** *Myioborus pictus*. Accidental

☐ ***Yellow-breasted Chat,** *Icteria virens*. Infrequent migrant, summer resident. Fairly common summer resident in southern and eastern Ohio

Tanagers

☐ ***Summer Tanager,** *Piranga rubra*. Rare-infrequent migrant, summer resident. Fairly common summer resident in unglaciated counties

☐ ***Scarlet Tanager,** *Piranga olivacea*. Fairly common migrant, summer resident. Common summer resident in southeastern Ohio

☐ **Western Tanager,** *Piranga ludoviciana*. Accidental

CARDINALS AND GROSBEAKS

☐ ***Northern Cardinal,** *Cardinalis cardinalis.* Common permanent resident
☐ ***Rose-breasted Grosbeak,** *Pheucticus ludovicianus.* Fairly common-common migrant; fairly common summer resident in northern Ohio, rare in southern Ohio
☐ **Black-headed Grosbeak,** *Pheucticus melanocephalus.* Accidental
☐ ***Blue Grosbeak,** *Guiraca caerulea.* Accidental migrant; accidental-rare summer resident in southern Ohio

BUNTINGS AND DICKCISSELS

☐ ***Indigo Bunting,** *Passerina cyanea.* Common migrant, summer resident; accidental in winter
☐ ***Dickcissel,** *Spiza americana.* Rare migrant, rare and erratic summer resident; accidental in winter

TOWHEES

☐ **Green-tailed Towhee,** *Pipilo chlorurus.* Accidental
☐ ***Rufous-sided Towhee,** *Pipilo erythrophthalmus.* Fairly common migrant, summer resident; infrequent in winter

SPARROWS

☐ ***Bachman's Sparrow,** *Aimophila aestivalis.* Accidental, probably extirpated
☐ **American Tree Sparrow,** *Spizella arborea.* Fairly common-common winter resident
☐ ***Chipping Sparrow,** *Spizella passerina.* Fairly common-common migrant, summer resident; accidental in winter
☐ **Clay-colored Sparrow,** *Spizella pallida.* Accidental
☐ ***Field Sparrow,** *Spizella pusilla.* Fairly common-common migrant, summer resident; infrequent in winter

☐ ***Vesper Sparrow,** *Pooecetes gramineus.* Infrequent migrant, infrequent-fairly common summer resident; accidental in winter

☐ ***Lark Sparrow,** *Chondestes grammacus.* Accidental-rare summer resident

☐ **Black-throated Sparrow,** *Amphispiza bilineata.* Accidental

☐ **Lark Bunting,** *Calamospiza melanocorys.* Accidental

☐ ***Savannah Sparrow,** *Passerculus sandwichensis.* Fairly common-common migrant; fairly common summer resident, most numerous in northern Ohio

☐ **Baird's Sparrow,** *Ammodramus bairdii.* Accidental

☐ ***Grasshopper Sparrow,** *Ammodramus savannarum.* Rare-infrequent migrant, summer resident

☐ ***Henslow's Sparrow,** *Ammodramus henslowii.* Rare-infrequent migrant, summer resident, most common in unglaciated counties

☐ **LeConte's Sparrow,** *Ammodramus leconteii.* Accidental

☐ **Sharp-tailed Sparrow,** *Ammodramus caudacutus.* Accidental-rare migrant most often seen along Lake Erie

☐ **Fox Sparrow,** *Passerella iliaca.* Infrequent-fairly common migrant, rare in winter

☐ ***Song Sparrow,** *Melospiza melodia.* Common migrant, summer resident; fairly common in winter

☐ **Lincoln's Sparrow,** *Melospiza lincolnii.* Infrequent-fairly common migrant, accidental in winter

☐ ***Swamp Sparrow,** *Melospiza georgiana.* Infrequent migrant, rare-infrequent summer resident; fairly common in northern Ohio. Infrequent in winter

☐ ***White-throated Sparrow,** *Zonotrichia albicollis.* Common migrant, rare summer resident northeastern Ohio; fairly common in winter

☐ **White-crowned Sparrow,** *Zonotrichia leucophrys.* Fairly common-common migrant, infrequent in winter

☐ **Harris' Sparrow,** *Zonotrichia querula.* Accidental migrant

JUNCOS AND LONGSPURS

☐ ***Dark-eyed Junco,** *Junco hyemalis.* Common migrant, winter resident; rare summer resident northeastern Ohio

☐ **Lapland Longspur,** *Calcarius lapponicus.* Rare-infrequent winter visitor except in northern Ohio where they can be locally fairly common

☐ **Smith's Longspur,** *Calcarius pictus.* Accidental-rare migrant, winter visitor

☐ **Snow Bunting,** *Plectophenax nivalis.* Infrequent-locally common winter visitor (fairly common-locally common in northern Ohio)

BLACKBIRDS, ORIOLES, AND ALLIES

☐ ***Bobolink,** Dolichonyx oryzivorus.* Rare-infrequent migrant, summer resident

☐ ***Red-winged Blackbird,** Agelaius phoeniceus.* Common migrant, summer resident; infrequent in winter except for occasional roosts

☐ ***Eastern Meadowlark,** Sturnella magna.* Infrequent-fairly common migrant, summer resident; rare in winter

☐ ***Western Meadowlark,** Sturnella neglecta.* Accidental-rare migrant, summer resident

☐ ***Yellow-headed Blackbird,** Xanthocephalus xanthocephalus.* Accidental-rare migrant, summer resident, most often seen in Lake Erie marshes

☐ **Rusty Blackbird,** *Euphagus carolinus.* Infrequent-locally common migrant, winter resident

☐ **Brewer's Blackbird,** *Euphagus cyanocephalus.* Accidental; infrequent migrant, winter visitor in Lake Erie marshes

☐ **Great-tailed Grackle,** *Quiscalus mexicanus.* Accidental

☐ ***Common Grackle,** Quiscalus quiscula.* Common migrant, summer resident; infrequent in winter except near roosts

☐ ***Brown-headed Cowbird,** Molothrus ater.* Common migrant, summer resident; infrequent in winter except near roosts

☐ ***Orchard Oriole,** Icterus spurius.* Infrequent migrant, summer resident, most numerous in southern Ohio

☐ ***Northern Oriole,** Icterus galbula.* Fairly common-common migrant, summer resident; accidental in winter

FINCHES, CROSSBILLS, AND ALLIES

☐ **Brambling,** *Fringilla montifringilla.* Accidental

☐ **Rosy Finch,** *Leucosticte arctoa.* Accidental

☐ **Pine Grosbeak,** *Pinicola enucleator.* Rare northern Ohio in winter; accidental elsewhere

☐ ***Purple Finch,** *Carpodacus purpureus.* Infrequent migrant, rare summer resident in northern Ohio. Rare-infrequent in winter

☐ ***House Finch,** *Carpodacus mexicanus.* Common permanent resident

☐ ***Red Crossbill,** *Loxia curvirostra.* Erratic and rare in winter, most numerous in northern Ohio. Accidental summer resident southeastern Ohio

☐ **White-winged Crossbill,** *Loxia leucoptera.* Rare migrant and winter visitor

☐ **Common Redpoll,** *Carduelis flammea.* Rare winter visitor, most common in northern counties

☐ **Hoary Redpoll,** *Carduelis hornemanni.* Accidental winter visitor

☐ ***Pine Siskin,** *Carduelis pinus.* Fairly common but erratic migrant, winter visitor; accidental-rare in summer

☐ ***American Goldfinch,** *Carduelis tristis.* Common migrant, summer resident; fairly common in winter

☐ **Evening Grosbeak,** *Coccothraustes vespertinus.* Infrequent-fairly common migrant, winter visitor, most numerous in northern and southeastern Ohio

☐ ***House Sparrow,** *Passer domesticus.* Common permanent resident

HYBRIDS

☐ **Brewster's Warbler,** *Vermivora leucobronchialis.* Rare-infrequent migrant, summer resident

☐ **Lawrence's Warbler,** *Vermivora lawrencei.* Accidental-rare migrant, summer resident

EXOTICS AND POSSIBLE ESCAPES

☐ **Greater Flamingo,** *Phoenicopterus ruber*
☐ **Lesser White-fronted Goose,** *Anser erythropus*
☐ **Bar-headed Goose,** *Anser indicus*
☐ **Barnacle Goose,** *Branta leucopsis*
☐ **Egyptian Goose,** *Alopochen aegyptiaca*
☐ **Common Shelduck,** *Tadorna tadorna*
☐ **Ruddy Shelduck,** *Casarca ferruginea*
☐ **Chukar,** *Alectoris chukar*

□ **Black Partridge,** *Francolinus francolinus*

□ **Elliot's Pheasant,** *Syrmaticus ellioti*

□ **Ringed Turtle-dove,** *Streptopelia risoria*

□ **Canary-winged Parakeet,** *Brotogeris versicolorus*

□ **Monk Parakeet,** *Myiopsitta monachus*

□ **Yellow-headed Parrot,** *Amazona ochrocephala*

□ **Troupial,** *Icterus icterus*

□ **Altamira (Lichtenstein's) Oriole,** *Icterus gularis*

□ **European Goldfinch,** *Carduelis carduelis*

□ **Eurasian Tree Sparrow,** *Passer montanus*

Appendix I:
Some Facts about Ohio

Ohio covers an area of 41,263 square miles with a width from east to west of about 215 miles, and a length from north to south of about 210 miles located between 42° and 38° 25' North latitude and 80° 30' and 84° 5' West longitude. Elevation ranges from a maximum of 1,550 feet above sea level at Campbell Hill near Bellfontaine in Logan County to 450 feet at the mouth of the Great Miami River in southwestern Hamilton County.

The climate is temperate with a mean annual temperature of 51.7° in the central part of the state, a January average of 26.4° and a July average of 73.2°. The mean annual rainfall is approximately 38 inches. Snowfall is greatest in the northeast counties because of the influence of Lake Erie, somewhat less in the northwest counties, and least of all in the southern counties. Over 6,000 streams and 18 larger watersheds drain the state. The northern third of Ohio lies within the Great Lakes–St. Lawrence watershed, and the southern two-thirds in the Ohio–Mississippi River watershed.

The eastern and southeastern sections of the state are typically described as belonging to the Appalachian or Allegheny Plateau. The western part of Ohio is within the Mississippi Valley Plain. The Allegheny Front Escarpment enters the state from Pennsylvania and extends from Ashtabula County southwest to Richland County then southward through Adams County and into Kentucky.

This escarpment delineates a fairly sharp division between the hill country of the Appalachian Plateau to the east and the more level terrain of the Mississippi Valley Plain to the west.

Before its settlement by non-native Americans, deciduous forests covered most of what is now Ohio, interspersed with occasional prairies, brushy and second growth areas recovering from fires and tornadoes, and marshes, most extensively bordering the western Lake Erie basin.

In 1790, there were approximately 3,000 pioneer settlers in the Ohio Country; there were 45,365 inhabitants by 1800. In 1850, the population was 1,980,329; in 1910 it was 4,767,121; by 1950 it was 7,946,627, and in 1990 it was estimated at 10,887,325.

During the first 150 years of this period, forests were cut and marshes and swamps drained for agricultural lands, home sites, villages, towns, and railroad rights-of-way. Most large animals and an appreciable number of birds became extinct, were extirpated, or were greatly reduced in numbers.

During the last 50 years, the greatest changes have involved the expansion of a network of cities, suburbs, and highways in direct proportion to increasing human population. Intensive and highly mechanized farming practices and the widespread use of chemicals in many parts of the state have left precious little "natural" habitat.

The good news is that organizations like the National Audubon Society and its local chapters, the Nature Conservancy, Metro Parks, the Ohio Department of Natural Resources and, especially, that department's Wildlife Division, and other environmental groups have made great progress in acquiring and setting aside or restoring appreciable amounts of land and remnant wetlands to something approaching their original condition.

Appendix II:
The Introduction of Peregrine Falcons to Ohio

DENIS S. CASE

Ohio Division of Wildlife

There are no historic records of peregrine falcons (*Falco peregrinus*) nesting in Ohio,[1] so a successful nesting attempt by a territorial pair in downtown Toledo in 1988 generated much interest. Both turned out to be birds that had been released in other urban areas as a result of efforts to reestablish peregrines in eastern North America. The male had been hacked (an old falconry technique for releasing raptors to the wild) in St. Louis, Missouri, and the female had been hacked in St. Catharines, Ontario. The Toledo birds produced two young.

This event sparked interest in getting breeding pairs established in other urban areas in Ohio, and a strategic plan was developed by the Ohio Division of Wildlife with two goals: to use the resources available in Ohio to contribute to the recovery of a viable peregrine population in the Midwest, and to take full advantage of educational and recreational opportunities created by the recovery effort. Specific objectives of the plan were to establish and maintain one nesting pair per city in Akron, Cincinnati, Cleveland, Columbus, Dayton, and Toledo, and to develop data on the amount of public interest in peregrines in Ohio.

The first management activity was to improve the nesting situation in Toledo. The birds had originally chosen a narrow ledge on a vacant building which did not provide adequate space for developing young to exercise or to gain necessary strength prior to fledging. Two nest boxes were constructed and placed on the building to provide a safer environment. The adult birds have used one or the other of the boxes each year since 1989. These birds have now produced a total of eight young through the 1992 breeding season.

To move further toward fulfillment of the strategic plan objectives, perc-

---

[1]There are several historical records of peregrines nesting in trees in the Midwest, but this behavior seems to have been unusual rather than common. If peregrines ever tree-nested in Ohio, occurrences went unrecorded.

grine hacking projects were carried out in Columbus (five birds released in 1989, eight in 1990, and seven in 1991), Cincinnati (six birds in 1990 and seven in 1991), and Akron (seven birds in 1992 and seven planned for 1993). Similar efforts had been planned for Cleveland and Dayton, but in each city, two birds showed up on their own.[2]

As a result of the releases in this state and other parts of the Midwest, Ohio ended up with a total of four territorial pairs of peregrines following the 1992 breeding season. These pairs were in Cincinnati, Cleveland, Dayton, and Toledo. Since then birds have also been routinely observed in Columbus, including two adults seen together in the downtown area in the fall and winter of 1992. There is some evidence that the female of the Cleveland pair is infertile (no eggs have been laid in two seasons, despite observed courtship and copulation). There are plans to capture and examine the bird.

Assuming the division is successful in establishing breeding pairs in each of the major urban areas, the following benefits are expected. The first is for the peregrines themselves. Ohio would be in the position of contributing six pairs to the Midwest population, where the goal is for a total of forty pairs. A second benefit is education. The division is not presented with many opportunities to reach a largely urban public with an endangered species project. The downtown environments give the projects high exposure, the resulting conservation message is delivered to millions. And finally, urban residents get a chance to observe and enjoy one of the most spectacular birds on earth.

One final word concerns funding for the project. The effort would not be possible without the support of Ohio citizens for the Nongame and Endangered Wildlife Checkoff on the state income tax form. The level of support has been consistently strong and has allowed the division to expand its programs for species such as peregrine falcons.

[*Author's Note:* In June of 1994, three out of four chicks were prospering in Columbus; there were four chicks in Cleveland, four eggs in a Cincinnati nest, and at least two chicks in a Toledo nest. The nest in Dayton did not produce any young birds in 1994.–TT]

[2] As in Toledo, these birds were the products of urban hacking programs in other cities. For instance, the Dayton male had been hacked in Cincinnati, the Dayton female in Columbus.

Appendix III:
Birding and Natural History Organizations

There are many organizations the birder can join. Local birding clubs are scattered fairly evenly around Ohio, and there are a number of national organizations. Many of the local clubs are affiliated with the National Audubon Society and offer joint memberships.

NATIONAL ORGANIZATIONS

The National Audubon Society

700 Broadway
New York, NY 10003
(212) 979-3000
Publications: *Audubon Magazine, American Birds, Audubon Activist*

American Birding Association

4 Swallow Drive
Colorado Springs, CO 80904
Publications: *Birding, Winging It*

American Ornithologists' Union

National Museum of Natural History
Smithsonian Institute
Washington, DC 20560
(612) 373-5643
Publication: *The Auk*

Wilson Ornithological Society

c/o Jerome A. Jackson
Department of Zoology
Mississippi State University
Mississippi State, MS 39762
Publication: *The Wilson Bulletin*

National Wildlife Federation

1412 16th Street NW
Washington, DC 20036
Publications: *National Wildlife, Ranger Rick*

Cornell Laboratory of Ornithology

159 Sapsucker Woods Road
Ithaca, NY 14850
Publications: *The Living Bird,*
members' newsletter

CANADIAN ORGANIZATIONS

Canadian Nature Federation

46 Elgin Street
Ottawa, Ontario K1P 5K6
Publication: *Nature Canada*

Canadian Wildlife Federation

1673 Carling Avenue
Ottawa, Ontario K2A 1C4
Publication: *International Wildlife*

REGIONAL ORGANIZATIONS

The Brooks Bird Club

707 Warwood Avenue
Wheeling, WV 26003
Tri-state membership: OH, WV, PA
Publications: *The Redstart, The Mailbag*
Meetings, field trips, and annual Foray

OHIO ORGANIZATIONS

Appalachian Front Audubon Society

P.O. Box 518
Hillsboro, OH 45133

Audubon Society of Greater Cleveland

The Park Bldg., 140 Public Square,
Cleveland, OH 44114
(216) 861-5093
Bulletin, meetings, field trips
Taped Bird News: (216) 861-2447

Audubon Society of Ohio

c/o Cincinnati Nature Center
4949 Tealtown Road
Milford, OH 45150
(513) 576-0305
Newsletter, field trips, meetings
Taped Rare Bird Alert: (513) 521-2847

Aullwood Audubon Center and Farm

1000 Aullwood Road (Center)
Dayton, OH 45414
(513) 890-7360
9101 Frederick Pike (Farm)
Dayton, OH 45414
(513) 890-2968

Beavercreek Wetlands Assocation

P.O. Box 42
Alpha, OH 45301-0042
(513) 426-4055

Blackbrook Audubon Society

5418 Vrooman Road
Mentor, OH 44060
(216) 352-0979

Black River Audubon Society

42750 Smith Road
Wellington, OH 44090

Brukner Nature Center

5995 Horseshoe Bend Road
Troy, OH 45373
(513) 698-6493
Nature center

Canton Audubon Society

P.O. Box 20068
Canton, OH 44701
Newsletter, meetings, field trips

Clark County Audubon Society

P.O. Box 2236
Springfield, OH 45501

Columbus Audubon Society

1065 Kendale Road North
Columbus, OH 43220
(614) 451-4591
Newsletter, meetings, field trips
Taped Rare Bird Alert: (614) 221-9736

Columbus Natural History Society

111 Richards Avenue
Columbus, OH 43214
(614) 263-2445
Meetings, field trips

Grant M. Cook Bird Club

c/o Lyle D. Miller
795 Mill Creek Boulevard
Youngstown, OH 44512

Dayton Audubon Society

Dayton Museum of Natural History
2629 Ridge Avenue
Dayton, OH 45414
(513) 299-4112
Newsletter, meetings, field trips
Taped Rare Bird Alert: (513) 277-6446

East Central Ohio Audubon Society

c/o Janet Schultz
2716 W. Dutch Lane NW
Newark, OH 43055
Meetings at Dawes Arboretum

Firelands Audubon Society

c/o Carol Andres
1137 New State Road
Norwalk, OH 44857
Newsletter, meetings, field trips

Forest Audubon Club

c/o Rosemarie Plant
314 South Bend Boulevard
Steubenville, OH 43952
(614) 282-3122

Glen Helen Association

405 Corry Street
Yellow Springs, OH 45387
(513) 767-7375
Trailside museum, outdoor education
center, raptor rehabilitation center, birding
and botany clubs

Greater Akron Audubon Society

P.O. Box 80056
Akron, OH 44308
Seiberling Nature Center
(216) 836-2185
Newsletter, meetings, field trips

R. B. Hayes Audubon Society

P.O. Box 92
Fremont, OH 43420
Newsletter, meetings, field trips

Hocking Valley Audubon Society

P.O. Box 43
Athens, OH 45701

Kirtland Bird Club

The Cleveland Museum of Natural History
Wade Oval, University Circle
Cleveland, OH 44106
(216) 231-4600
Newsletter, meetings, field trips
Taped Rare Bird Alert: (216) 321-7245

Maumee Valley Audubon Society

c/o Side Cut Metro Park
P.O. Box 1009
Maumee, OH 43537
(419) 837-5531

Mahoning Valley Audubon Society

P.O. Box 3214
Youngstown, OH 44513
Hotline: (216) 742-6661

Oxford Audubon Society

P.O. Box 556
Oxford, OH 45056

Shawnee Nature Club P.O. Box 1432

Friendship, OH 45630
Schedule, meetings, field trips

Toledo Naturalists' Association

Bulletin, meetings, field trips
Taped Rare Bird Alert: (419) 875-6889

Tri-Moraine Audubon Society

P.O. Box 5216
Lima, OH 45802
Newsletter, meetings, field trips

Western Cuyahoga Audubon Society

510 Humiston Blvd.
Bay Village, OH 44140

Wayne Nature Club

c/o Robert M. Bruce
1457 Cleveland Road
Wooster, OH 44691

Zanesville Audubon Society

P.O. Box 2464
Zanesville, OH 43701
Newsletter, meetings, field trips

Appendix IV:
Taped Rare Bird Alerts

OHIO

Cincinnati	(513) 521-2847
Cleveland	(216) 696-8186
Cleveland	(216) 861-2447
Columbus	(614) 221-9736
Toledo	(419) 875-6889
SW Ohio	(513) 277-6446
Youngstown	(216) 742-6661

NEIGHBORING STATES

Detroit	(313) 477-1360
Michigan	(616) 471-4919
Indiana	(317) 259-0911
Kentucky	(502) 894-9538
Philadelphia	(215) 567-2473

OTHER HOT SPOTS

Cape May	(609) 884-2626
Boston	(617) 259-8805
Los Angeles	(213) 874-1318
S. Carolina	(704) 332-2473
Texas	(713) 992-2757
Rio Grande	(210) 565-6773
Virginia	(804) 929-1736
Ottawa	(613) 761-1967
Vancouver	(604) 737-9910

Bibliography

American Birding Association
  1990 *Checklist: Birds of the Continental United States and Canada.* Fourth ed., Austin, TX.
Arhib, Robert
  1979 The Blue List for 1980. *American Birds* 33:830–835.
Audubon Field Notes
  1947–1981 Bimonthly periodical, National Audubon Society, New York, NY.
Auk, The
  1923–1981 Bimonthly periodical, American Ornithologists' Union, Washington, D.C.
Bailey, David
  1975 *The Birds of Cedar Bog, Spring of 1975.* Nat. Hist. Dept., Ohio Historical Society, Vol. 4.
Balch, Lawrence G.
  1979 Identification of Groove-billed and Smooth-billed Anis. *Birding* 11:295–297.
Bent, A. C.
  1919–1958 *Life Histories of North American Birds.* United States National Museum, Bull. 107, 113, 121, 126, 130, 135, 142, 146, 162, 167, 170, 174, 176, 179, 191, 195, 196, 197, 203, and 211 (Also available in reprints from Dover, New York, NY).
Bingaman, Ann
  1975 *Wahkeena Breeding Bird Census.* Nat. Hist. Dept., Ohio Historical Society, Vol. 4.
Bird Lore
  1921–1940 Bimonthly periodical, National Audubon Society, New York, NY.
Blincoe, Benedict J.
  1967 *The Birds of Dayton and the Central Miami Valley.* Ohio Biological Survey, Biol. Notes #1 (Revised edition).
Borror, Donald J.
  1950 A Check List of the Birds of Ohio with the migration dates for the birds of central Ohio. *Ohio Journal of Science* 50:1–32.
Braun, Lucy E.
  1961 *The Woody Plants of Ohio.* The Ohio State University Press, Columbus, OH.
Buchanan, Forest W.
  1980 *The Breeding Birds of Carroll and Northern Jefferson Counties, Ohio.* Ohio Biological Survey, Biol. Notes #12, Columbus, OH.
Bull, John
  1975 *Birds of the New York Area.* Dover Press, New York, NY.
Campbell, Louis W.
  1940 *Birds of Lucas County.* Toledo Museum of Science Bulletin #1.

1968   *Birds of the Toledo Area.* The Toledo Blade Co.
Cedar Bog Symposium
1973   Ohio Biological Survey, Circ. #4.
Clark, Clarence F. and James P. Sipe
1970   *Birds of the Lake St. Marys Area.* Ohio Dept. Nat. Resources, Publ. #350.
Cleveland Bird Calendar
1950–1980   Kirtland Bird Club. Quarterly periodical. Cleveland, OH.
Columbus Audubon Society Newsletter
1960–1982   Columbus Audubon Society, monthly periodical, Sept.–May.
Courser, William D.
1979   Continued Breeding Range Expansion of the Burrowing Owl in Florida. *American Birds* 33:143.
Davie, Oliver
1882   *Naturalist's Manual.* Columbus, OH.

_____

1898   *Nests and Eggs of North American Birds.* 5th ed. McKay, Philadelphia, PA.
Dawson, William L.
1903   *The Birds of Ohio.* Wheaton Publishing Co., Columbus, OH.
Folzenlogen, Robert
1988   *A Birder's Guide to the Cincinnati Tristate.* 142 pp. Willow Press, Glendale, OH.
Geffen, Alice M.
1978   *A Birdwatcher's Guide to the Eastern United States.* Barron's, Woodbury, N.Y.
Godfrey, W. Earl
1979   *The Birds of Canada.* National Museums of Canada, Ottawa, Canada.
Henninger, W. F.
1909   A Preliminary List of the Birds of Middle and Southern Ohio. *Wilson Bull.* 14:77–93.
Hicks, Lawrence E.
1928   Some interesting Ohio records. *Wilson Bull.* 41:43–44.

_____

1935   Distribution of the Breeding Birds of Ohio. *Ohio Biol. Surv. Bull.* 32:125–90.

_____

1937   An Ohio Invasion of LeConte's Sparrows. *Auk* 54:545–46.
Hochbaum, H. Albert
1955   *Travels and Traditions of Waterfowl.* University of Minnesota Press, Minneapolis.
Jones, Lynds
1903   *The Birds of Ohio.* Ohio Acad. Sci. Spec. Paper #6.
Keller, Charles E., Shirley A., Timothy C.
1979   *Indiana Birds and Their Haunts.* Indiana University Press, Bloomington, IN.
Kemsies, Emerson, and Worth Randle
1953   *Birds of Southwestern Ohio.* Edward Bros., Ann Arbor, MI.
Kirby, Edna L.
1976   *Wahkeena Spring Flowers.* Nat. Hist. Dept., Ohio Historical Society, Vol. 5.
Kline, Dennis
1988   *Birds of Holmes and Wayne Counties, Ohio (Checklist).* Dennis Kline, Shreve, Ohio 44676.
Lauro, Anthony J., and Barbara J. Spencer
1980   A method for separating juvenal and first-winter Ring-billed Gulls and Common Gulls. *American Birds* 34:111–117.

Lincoln, Frederick C.
  1950   *Migration of Birds.* U.S. Dept. Agr. Circ. 16.
Lowery, Jr., George H.
  1955   *Louisiana Birds.* Louisiana State University Press, Baton Rouge, La.
Mackenzie, John P.S.
  1977   *Birds in Peril.* Pagurian Press Limited, Toronto, Canada.
Matthiessen, Peter
  1959   *Wildlife in America.* Viking Press, New York, NY.
McLaughlin, Vincent P.
  1979   Occurrence of Large-billed Tern *(Phaetusa simplex)* in Ohio. *American Birds*
         33:727.
Melvin, Ruth W.
  1970   *A Guide to Ohio Outdoor Education Areas.* Ohio Dept. Nat. Resources and the
         Ohio Academy of Science. Columbus, OH.
Newman, Donald L.
  1969   *A Field Book of Birds of the Cleveland Region.* Cleveland Museum of Natural
         History.
Oberholser, H. C.
  1896   A Preliminary List of the Birds of Wayne County, Ohio. Bull. of the Ohio
         Agr. Exp. Sta. Tech. Ser. 1:243–353.
Peterjohn, Bruce G., R. L. Hannikman, J. M. Hoffman, and E. J. Tramer
  1987   *Abundance and Distribution of the Birds of Ohio.* Ohio Biological Survey, Biological
         Notes No. 19. 52 pp.

———
  1989   *The Birds of Ohio.* Indiana University Press. 237 pp.
——— and Daniel L. Rice
  1991   *The Ohio Breeding Bird Atlas.* The Ohio Department of Natural Resources,
         Division of Natural Areas and Preserrves. 416 pp.
Peterson, Roger Tory
  1961   *A Field Guide to Western Birds.* Houghton Mifflin, Boston, Mass.
Peterson, Roger Tory, Guy Mountfort, and P.A.D. Hollum
  1967   *A Field Guide to the Birds of Britain and Europe.* Houghton Mifflin, Boston, Mass.
Peterson, Roger Tory
  1980   *A Field Guide to the Birds East of the Rockies.* Houghton Mifflin, Boston, Mass.
Pettingill, Jr., Olin Sewall
  1962   *A Guide to Bird Finding East of the Mississippi.* 4th ed. Oxford University Press,
         New York, N.Y.

———
  1970   *Ornithology in Laboratory and Field.* Burgess, Minneapolis, Minn.
Redstart, The
  1957–1980   Quarterly publication, the Brooks Bird Club, Wheeling, W. Va.
Rosche, Larry (ed.)
  1988   *A Field Book of Birds of the Cleveland Region.* Second Edition. The Cleveland
         Museum of Natural History.
Savaloja, Terry
  1981   Yellow Rail. *Birding* 13:80–85.
Smith, H. G., R. K. Burnard, E. E. Good, and J. M. Keener
  1973   Rare and Endangered Vertebrates of Ohio. *The Ohio Journal of Science* 73:257–
         271.

Tate, Jr., James
  1981   The Blue List for 1981. *American Birds* 35:3–10.
Terres, John K.
  1980   *The Audubon Society Encyclopedia of North American Birds.* Alfred A. Knopf, New York, N.Y.
Thomas, Edward S.
  1928   The Chickadees of Central Ohio. *Ohio State Museum Sci. Bull.* 1:76–77.

———
  1939–1981 Nature column, weekly. *Columbus Sunday Dispatch.* Thomson, A. L. (editor).
Thomson, Tom
  1974   *Checklist of the Birds of Ohio.* The Columbus Audubon Society.

———
  1983. *Birding in Ohio.* First Edition. Indiana University Press.
Trautman, Milton B.
  1940   *The Birds of Buckeye Lake, Ohio.* University of Michigan Museum of Zoology, Misc. Publ. No. 44.
Trautman, Milton B., and Mary A.
  1968   Annotated List of the Birds of Ohio. *The Ohio Journal of Science* 68:257–332.
Trautman, Milton B.
  1979   Experiences and thoughts relative to Kirtland's Warbler. *The Jack Pine Warbler* 57:135–140.
Walker, Charles F.
  1928   The Seasons of Birds in Central Ohio. The Ohio State Museum Sci. Bull. 1:9–23.
Walton, Debra, et al.
  N.D. *A Guide to the Ohio Preserves of the Nature Conservancy,* with a forword by George Laycock. 59 pp.
Wheaton Club Bulletin
  1956–1980 Annual publication of the Wheaton Club. Columbus, OH.
Wheaton, J. M.
  1882   Report on the Birds of Ohio. *Geol. Surv. Ohio* 4:187–628.
Williams, Arthur B.
  1950   *Birds of the Cleveland Region.* The Cleveland Museum of Natural History.
Wilson Bulletin, The
  1925–1980 Quarterly publication of the Wilson Ornithological Society, Ann Arbor, MI.

About the Contributors

John A. Shrader, M.D., regional editor and major contributor for the Miami Valley and Dayton Area in southwestern Ohio, is the program director for the Transitional Year residency program and senior associate program director for the internal medicine residency program at Kettering Medical Center in Kettering, Ohio. In addition to internal medicine, he is particularly interested in the use of computers in medicine and has been involved in computerization of medical records for about eleven years.

John is on the Board of Directors and is a past president of the Dayton Audubon Society. He was bitten by the birding bug over 16 years ago. Although he is primarily interested in birding the American Birding Association area (he has an ABA life list of over 700 species) as well as in "world birding," he also enjoys keeping up with birds on the local scene. He is the birding editor for the Dayton Audubon Society's *Yellow Warbler* and writes a regular column for the publication entitled "Seasonal Sightings," covering observations in southwest Ohio. In addition to birding and traveling, he is also a Master Bird Bander and enjoys giving talks about both birding and banding. He is married to **Karen Schrader**, who is also an avid birder and world traveler.

The following individuals assisted John Shrader in updating existing site descriptions in southwestern Ohio as well as providing information regarding new locations included in this book for the first time. Many thanks to **Betty and Charles Berry**, **Cliff Cathers**, **Carolyn and Jim Garber**, **Jim Hickman**, **Jim Hill**, **Charlotte Mathena**, and **Sue Utterback**, who reviewed all of the material. **Larry Gara** worked on the Cowan Lake and Fort Ancient sections. **Bob Heidelberg** submitted material on the Bruckner Nature Center. **Tom Hissong** updated the birding and natural history organizations in the southwest part of the state. **John Howard** worked on the Beaver Creek Wetlands and Indian Mound Reserve descriptions. **Dave Knoop** submitted data on Eastwood Lake. **Tim Little** contributed information on the Middletown area. **Chris McKay** provided material on the Miami County Park District. **Dane Mutter** furnished data on the Beaver Creek Wetlands. **Frank Renfrow** helped with the Gilmore Ponds account, and **Billy Taylor** provided material on Hills and Dales Park.

Tom Kemp was a major contributor of material on the Oak Openings and several other sites in the Toledo area. A high school biology teacher who has been studying birds for 29 years, Tom is a member of the Ohio Bird Records Committee and a long-time member of the Toledo Naturalists' Association. He is a former editor of the latter organization's publication, *The Ohio Cardinal*. At the present time, he coordinates the rare bird alert for the Toledo area.

Charles H. Gambill created the line drawings for both editions of *Birding in Ohio*. He teaches high school art in the Columbus school system. Charles's interest in birds dates back to 1975, and his North American life list stood at 730 species in the spring of 1993. The North American life lists of his father and mother, "Red" and Louise Gambill, number somewhere around 768; Charles's son, Brad, has seen 526 species. They are the only three generations of one family in the ABA's membership who have all seen over 500 species.

Bruce Stehling coordinated contributions on areas in southwest Ohio, including Winton Woods, Lunken Airport, East Fork State Park and Reservoir, the Miller Brewery Company Fields, and Gilmore Ponds. Bruce has been an active birder for 22 years and has contributed to *American Birds* and *The Ohio Cardinal*.

Jay Stenger and **Ned Keller** updated southwest Ohio sites that were included in the first edition and contributed notes on a number of new locations in the Cincinnati area. Both men are expert birders and have kept notes and collected migration data for many years.

Marcella and Howard Meahl contributed notes on Conneaut Harbor and Ashtabula's Walnut Beach. They are enthusiastic birders and banding instructors and have been banding birds for over three decades.

John Pogacnik contributed valuable data on the Lake County Metro Parks, Geneva State Park, and Kelley's Island. He started birding in 1977 while a student at The Ohio State University. "Being from Lorain, I have birded that area heavily which gave me my knowledge of gull identification," he says. John worked as a ranger at Crane Creek State Park from 1980 to 1991 and is now a ranger for the Lake Metroparks in Lake County. His Ohio life list is presently at 352, and of these he has photographed 319–all in Ohio, of course. He was also part of the May 11, 1987, Big Day team that tallied a record 205 species.

Glen Kitson of Ashtabula was one of several experienced birders who contributed notes on the birding hot spots of northeastern Ohio.

Gildo M. Tori is the wetland wildlife project leader for the Ohio Division of Wildlife's Crane Creek Wildlife Experiment Station. He has a Master of Science degree in Zoology from The Ohio State University and a Bachelor of Science degree in Wildlife Biology from Michigan State University. Gildo has worked for the Division of Wildlife for 10 years. He contributed notes on Magee Marsh, the Mallard Club Marsh Wildlife Area, and the Pipe Creek Wildlife Area.

Darlene Sadler was kind enough to furnish material about Gilmore Ponds and provide information about the Gilmore Ponds Conservancy, which was formed to protect this valuable wetland.

Tod Dawson was a birder's birder. His identification skills were of the highest order, and his energy and enthusiasm in the field could be vouched for by his birding companions, **John Stritmatter** and **Keith Archibald**. Tod contributed notes on Scioto Trail State Park and Forest, one of the trio's favorite places to find early migrating spring warblers.

Denis Case is the Assistant Administrator of Wildlife Management and Research for the Ohio Department of Natural Resources. He is one of the leading authorities on nesting birds of prey in the United States. He contributed the article on the introduction of Peregrine Falcons to Ohio.

Harry and Elsie Knighton contributed to the accounts on Lake White and the Scioto River bottoms. They were married in 1937 and have been active in natural history circles for many years. They founded the North American Mycological Association in 1959 and served as executive officers for many years. Both have participated in their local Christmas Bird Count since 1950 and have been compilers since 1954.

Lynn Barnhart lives in Marietta, Ohio, and works as an outdoor education camp naturalist for the Marietta, Washington, and Morgan county schools and as a naturalist at Burr Oak State Park Resort Lodge. A bird bander, he also maintains a 25-mile-long bluebird trail. His contributions included information on the fascinating and little-known Newell's Run and Leith Run embayments.

Pete Whan manages a system of preserves for the Nature Conservancy on Long Island. A life-long birder, he was until recently manager of the Edge of Appalachia Preserve in Adams County for the Cincinnati Museum of Natural History and the Nature Conservancy. He has led nature tours into the Everglades, done ornithological research at Manomet Bird Observatory in Massachusetts and for the Ohio Department of Natural Resources. His work has appeared in professional journals and birding magazines.

Bill Whan, brother of Pete, is a Columbus writer. He has graduate degrees from the University of Michigan and Trinity College in Dublin. Although he has been a teacher and a counselor, Bill is a perpetual student with special interests in natural history and has been an enthusiastic birder for over 16 years. He contributed material on the Big Island Wildlife Area.

Charles A. Bombaci, B.S., A.S.A. Bentley College, is the author of *A Birder's Guide to Columbus and Central Ohio,* 1991. He is a volunteer naturalist and a member of the Executive Board of the Columbus and Franklin County Metropolitan Parks, Inc., a volunteer naturalist of the Hoover Nature Preserve, and member of the Nature Conservancy, Cornell Laboratory of Ornithology, and the National Wildlife Federation. Charles is also an amateur nature photographer and compiler for the Hoover Reservoir, Ohio, Christmas Bird Count.

Index to the Birds

Page numbers refer to the various species as they are listed in the expanded Checklist of Ohio Birds commencing on page 217. There, the common names are followed by the scientific names and a brief description of the status of the species in Ohio.

Site Index